SMOOTH RIDE GUIDES

SMOOTH RIDE GUIDES

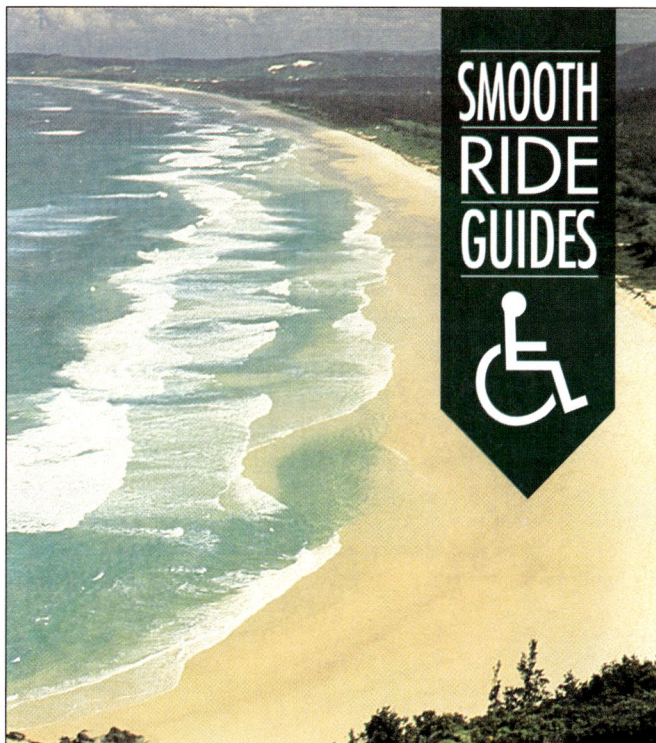

AUSTRALIA
& NEW ZEALAND

FREEWHEELING MADE EASY

FT PUBLISHING

SMOOTH RIDE GUIDES
AUSTRALIA AND NEW ZEALAND
by July Ramsey

Researchers: July Ramsey and Elizabeth Meadows
Series Adviser: Malcolm Gorman
Editor: John Bailey
Designed by Design 23
Printed by Graficromo, SA., Spain
Publicity: Jacqueline Richardson Press & PR Consultants
Photography courtesy of Australian and New Zealand
Tourist Commissions

ISBN 0 9521982 0 7

First published: 1994 Copyright © FT Publishing

ACKNOWLEDGEMENTS
The publisher should like to thank the many
organisations and individuals who have contributed to
this edition. In particular JETSET EUROPE who have given
substantial financial and publicity support; the
AUSTRALIAN TOURIST COMMISSION and THE HOLIDAY
CARE SERVICE CHARITY for their sponsorship and
expertise; and the SPINAL INJURIES ASSOCIATION and
TRIPSCOPE for their invaluable help and assistance.
Substantial personal contributions, for which we are very
grateful, were made by John Bond, Pia Byrne, Theresa
Carey, Diane Clements, Lynette Cowan, Adrian Drew,
Brian Howard, John MacPherson, Ian Milligan, Kate
Osborne, David Phillips, Lyn Punchard, Gaby Richardson
and Maundy Todd.

The contents of this publication are believed correct at
the time of going to press. Suggestions for future
editions should be addressed to July Ramsey, FT
Publishing, 44 Talbot Road, Highgate, London N6 4QP.

"A BOOK SHOULD TEACH US TO ENJOY LIFE, OR TO ENDURE IT."
attrib. Samuel Johnson.
The publisher of *Smooth Ride Guides* hopes it will be the former.

CONTENTS

AUSTRALIA

NEW ZEALAND

UNTAPPED HOLIDAY MARKETS

"Ignoring the disabled costs £22.4 billion." So began a report in *The Times* of 28 October 1993, following the Tourism for All conference in London organised by the Holiday Care Service.

"Many handicapped people who find it difficult to travel, would do so if they were better catered for by the industry….Wheelchair access is one of the big difficulties faced by many disabled people who want to travel…."

The report continued on the theme that few disabled people travelled because of a lack of suitable accommodation, access and guides. Management consultants Touche Ross identified a potential new market of 14 million people in Europe who would take a holiday trip if better facilities were available and said it was a myth that they stayed at home because they had no disposable income.

The Touche Ross report advised that five million people with disabilities already travelled and made up three percent of all tourists, accounting for £5.7 billion annual spend.

The report suggested that the extra effort required and the absence of accessible destinations and reliable information were the biggest difficulties rather than income restraint. The study estimated that 14 million people with impaired mobility, 28 percent of the disabled population, would not be able to afford to travel. However, six million would want to travel abroad.

The author of the Touche Ross report, Mr Hugh Cade, said: "For disabled people, the unknown travel experience can be fraught with so many more problems and hazards than for the able-bodied. The majority require facilities that have advantages for other travellers. Wide doors needed for those with poor mobility are also useful for people with lots of luggage and pregnant women. Hand rails make slippery baths and showers safer for all customers.

"Some disabled travellers will pay extra for the peace of mind that comes from staying in a better quality hotel and travelling first class. Not all such tourists are low spenders." The survey concluded that simple, low-cost measures could attract these travellers.

The aim of the Smooth Ride series of guides is to take away some of the continuing huge and daunting difficulties, open new doors for travellers with impaired mobility around the world and increase travelling opportunities for those who use wheelchairs.

July Ramsey
PUBLISHER

FOREWORD BY THE SPINAL INJURIES ASSOCIATION

When Baroness Masham founded the Spinal Injuries Association 20 years ago, she recognised the need for spinal-cord-injured people to have access to the best possible information to enable them to live their lives independently.

The Spinal Injuries Association is the only national charity providing services for spinal-cord-injured people. It is run by and for its members, ensuring that people's needs are met through the services it can provide.

Spinal-cord-injured people are as keen to travel as anyone else, but they need to know before they set off on their journey that they will be able to cope with the physical barriers imposed by society. For this reason SIA has created a database of information on holiday facilities that other people have tried, tested and found to be satisfactory. This includes information on hotels, caravans, narrow boats and self-catering cottages in the UK and abroad.

Although many SIA members have proved to be pioneers in the field of travel and have visited some far away places, there is naturally less information about distant countries than about Europe. We therefore welcome the publication of this guide to Australia and New Zealand and feel confident in commending it to all disabled people as a basis for holiday planning. The researchers have listened to our views and those of other disability organisations in making their assessments on the suitability of accommodation to be included.

You can use this guide with confidence, but remember you should always check that your own specific needs can be met before you make your booking.

7

Further information about the Spinal Injuries Association can be obtained by writing or telephoning:
Spinal Injuries Association
76 St. James's Lane
Muswell Hill
London N10 3DF
Tel: 081-444 2121 Fax: 081-444 3761

> *"And now am I in Arden, the more fool I. When I was at home, I was in a better place, but travellers must be content."*
>
> *Touchstone,*
> *"As You Like It Act" I, Sc IV*
> *William Shakespeare*

A smooth ride for all holidaymakers can be guaranteed by consulting the right guide books.

HOLIDAY CARE SERVICE

Holiday Care Service, a national charity, is the UK's central resource of holiday information and support for disabled and disadvantaged people.

With a potential new tourism market of approximately 14 million disabled Europeans, the service works closely with the tourism industry to assist them in recognising the market and meeting the needs of those tourists.

In 1993 Holiday Care Service assisted around 30,000 individual enquirers, and many thousands more through information contained in its colourful guides. Nevertheless, this represents the tip of the iceberg so far as potential business goes for the tourism industry.

Dissemination of information that is accurate and reliable is one of the most important aspects of reaching that market. Disabled people need information that they can trust and rely on, and Holiday Care Service are the most comprehensive resource of that information in Europe, maybe even the world.

We hold some 200 information databases. Our UK regional Accessible Accommodation Guides set the standard for Europe. Every establishment listed has been inspected against the National Accessible Standard for the UK as operated by ourselves and the tourist boards. This gives disabled people reassurance and confidence that when they book into a hotel, bed and breakfast or self-catering establishment, it will be as accessible as identified by the symbol.

We now operate a Reservations Service, offering discounted rates at some 250 accessible properties throughout the UK and we hope to expand this to include Europe.

Our information includes every European country and the USA where we also inspect. Farther afield it is difficult for us to obtain reliable information and certainly impossible to inspect. We therefore welcome the new *Smooth Ride Guide to Australia and New Zealand*.

Holiday Care Service acts as a catalyst to bring about change in tourism and to assist the industry in understanding that all people would like the opportunity of choice, to book the holiday they want when they want and where they want.

We therefore positively encourage providers of activity holidays, sailing, fishing, riding or whatever to ensure their facilities are accessible to all, and that their information provision states the level of facilities and accessibility.

Our range of assistance also includes people on low income, one-parent families, carers of disabled people, older people and those on their own.

We operate very low-cost holidays for people on benefits under the Tourism For All holidays scheme. We welcome partnerships with the tourism industry to enable many more of the thousands who can have no break from an often stressful life, to take a holiday. People on low incomes sometimes also have disability in the family, and carers, of which there are some six million in the UK, also need a break.

Last year we produced a new guide called *Care for Carers,* giving information about holiday opportunities.

Our main guides and publications are: 14 Regional Accessible Accommodation Guides UK; A guide to holidays for One-Parent Families; A guide to financial help towards the cost of a holiday; *Care for Carers* plus 200 other incidental sheets.

Holiday Care operates a Friends of Holiday Care Service scheme; members receive free sets of guides as new ones are published, a newsletter and preferred booking at hotels, and various other benefits. The membership fee is £10.

If you would like assistance from Holiday Care Service, or would like to support our work by becoming a Friend or giving a company donation, please contact us at:

> Holiday Care Service
> 2 Old Bank Chambers
> Station Road
> Horley, Surrey RH6 9HW
> Tel: 0293 774535
> Fax: 0293 784647
> Minicom: 0293 776943

> *"As the Spanish proverb says — he who would bring home the wealth of the Indies, must carry the wealth of the Indies with him. So it is with travelling; a man must carry knowledge with him, if he would bring home knowledge."*
>
> Boswell's "Life of Johnson" 1778

Many organisations exist to make sure your holiday snaps tell a happy story.

TRIPSCOPE

Travelling for the first time to or in a strange country can be very stressful and travelling on your own can be doubly worrying, but if you also have a mobility handicap that anxiety can be multiplied many times. Such journeys should be pleasant and comfortable at the very least and, at best, travelling should be an invigorating and stimulating experience.

With the right preparation it can be!

TRIPSCOPE is a UK-based, international travel and transport information service for those with a mobility problem. Wherever you live and wherever you want to travel, TRIPSCOPE's unique service can help with the often difficult task of planning and organising journeys whatever the distance involved and whatever your mobility handicap. We can help with journeys to Australia and New Zealand just as we can help visitors with mobility handicaps organise their travel to and around the UK.

Our service is available to individuals, families or larger groups, whatever the reason for the trip. We can also help with information about the problems you may experience getting from place to place, whether you plan to use public or private transport or both. We can also point the way to assistance with all those other matters that may be a bother – from where to find accessible WCs to hiring wheelchairs.

TRIPSCOPE is a registered charity so all this information comes free of charge – although donations are always welcome to help maintain and expand our service. If the cost of telephoning is a matter of concern we are always happy to return calls immediately to help keep your telephone bill as low as possible.

11

The most important aspect of our service is the opportunity to talk over your needs with one of our professional and friendly information staff on the telephone, although your enquiry also can be dealt with by letter, tape or minicom. Whilst we rely on our comprehensive computerised database to provide up-to-date, accurate information, personal contact by telephone means we can give you the support, confidence and encouragement you may need to have a successful and enjoyable trip. We can help you to prepare for your travels abroad as fully as possible, and for visitors to Britain we can also offer a reassuring point of contact for travel information.

Contact us in London on 081-994 9294 (UK, international and minicom)
Fax: 081-994 3618

or Bristol on 0272 414094 (for the south west and South Wales)
Fax: 0272 414024

or write to: TRIPSCOPE, The Courtyard, Evelyn Road, London W4 5JL

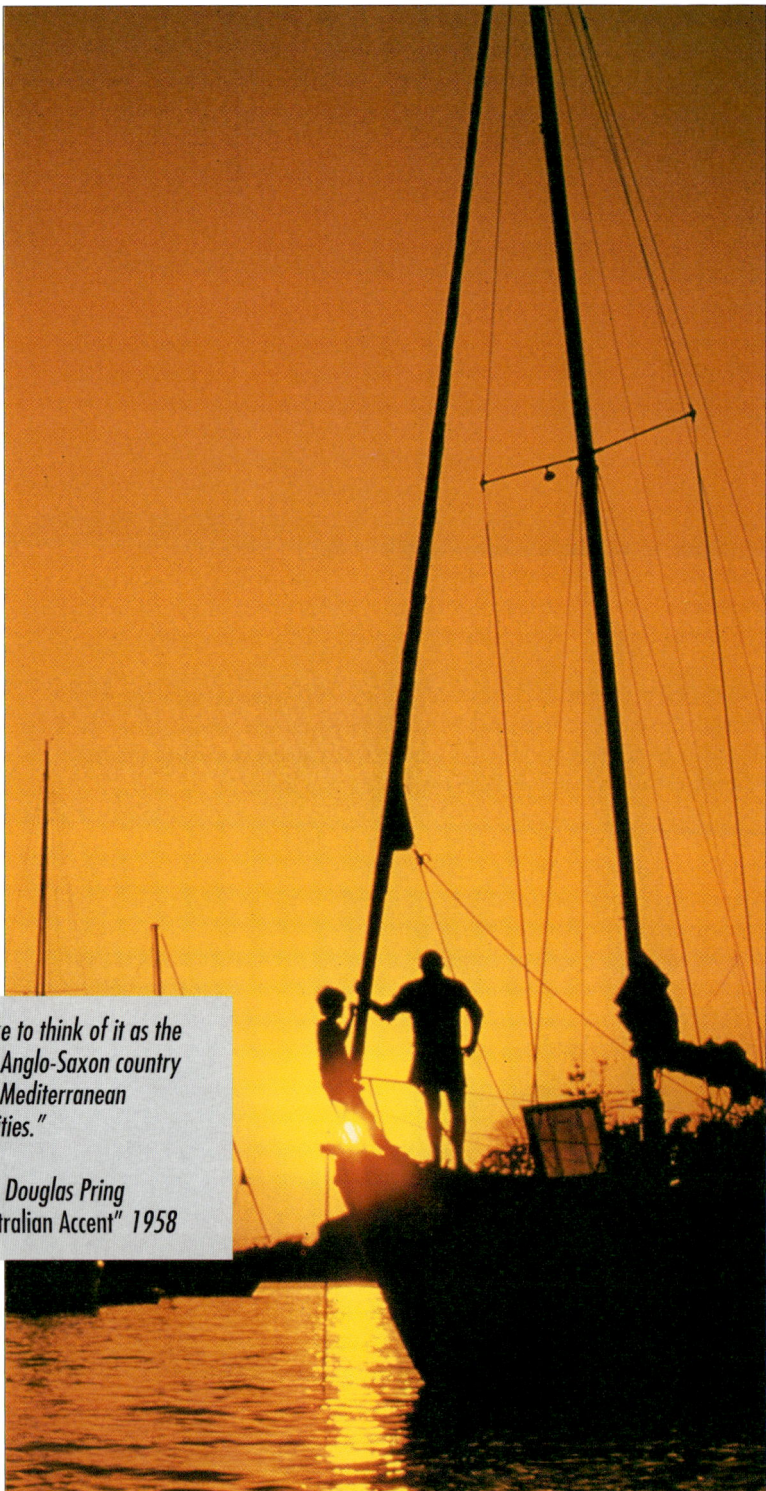

"I like to think of it as the only Anglo-Saxon country with Mediterranean qualities."

John Douglas Pring
"Australian Accent" 1958

Sailing by sunset.

AUSTRALIAN TOURIST COMMISSION

The demand for information on travel for people with impaired mobility has never been greater. To participate independently in community life, including the enjoyment of travel, these people need – and are demanding – barrier-free environments. This includes seemingly simple requirements such as easy access to public transport, buildings and footpaths, and thoughtfully designed facilities and services from airports to accommodation.

In the past, the needs of people with disabilities were largely ignored, but in recent years various companies and organisations in Australia have been made aware of the necessity of having accessible facilities for all people. As a result, travel in Australia for those with impaired mobility is progressing year by year. Many of the hotels, restaurants, cinemas, theatres and shops in Australia's major cities have accessible facilities, although not all of them cater for those in wheelchairs. *Smooth Ride Guides*, however, are specifically for those travellers in wheelchairs.

Australia is now, therefore, very aware of the need for facilities for all travellers with disabilities. Advance notice is the best way to ensure the finest possible assistance from airlines, hotels and transport offices.

Almost equal in size to the mainland United States, Australia is the world's third largest island, or smallest continent. Covering almost three million square miles, it is divided into six states and two territories. Though vast, Australia is relatively unpopulated; its population of 17 and a half million is only a little more than that of the Netherlands.

Among the waters that lap 23,021 miles of coastline are the South Pacific and Indian Oceans and the Timor and Arafura Seas. Off the Queensland shore extends the Great Barrier Reef, the world's longest and most spectacular coral formation.

The Australian countryside is unique – both the isolation and age of this continent have contributed to the survival of flora and fauna found nowhere else. Only 30 percent of the land is inhabited and there is much wild and unusual beauty.

It is a country of fascinating contrasts: from the glorious harbour at Sydney, with its opera house, to the isolated Outback and the huge canyons of the Blue Mountains in New South Wales, to the Gold Coast with its luxury hotels, there is something here for everybody. Residents include various animal species, many of them marsupials, including the kangaroo and the koala. The largest bird, the non-flying, but fast-running emu, is also indigenous to Australia.

The first Aborigines arrived here at least 30,000 years ago. Wall paintings that may be 5,000 years old still exist in the Northern Territory. These tribes of native peoples survived for thousands of years without outside contact and developed their own mythology and a complex social order. There are today many aboriginal reserves all over Australia.

It is generally believed that a 16th century Dutch navigator, Willem Janszoon, was the first European to make contact with Australia. Captain James Cook's expedition along the east coast in 1770 was the start of English colonisation and of Australia's modern history. Eighteen years after his arrival, Australia's first settlement at Sydney was founded under Captain Arthur Phillip. An infamous town, Sydney was built by British and Irish convicts to house prisoners sentenced to transportation. Old Sydney has been restored and at The Rocks many convict-built warehouses and pubs can still be seen and visited today.

Both the successful breeding of Merino sheep for their fine wool and the discovery of gold in 1851, contributed to the rapid growth of Australia, particularly in the state of Victoria, where there are many gold rush towns such as Ballarat. In 1854 the Eureka Stockade took place there; it was Australia's only bloody rebellion – now a legend of the underdog against authority.

There is, today, nowhere quite like Australia. It is a land of new experiences – a huge island continent brimming with thriving modern elegant and cosmopolitan cities, vast farmlands, rolling hills, spectacular mountain ranges, vast red deserts and rich pastoral country. There are sandy beaches, rainforests, unique birds, animals and wildflowers.

Discover Aboriginal art, explore Australia's colonial past through its grand Georgian and Victorian buildings as well as the ruins of stark penal settlements. Adventure into the Outback, which is rugged and unspoilt. Uluru (Ayers Rock), in Central Australia, is sacred to the Aborigines and ancient paintings can be seen in the caves around its vast base. In contrast, dine at fine restaurants, shop in style and enjoy harbour or river cruises.

Australia offers many wonderful choices for travellers, with each state and territory providing its own special attractions. Queensland, with its lush, tropical rainforests and the Great Barrier Reef; New South Wales, with its vibrant capital, Sydney, straddling a magnificent harbour; and Canberra, the nation's capital, with its futuristic architecture and picturesque parklands. Victoria's capital, Melbourne, is noted for its cultural life, grand Victorian-era buildings and parks and gardens. Tasmania has splendid wilderness and early colonial buildings. South Australia's wine-growing regions and opal mines are world famous. Western Australia's vastness encompasses sandy beaches, remote mountains and unique wildflowers. And the Northern Territory, stretching from the tropical "Top End" to the rugged Red Centre, famous for Alice Springs and Uluru (Ayers Rock), adds a new dimension to adventure travel.

Why don't you come and say G'Day?

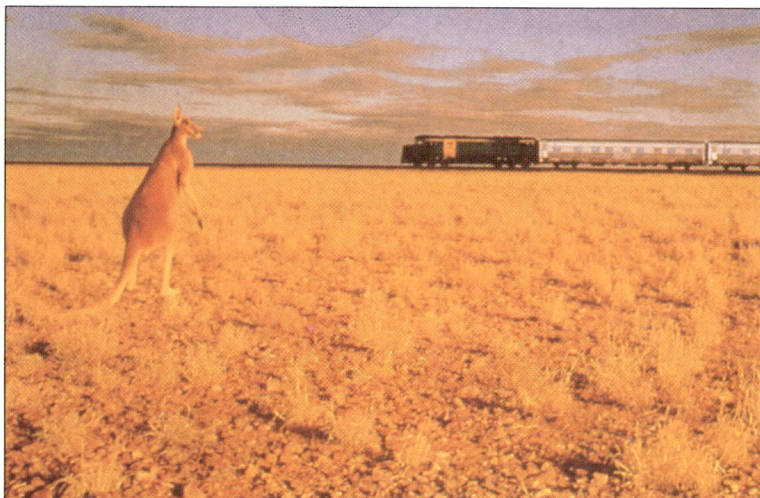

FINDING YOUR WAY

To make your journey as easy as possible, it is important to understand that many people who do not have physical disabilities frequently will need to be guided. Your local travel agent, for example, will need a checklist covering accessible transport to and from departure and arrival airports; assistance at both airports including boarding and deplaning; and information on accessible accommodation.

Make sure your travel agent is a member of ABTA and that they ensure everyone concerned with all aspects of your holiday is aware of your special needs.

SPECIALIST ASSOCIATIONS

These include travel associations and organisations carrying information on holidays for people with disabilities.

HOLIDAY CAR SERVICE
2 Old Bank Chambers
Station Road
Horley
Surrey RH6 9HW
Tel: 0293 774535 Fax: 0293 784647

TRIPSCOPE (London)
The Courtyard
Evelyn Road
London W4 5JL
Tel: 081-994 9294 Fax: 081-994 3618

TRIPSCOPE (Bristol)
Pamwell House
160 Pennywell Road
Bristol
Avon BS5 0TX
Tel: 0272 414094 Fax: 0272 414024

ACCESS TRAVEL (LANCS) LTD
16 Haweswater Avenue
Astley
Lancashire M29 7BL
Tel: 0942 891811 Fax: 0942 891811

The Indian Pacific on its 3-day journey from Sydney to Perth.

ATS TRAVEL
ATS House
1 Tank Hill Road
Purfleet
Essex RM16 1SX
Tel: 0708 863198 Fax: 0708 860514

CHALFONT LINE HOLIDAYS
4 Medway Parade
Perivale
Middlesex UB6 8HA
Tel: 081-997 3799 Fax: 081-991 2892

RADAR
25 Mortimer Street
London W1N 8AB
Tel: 071-637 5400 Fax: 071-637 1827

SPINAL INJURIES ASSOCIATION
76 St. James's Lane
London N10 3DF
Tel: 081-444 2121 Fax: 081-444 3761

Spinal Injuries Association is the leading national organisation of, and for, people with spinal cord injuries in the UK. Its wide range of services gives members an opportunity to experience life to the full. A quarterly journal gives personal reports on holidays and using information supplied by visiting members the association has compiled a comprehensive report on the suitability or otherwise for guests in wheelchairs in hotels throughout the world. Telephone for a free information pack.

MEDICAL ALERT FOUNDATION
12 Bridge Wharf
156 Caledonian Road
London N1 9UU
Tel: 071-833 3035 Fax: 071-278 0647

The Medical Alert identification system (a bracelet or necklet engraved with your medical condition) ensures that wherever you are your condition can be identified. It is particularly relevant in case of major accidents. Life membership costs £30.

15

PHAB
Tavistock House North
Tavistock Square
London WC1H 9HJ
Tel: 071-388 1863
PHAB organises holidays and group
activities in UK and abroad for able-bodied
young people and those with disabilities.

WINGED FELLOWSHIP TRUST
Angel House
Pentonville Road
London N1 9XD
Tel: 071-833 2594

MOBILITY INTERNATIONAL
228 Borough High Street
London SE1 1JX
Tel: 071-403 5688

DISAWAY TRUST
2 Charles Road
Merton Park
London SW19 3BD
Tel: 081-543 3431

ABILITY SOLUTIONS
3 Mossfield
Cobham
Surrey KT11 1DF
Tel and Fax: 0932 866333
Minicom: 0932 862280

DISABILITY NOW
12 Park Crescent
London W1N 4EQ
Tel: 071-636 5020 Fax: 071-436 2601

BRITISH RED CROSS SOCIETY
9 Grosvenor Crescent
London SW1X 7EJ
Tel: 071-235 5454
For information on essential aids.

DISABLED LIVING FOUNDATION
380-384 Harrow Road
London NW9 2HU
Tel: 071-289 6111
For information on essential aids.

CONSULATES

UNITED KINGDOM
HIGH COMMISSION OF THE
COMMONWEALTH OF AUSTRALIA
Australia House
The Strand, London WC2B 4LA
Tel: 071-379 4334 (general) 071-438 8818
(visa) Fax: 071-240 5333. Open weekdays
0900-1700; 1000-1600 for visas

AUSTRALIAN CONSULATE
Chatsworth House
Lever Street, Manchester M1 2DL
Tel: 061-228 1344 Fax: 061-236 4074

AUSTRALIAN CONSULATE
Hobart House
80 Hanover Street, Edinburgh EH2 2DL
Tel: 031-226 6271 Fax: 031-225 1078

NEW ZEALAND HIGH COMMISSION
New Zealand House
80 Haymarket, London SW1Y 4TQ
Tel: 071-930 8422 Fax: 071-839 4580
Open Monday-Friday 1000-1200 and
1400-1600

AUSTRALIA
BRITISH HIGH COMMISSION
Commonwealth House
Yarralumla Canberra ACT 2606
Tel: 06 270 6666
Fax: 06 273 3236
British Consulates in Adelaide, Brisbane,
Darwin, Melbourne, Perth and Sydney are
detailed under each city

**EMBASSY OF THE UNITED
STATES OF AMERICA**
Moonah Place, Canberra ACT 2600
Tel: 06 270 5000 Fax: 06 270 5970
US Consulates in Brisbane, Melbourne, Perth
and Sydney

NEW ZEALAND
AUSTRALIAN HIGH COMMISSION
72-78 Hobson Street, Thorndon
(PO Box 4036), Wellington
Tel: 04 473 6411

AUSTRALIAN CONSULATE GENERAL
Union House
32-38 Quay Street, Auckland
Tel: 04 932 429

BRITISH HIGH COMMISSION
PO Box 1812, 44 Hill Street
Wellington 1
Tel: 04 726 049 Fax: 04 711 974

EMBASSY OF THE UNITED
STATES OF AMERICA
PO Box 1190, 29 Fitzherbert Terrace
Wellington
Tel: 04 722 068 Fax: 04 781 701

CANADIAN HIGH COMMISSION
PO Box 12049, 61 Molesworth Street
Wellington 1
Tel: 04 738 577 Fax: 04 712 082

UNITED STATES OF AMERICA
EMBASSY OF THE
COMMONWEALTH OF AUSTRALIA
1601 Massachusetts Avenue
Washington DC 20036-2273, USA
Tel: 202 797 3000
Fax: 202 797 3168

AUSTRALIAN CONSULATE GENERAL
International Building
635 5th Avenue, New York NY 10020
Tel: 212 245 4000

AUSTRALIAN CONSULATE GENERAL
Suite 2930
321 North Clark Street, Chicago IL 60610
Tel: 312 645 9440

AUSTRALIAN CONSULATE GENERAL
1000 Bishop Street
Honolulu HI 96813
Tel: 808 524 5050

AUSTRALIAN CONSULATE GENERAL
Qantas Building, 360 Post Street
San Francisco CA 94108-4979
Tel: 510 362 6160

AUSTRALIAN CONSULATE GENERAL
Suite 800, 3 Post Oak Central
1990 South Post Oak Boulevard
Houston TX 77056-99976
Tel: 713 629 9131

AUSTRALIAN TOURIST COMMISSION
Suite 1200, 2121 Avenue of the Stars
Los Angeles CA 90067
Tel: 213 552 1988
Fax: 213 552 1215

CANADA
AUSTRALIAN HIGH COMMISSION
Suite 710, 50 O'Connor Street
Ottawa
Ontario K1P 6L2
Tel: 613 236 0841
Fax: 613 236 4376

AUSTRALIAN CONSULATE GENERAL
Suite 314, 3rd Floor, 175 Bloor Street East
Toronto
Ontario M4W 3R8
Tel: 416 323 1155
Fax: 416 323 3910

AUSTRALIAN CONSULATE GENERAL
Trade Office Complex
802-999 Canada Place
Vancouver BC V8C 3E1
Tel: 604 684 1177

AUSTRALIAN TOURIST COMMISSION
2 Bloor Street West
Toronto
Ontario M4W 3E2
Tel: 416 925 9575
Fax: 416 925 9312

NEW ZEALAND HIGH COMMISSION
Suite 727, Metropolitan House
99 Bank Street
Ottawa
Ontario K1P 6G3
Tel: 613 238 5991
Fax: 613 238 5707

17

TRAVEL DETAILS AND GENERAL INFORMATION

AUSTRALIA

Passport and visa requirements
A ten-year passport and a visa is required for all visitors, including USA and Canadian citizens, except NZ passport holders. Apply to the Australian High Commission. Requirements include application form, passport-size photographs, proof of funds for length of stay and return ticket.

Currency
The Australian dollar (A$) = 100 cents. There are no currency restrictions. Most major currencies in traveller-cheque form and major credit cards are accepted.

Climate
Between November and March (spring-summer) it is warm or hot everywhere; tropical in the north and warm with mild nights in the south. From April to September (autumn-winter), north and central areas have warm days, cool nights. In the south there is plenty of sunlight, cool days and some rain. It snows only in the mountainous area of the south-east.

Time
Australia spans three time zones:
NE-SE.   GMT + 10 hours
Central   GMT + 9.5 hours
West   GMT + 8 hours
Specific times are listed for each state.

Electricity
As UK; voltage – 240; frequency – 50Hz. An adaptor is needed for travel items.

MEDICAL NOTES

Equivalent to the UK's National Health Service, Australia's Medicare system covers short-term visitors from the UK, except for pre-existing conditions. To qualify for Medicare you must register at a Medicare office and produce your passport and visa. If urgent treatment is required in hospital registration may be effected afterwards, but it is advisable to register directly upon arrival. Medicare offices are in all major cities, or you can apply by post to PO Box 9822 in any capital city. You will need an internal mailing address and the card will take about three weeks to arrive. Medicare treatment at a public hospital is free, except a nominal charge for prescriptions. If consulting a GP find a practice that Bulk Bills and there will be a small charge. Dental treatment is not covered by Medicare and may be expensive. A check-up prior to departure is recommended. The Marine Stinger and the potentially lethal box jellyfish (sea wasp) are common to the Queensland and Northern Territory coasts from October to May. The best antidote is to apply vinegar within minutes, tie a tourniquet and get to hospital quickly for an anti-venom jab. Saltwater crocodiles are found along the northern coastline. Do not swim in areas about which you are unsure, nor camp near a riverbank in the Outback. If you are confronted in the water, swim away in a zig-zag fashion. If bitten by a venomous snake, apply a bandage firmly above and below the bite. Serum is available at all hospitals. Don't scratch insect bites and always carry an insect repellant. Few spiders bite but the Funnel Web and Black Widow can be nasty. Always seek medical help if bitten. There have been some outbreaks of malaria, especially in Queensland. Keep screens on doors and windows closed, wear long sleeves and trousers at night and use a repellant.

Medications
If you take prescribed drugs (except contraceptives) take a doctor's letter explaining why you need them. It is your responsibility to ascertain what may be taken in and out of countries. The embassy or representatives of the country you are visiting can advise on that country's drug regulations and the Home Office Drugs Branch will advise on UK regulations. (Tel: 071-273 3806). Do not carry non-prescribed drugs without a doctor's letter. Some drugs available over the counter in the UK may be available only on prescription in Australia. Always carry medication with you, do not leave it in the hold in case luggage gets lost. Taking a spare urinal or bed pan might be sensible for emergency use. For wheelchair

breakdown take a spare inner tube, repair kit and a set of wheelchair castors.

Medical Directory

For information, advice and details of immunisation requirements contact:

BRITISH AIRWAYS
Immunisation Service
156 Regent Street, London W1R 5TA
Tel: 071-439 9584/5
Open Monday-Friday 0900-1615, Saturday 1000-1600 No appointment is necessary

BA TRAVEL SHOP
101 Cheapside, London EC2V 6DT
Tel: 071-606 2977
An appointment is necessary

BA TERMINAL
First Floor, Victoria Station
Victoria Place, London SW1W 9SJ
Tel: 071-233 6661
An appointment is necessary
For information only call Regent Street office.

VACCINATION CENTRE
Hospital for Tropical Diseases
4 St. Pancras Way, London NW1 0PE
Tel: 071-388 9600/8989

DEPARTMENT OF HEALTH
International Branch, Hannibal House
Elephant & Castle, London SE1 6TE
Tel: 071-972 2000, ext 6749

MASTA
Medical Advisory Service for Travellers Abroad
Keppel Street, London WC1E 7HT
Tel: 071-631 4408

INSURANCE
TRAVELCARE LIMITED
Tamarville House, 35A High Street
Chislehurst, Kent BR7 5AE
Tel: 081-295 1797 Fax: 081-467 2467
Offers a comprehensive policy, but general travel cover doesn't include wheelchair cover.

DEREK KETTERIDGE & ASSOCS. LTD
2nd Floor, 7A Middle Street
Brighton, East Sussex BN1 1AL
Tel: 0273 720222 Fax: 0273 722799

DKA is a long-established and highly individual company specialising in insurance within the travel industry. They advise that there is no increase in the standard premium for travellers with disability, nor is anyone with a pre-existing medical condition excluded from cover, other than those with a terminal illness. A GP's letter is not normally required. Wheelchairs must be covered under a separate policy.

LEISURECARE INSURANCE SERVICES LTD
Shaftesbury Centre, Percy Street,
Swindon, Wilts SN2 2AZ
Tel: 0793 514199 Fax: 0793 481333
Registered brokers run by travel specialists who offer a Special Care policy for medically disadvantaged travellers, including carer for daily needs; replacement carer where necessary; wheelchair cover up to £1,000 plus normal personal effects; medical equipment on a one-off basis for special items, plus hire charge if items are stolen or damaged beyond use; pre-existing medical conditions are accepted.

HOLIDAY CARE SERVICE
2 Old Bank Chambers, Station Road,
Horley, Surrey RH6 9HW
Tel: 0293 774535 Fax: 0293 784647
Minicom: 0293 776943
Has agreed an insurance policy with a reputable company and can offer advice.

EXTRA SURE HOLDINGS LTD
6 Lloyds Avenue, London EC3N 3AX
Tel: 071-488 9341

M. J. FISH & CO.
3 Riversway Business Village
Navigation Way, Aston, Preston, Lancs PR2 2YP
Tel: 0772 724442

PD ASSOCIATES GROUP LTD
5 Ancells Court, Ancells Business Park
Fleet, Hants GU14 8UY
Tel: 0252 629161
Disabled cover and wheelchair insurance.

PJ HAYMAN TRAVEL INSURANCE
17 Isolly Lane, Petersfield, Hants GU31 4AU
Tel: 0730 260222

19

UK AIRPORTS AND TRANSPORTATION

HEATHROW AIRPORT
HEATHROW TRAVEL-CARE
Room 1214, First Floor
Queen's Building, Heathrow Airport
Hounslow Middx TW6 1JH
Tel: 081-745 7495 (24-hour service)
Office hours: weekdays 0900-1800
weekends 0930-1630

An independent agency with professional
staff and experienced volunteers who are
familiar with the airport environment.
They will assist in any way possible.
Located in the Queen's Building between
Terminal 1 and Terminal 2, their booklet
is well worth obtaining.

Car parking
There are special parking bays at short-
term car parks, long-term parks are
served by a special coach service to
terminals.

Car Park 1: Access to the terminal is via
levels 2 and 6. Spaces for orange badge
holders are situated on level 2 at northern
and southern ends of the car park.

Car Park 1A: Access to terminal is via
level 2. Parking spaces for orange badge
holders are situated on level 2 next to the
walkway bridge to the terminal.

Car Park 2: Access to the terminal is via
level 2. Parking spaces for orange badge
holders are situated on the ground floor,
immediately to the left upon entering the
covered portion of the car park.
A Help Point is available to summon
assistance and is located immediately
beside the parking bays.

Car Park 3: Access to the terminal is via
level 2. Parking spaces for orange badge
holders are situated on the ground floor,
immediately to the left of the kiosks on
the left hand side.
A Help Point is available and is located
immediately to the right hand side of the
parking bays.

Car Park 4: Access to the terminal is via
levels 1 and 4. Parking spaces for orange
badge holders are situated on Level 4 to
the left of the entry landing. A Help Point
is found next to the car park pay station
directly opposite the parking bays.

*For latest details of all car parking facilities at
Heathrow phone 081-745 7160.*

Passenger Services
There are specially trained BAA Passenger
Services Staff at the airport who offer free
assistance. They can be called from one of
the Help Points situated outside all the
terminal buildings. There are two phones,
a red one to call a Skycap porter, and a
grey/ beige telephone for passenger
services. If you require special assistance
lift the grey phone; if assistance with
luggage is needed the Help Point staff will
arrange for Skycap assistance free of
charge. This is a dedicated portering
service for all passengers, and operates in
all four terminals.

Facilities
Each terminal is equipped with ramps
and lifts located close to stairs or
escalators. Special WC facilities are
accessible and clearly sign-posted. Public
telephones in each terminal are at a
practical height.
Each airline makes its own arrangements
for the care of passengers in wheelchairs,
so contact with the airline should be
made well in advance of travel date.

Terminal 1
Departures: Check-in desks are in the
centre of the floor. All desks are at quite a
low level. Departures for international
flights are on the right where there is a
24-hour Thomas Cook bureau de change.
On the far left-hand side are post boxes
and Cafe One that sells beers and wines,
meals and snacks and a bar, all easily
accessible to wheelchair users. The
restaurants are on a mezzanine floor

above departures, reached by a lift located on the left-hand side behind the retail outlet, currently Shirt Factory. A unisex, accessible WC is adjacent to Cafe One.

Arrivals: International passengers arrive on the right-hand side. The information desk (open 0700-2230) is on the left-hand side. Left luggage is on a mezzanine floor and accessible by a lift near the restaurant area. There is a unisex WC in landside arrivals hall, and also in airside international baggage reclaim hall.

Terminal 2

Departures: Check-in on the ground floor. There is a lift on the right-hand side to first floor departures.
On the first floor the information desk (open 0700-2200) is in the centre next to the meeting point.
There is a bank in the centre of the first floor behind the stairs. To the right of the stairs are branches of WH Smiths and Boots, in which there is a pharmacy. Restaurants and the main shopping area are in the Plaza up the stairs in the centre of the first floor. You can reach this area by lifts situated to the left and right of the stairs. In this area there are accessible WCs but assistance may be needed.

Arrivals: Are also on the first floor with departures with lifts and ramps down to the ground floor for exit, on your right as you come out of the arrivals door. The meeting point is on your right.

Terminal 3

Terminal 3 is divided into two adjacent buildings, one covers departures and the other arrivals.

Departures: Check-in is on the ground floor, with departure gates, shops and restaurants on the first floor.
Lifts are situated at each end of the building, and the information desk is on the ground floor in Block B on the left-hand side. It is not very conspicuous. There is a bureau de change located on the first floor.

Arrivals: Passengers arrive on the ground floor and people with mobility problems may wait there rather than in the upstairs waiting area. The information desk is located in the centre of the ground floor next to the post boxes.
On the right-hand side is a bar and self-service restaurant where everything, except a smokers' corner, is situated on one level.

Terminal 4

Departures: The departure area consists mainly of check-in desks. BA passengers with a disability may check-in at desk 78 on the right-hand side. All desks are quite low-level. The Travelex bureau de change has a Barclays Bank cash dispenser open 0900-1730 Monday to Saturday and 0900-1300 Sundays.
There is a pharmacy on the right-hand side and a bar and restaurant in the main refreshment area on the mezzanine floor. For departing passengers there are more extensive facilities airside, and it is worth going straight through passport control once you have checked-in.

Arrivals: The information desk is located at the arrivals area on the ground floor. On the left-hand side of the arrivals area, next to left baggage, there are post boxes and nearby a small cafe/bar. There is also a cafe on the right-hand side.

Going airside

In Terminal 1 there is a considerable distance to travel between check-in and the gaterooms. In Terminal 2, there are accessible WCs between check-in and departure gates. In Terminal 3 the distance between the departure lounge and the gates is particularly long. No problems envisaged airside in Terminal 4.

Transfer

The Help Bus with wheelchair lift connects all terminals between 0600-2300. Call 5185 on the Help Bus phones. There are a limited number of Help Buses so allow time for possible delays.

Airbus service

All buses on the Airbus routes between Heathrow and central London are equipped with hydraulic lifts and have space for wheelchair passengers. Victoria, Paddington, Euston, King's Cross, Liverpool Street and Waterloo are all linked on this service. Contact London Transport Unit for Disabled Passengers on 071-227 3312/3299.

Underground service

London Underground advise that people with disabilities can use the Underground, but only 40 stations are wheelchair accessible. For information telephone 071-918 3312.

GATWICK AIRPORT
GATWICK TRAVEL-CARE
Gatwick Airport
West Sussex RH6 0NP
Tel: 0293 504283 or dial 4283 on any white or grey Helpline telephone in the airport.
Open 0930-1730 weekdays, 0930-1630 weekends.

Car parking

For short- or long-stay parking passengers are advised to seek advance information:
North Terminal, Europarks Tel: 0293 502737
South Terminal, APCOA Parking. Tel: 0293 502896.
Bays are reserved in both multi-storey car parks giving level access into terminals. Courtesy phones are available.

Facilities

For wheelchair passengers, ramps and/or lifts are provided in both terminals. There is reserved seating in the check-in areas, accessible Unisex WCs in both terminals and telephones are at an accessible height. Any queries, contact Disabled Assistance:
British Airways Tel: 0293 666291
Gatwick Handling South:
Tel: 0293 502337
Gatwick Handling North:
Tel: 0293 507147
Servisair: Tel: 0293 507320.

British Rail

The Gatwick Express service from London Victoria to Gatwick is fully accessible to those in wheelchairs. Advance notice is not required. NO ACCESSIBLE WC. Refreshments can be brought to your seat when there is a buffet. The service runs every 15 minutes during the day with a journey time of 30 minutes and hourly at nights taking 45 minutes. British Airways and Air New Zealand luggage can be checked in at the airlines' offices at Victoria.

Stationlink

Stationlink is a circular service operating between all major London rail terminii.

Coach and bus

Gatwick Coach Station is located on the ground floor of the South Terminal. Courtesy phones to handling agents are near to set-down points.
Flightline 777 from London Victoria Tel: 081-668 7261.
Flightlink from Birmingham Tel: 021-554 5232.
National Express 825 from Manchester Tel: 071-730 0202.
For details call Bus and Coach Council Tel: 071-831 7546.

Accessible taxis for home/airport transfer

These taxi companies take people sitting in wheelchairs and no transfer from chairs is required.

LONDON AREA
GATWICK AIRPORT CARS
Tel: 0293 562291

COMPUTER CAB
Tel: 071-286 7009

BLACK RADIO TAXIS
Tel: 081-209 0266

DIAL-A-CAB
Tel: 071-253 5000

Prior notice, a suitable vehicle and the right price equals smiles all round.

BIRMINGHAM
BB TAXIS
Tel: 021-233 3030

TAO TAXIS
Tel: 021-427 8888

BRISTOL
ACE TAXIS
Tel: 0272 777477

PETER TAXIS
Tel: 0272 714141

EDINBURGH
CENTRAL RADIO TAXIS
Tel: 031-229 2468

CAPITAL CASTLE CABS
Tel: 031-228 2555

GLASGOW
TAO TAXIS
Tel: 041-332 7070

LEEDS
STREAMLINE TAXIS
Tel: 0532 443322

LIVERPOOL (MERSEYSIDE)
DAVEY LIVER CABS
Tel: 051-709 4646

MERSEY CABS
Tel: 051-733 3393

LUTON
HALFWAY TAXIS
Tel: 0582 562 562

MANCHESTER
MANTAX
Tel: 061-236 5133

NORWICH
JOHN ARMSTRONG WIGGINS TAXIS
Tel: 0603 762222

NOTTINGHAM
STREAMLINE TAXIS
Tel: 0602 475964

PLYMOUTH
PLYMOUTH TAXIS
Tel: 0752 606060

US AND CANADIAN AIRPORTS WITH DIRECT SERVICE TO AND FROM AUSTRALASIA

HONOLULU INTERNATIONAL AIRPORT
Tel: 808 836 6411

Car Parking
Designated spaces are reserved in the international and inter-island car parks.

Facilities
Terminal: Carriers use Skycap (porter) services to assist passengers with special needs. WCs include wide stand and grab bars. All telephones are accessible. There is a 24-hour medical clinic in the garden area on the ground floor, telephone: 808 831 5025. Loading bridges are used in both terminals. The following offer suitable vehicles, but require prior notice.

HANDI-CABS OF THE PACIFIC
PO Box 22428, Honolulu HAW 96823
Tel: 808 524 3866

AVIS RENT-A-CAR
417 Lel Street, Honolulu HAW 96820
Tel: 808 834 5536

HERTZ RENT A CAR
PO Box 29240, Honolulu HAW 96820
Freephone: 1-800 654 3011

LOS ANGELES AIRPORT
Tel: 310 646 5260

Car Parking
Extra-wide, specifically designed spaces in all parking lots on every level adjacent to lifts. A free shuttle service to and from terminals is available at Lot C on 96th Street, east of Sepulveda Boulevard and Lot B at 11th Street and La Cienaga. Lift-equipped shuttles operate between Lots B and C and terminals. On request a van with hydraulic lift is available from Lot C.

Facilities
Transfer: A lift-equipped free shuttle bus is on a continuous loop around the Central Terminal, tel: 310 646 6402 or 310 646 8021. Terminals: There are rampways from street to pavement level in front of terminals. Lifts are near public stairways and escalators inside the terminals. All terminals provide public phones wide enough for a wheelchair. There are male and female WCs in all terminals with extra-wide stalls and grab bars. There are unisex accessible restrooms in Terminal 2 on the departure level and Terminal 6 on the arrival level. In all terminals coffee shops and snack bars are accessible and designed for easy wheelchair access to counters and tables. There is a first aid station on the departure level of the Tom Bradley International Terminal open daily from 0700-2300, tel: 310 215 6000. There is a Travellers' Aid facility at several booths on the arrival level, tel: 310 646 2270. All buses on the FlyAway Bus Service between San Fernando Valley and the airport have wheelchair lifts.

Carriers within Central Terminal Area
Tom Bradley International: Air France, Air New Zealand, Alitalia, British Airways, Canadian Airlines, Cathay Pacific, Garuda, Iberia, JAL, Lufthansa, Malaysia, Philippine, Qantas, SAS, Singapore, Swissair, Thai.
Terminal 1: USAir
Terminal 2: Air Canada, KLM, Northwest, Virgin Atlantic
Terminal 3: TWA
Terminal 5: Delta
Terminal 6: Continental
Terminal 7: United
Domestic carriers are in Terminal 4

SAN FRANCISCO AIRPORT
Tel: 415 761 0800
Fax: 415 876 7875

Car Parking
There is limited short-term parking (72 hours) in the designated terminal courtyards

– No.1 (South Terminal) and No. 3 (International Terminal). There are 39 reserved spaces on level 2 of the garage, grouped at each of the seven lift areas. (Directions signposted on approach road.)

SOUTH TERMINAL AIRLINES
Area A: Air Canada, Southwest, USAir.
Area B: Alaska domestic, America West, American Airlines, Reno Air, TWA.
Area C: Delta, Northwest domestic.

INTERNATIONAL TERMINAL AIRLINES
Area D: Aeroflot, Air China, Air France, British Airways, Japan Airlines, Lufthansa, Mexicana, Northwest International, Qantas, Philippine, Singapore, United International.

NORTH TERMINAL AIRLINES
Area E: American and Canadian Airlines.
Area F: United domestic.

Facilities
All terminals: All telephones and white courtesy telephones, plus all lifts and WCs are accessible. There is a medical clinic on the International Terminal lower level, open 24 hours every day. Dial 7 0444 on a white courtesy phone. Several carriers offer disabled services between the airport and downtown. Yellow Van Service tel: 415 282 2300; Medi-Van tel: 415 468 4300; Super Shuttle tel: 415 558 8500; Sam Trans 3B, connects with Daly City BART. Most carriers require several hours' notice, as not all vehicles are lift-equipped. Reserve in advance.

VANCOUVER INTERNATIONAL AIRPORT
Tel: 604 276 6500
North America's most accessible airport for those with disabilities. A barrier-free consultant was involved in the design of the new international terminal.

Car Parking
There are 12 designated spaces in the main parking lot, 12 in economy; four on level 3 departures; two on level 2 arrivals and two on level 1 international arrivals.

Facilities
Terminals: All bars, restaurants, toilets, lifts, telephones and shops are wheelchair accessible. Wheelchairs are available from the carriers. There are no medical facilities, but an emergency response team is two minutes from the terminal. All 120 passenger check-in counters at the new terminal will have slide-out shelves for those in wheelchairs, distances between vital areas will be minimal and narrow wheelchairs available for airplane access. The terminal is scheduled for completion in June 1996.

25

INTERNATIONAL AIRLINES

INCAD – Incapacitated Passengers Handling Advice – is now normally required by long-haul airlines for passengers in wheelchairs. Part One covers operations – whether individual help is required to get on and off planes and assistance required at your destination. Part Two covers medical clearance.

BRITISH AIRWAYS
Head Office: PO Box 10
Heathrow Airport
Hounslow Middx TW6 2JA
Tel: 081-759 5511 (administration)

081-897 4000 (reservations)
BA offer a wheelchair and expert lifting facility that must be booked in advance. On Boeing 737, 747 and 757s seats with lifting armrests at certain aisle positions are being fitted. 747s carry a wheelchair for use in the passenger cabin. Contact BA's Medical Officer for Passenger Services on 081-562 5208 at Heathrow and 0293 27890 at Gatwick.
Care in the Air by the Air Transport Users Committee gives useful advice for wheelchair users.
Copies are free, tel: 071-242 3882.

BRITISH AIRWAYS OFFICES WITHIN AUSTRALIA

ADELAIDE: Tel: 238 2138
ALICE SPRINGS: Tel: 505 222
BRISBANE: Tel: 223 3123
BROOME: Tel: 921 101
CANBERRA: Tel: 081 13722
DARWIN: Tel: 801 222
HOBART: Tel: 347 433
KALGOORLIE: Tel: 212 277
MELBOURNE: Tel: 603 1133
PERTH: Tel: 483 7711
PORT HEDLAND: Tel: 731 777
SYDNEY: Tel: 258 3300

BRITISH AIRWAYS OFFICES WITHIN NEW ZEALAND

AUCKLAND: Tel: 367 7500
CHRISTCHURCH: Tel: 79 2503
WELLINGTON: Tel: 472 7327

QANTAS AIRWAYS LTD
Head Office, UK administration and reservations:
395-403 King Street, London W6 9NJ
Tel: 081-846 0466 (administration)
0345 747767(reservations) Fax: 081-748
8551 Ticketing Office: 91 Regent Street,
London W1. Tel: 071-846 0466
Try to obtain a copy of the Qantas Travel
Care booklet. Passengers with disabilities
are identified by the computer code
WCHC on their reservation, and your GP
must complete a medical form. Large
wheelchairs must be carried in the hold,
but wheelchairs are provided on board.
Power-driven wheelchairs with spillable
batteries are restricted articles and can be
carried only under certain conditions.
Passengers with disabilities are allocated
aisle seats where possible because some
have lifting armrests that allow
passengers to slide from wheelchair
directly onto aircraft seat. Specially
designed toilets are provided on the
Longreach (Boeing 747-400), Extended
Upper Deck (Boeing 747-300) and all Boeing
767 aircraft. Ground staff at all airports will
meet you with a wheelchair. Early boarding
is customary and baggage has Special
Assistance tags. Most airports have skychairs for boarding and disembarking
where aerobridges are not available.

QANTAS OFFICES WITHIN AUSTRALIA

ADELAIDE: Tel: 237 8541
BRISBANE: Tel: 234 3747
CAIRNS: Tel: 008 177 767*
CANBERRA: Tel: 250 8211
DARWIN: Tel: 008 802 710*
GEELONG: Tel: 008 112 121*
HOBART: Tel: 008 112 121*
MELBOURNE: Tel: 805 0111
NEWCASTLE: Tel: 008 112 121*
PERTH: Tel: 225 2222
SURFERS PARADISE: Tel: 008 177 767*
SYDNEY: Tel: 957 0111
TOWNSVILLE: Tel: 008 177 767*
WOLLONGONG: Tel: 282 318
*These numbers are available toll-free
only when dialling within Australia.

AIR NEW ZEALAND
Head Office: Air New Zealand House
1 Queen Street, Auckland
Tel: 09 379 7515 Fax: 09 388 0575

London: New Zealand House
Haymarket, London SW1Y 4TE
Tel: 081-846 9595 (administration)
071-741 2299 (reservations)
Fax: 071-741 4645
An entry permit is required for tourists
with any kind of disability.
Medical clearance is not normally
required for either Air New Zealand or
Mount Cook airlines, but if passengers
are undergoing medical treatment or
rehabilitation, a Medical Fitness Form
(MEDA) will have to be completed. Fully
rehabilitated paraplegics will not require
a MEDA form. Quadriplegics need prior
clearance for all international flights and
MUST BE INDIVIDUALLY ESCORTED.
Special requirements should be notified
at time of reservation. Passengers should
check in at least 30 minutes prior to
normal check-in time. Cabin crews are
trained to help and wheelchairs for
inflight mobility are standard equipment
on Air New Zealand 747 and 767 aircraft.
The Newton Skychair has been designed
for in-flight use and enables passengers
to move easily to and from their seats and
to WC facilities. Seat belt extensions,

quadriplegic harnesses and padded leg rests are also helpful. Movable armrests are installed in certain seats on board 747, 767 and 737 aircraft. All 744/762 and 762 aircraft have specially adapted WC facilities. Specially designed stretchers can be fitted in the aircraft and curtained off.

Wheelchairs are provided at all airports served by Air New Zealand. Wheelchairs must be clearly labelled and non-spillable batteries disconnected and terminals insulated to prevent accidental short circuit. If a chair cannot be stowed in an upright position, the battery must be removed and stowed separately.

Contact Air New Zealand for a copy of Air Travel for People with Disabilities.

SINGAPORE AIRLINES
London Office:
580-586 Chiswick High Road
London W4 5RB
Tel: 081-995 4901 (administration)
081-747 0007 (reservations)

Singapore Airlines offers passengers with disabilities seating in a specific section of the aircraft that allows for ease of movement without inconveniencing other passengers. The airline provides ambulances, wheelchairs and oxygen tanks, but asks that bookings and requests for extra requirements be made as far in advance as possible.

There is no special check-in for passengers in wheelchairs, except at Singapore Changi Airport.

Wheelchairs are provided at all airports to transfer passengers from the check-in counter to the aircraft. Passengers may also travel between check-in and aircraft in their own wheelchairs if they prefer. Aerobridges are used wherever available. Skychairs are currently available on seven of the Megatop aircraft – Boeing 747-400. There are plans to introduce skychairs to the rest of the Megatop fleet. Seat-belt extensions are available and leg rests in first and business class.

There are certain rows of seats on the aircraft that have removable armrests. At present, WCs on board are NOT

designed to accommodate skychairs.
IF AT THE TIME OF RESERVATION A MEDICAL FORM NEEDS TO BE COMPLETED, THE FORM MUST BE COMPLETED BY THE PASSENGER'S DOCTOR AND SUBMITTED TO SINGAPORE AIRLINES' COMPANY DOCTOR FOR CLEARANCE.

GARUDA INDONESIA
Room 623, North Office Block
Gatwick Airport, Gatwick Sussex RH6 0NP
Tel: 0293 502035 (administration)
071-486 3011 (reservations)
Fax: 0293 567719

Garuda do not produce special literature for disabled passengers. Medical forms are required. All types of wheelchair may be transported in the aircraft hold. All passengers requiring assistance can request this upon check-in, and no earlier check-in time is required. The airline provides either wheelchair assistance or a buggy from check-in to boarding. Skychairs are not available on the aircraft, neither do any of the armrests lift to enable lateral transfer from wheelchair to seat. There are no extended seat belts or quadriplegic belts available. None of the aircraft has specially designed WC facilities.

Stoma masks and leg support bridges are available only in club class.

UNITED AIRLINES
United House
Southern Perimeter Road
Heathrow Airport
Hounslow Middx TW6 3LP
Tel: 081-990 9900 Fax: 081-759 7019

United fly from Los Angeles to Sydney and Auckland. Connecting flights also for Brisbane and Melbourne. A medical form is not required for non-ambulatory wheelchair passengers, but medical clearance is required through the airlines' local company doctor. Extra time is required at check-in if passengers have wet-cell, battery-driven wheelchairs to allow for special stowage of the battery. Passengers may either transfer to a United-supplied wheelchair at check-in or

27

remain in their own chair until the departure gate.
Assistance is available at check-in but not at roadside. Assistance is also available to get passengers comfortably settled in their seats, but not once on board. Skychairs are available on all United aircraft. Adapted WC facilities are available on 747, 757, 767 and DC10 aircraft but not on 727 and 737 aircraft.

CANADIAN AIRLINES INTERNATIONAL
1st Floor, Rothschild House
Whitgift Centre
Croydon
Surrey CR9 3HN
Tel: 081-667 0666 Fax: 081-688 2997
CAI operate from Vancouver to Sydney, Melbourne and Auckland.
CAI's entire fleet has retractable arm rests in economy class, and all aircraft on international routes have specially equipped washrooms (except DC10s). They are on the left-hand side of the main passenger cabin and equipped with features allowing for transfer from a folding wheelchair including special doors, fixed grab handles, fold-down assist handles with which to operate mirror light, lever taps and privacy curtains.
When making reservations, CAI agents will advise on optimum travel schedule, routeing and facilities.
Once checked in, passengers are escorted by CIA personnel (at Toronto and Vancouver) or in conjunction with local airport agents. CIA hold a stock of wheelchairs for passengers unable to use airport buggies. Travellers in manually operated wheelchairs may remain seated in them until the boarding gate.

CRITERIA FOR LISTED HOTELS AND CODES

The publishers are extremely grateful for assistance given by the Spinal Injuries Association, Holiday Care Service, PHAB, and RADAR in putting together the stringent criteria form that was sent to over 500 hotels in the Australasia region. Many of the hotels courteously responded advising that they did not meet all the criteria and others simply did not reply indicating that they were not suitable, although initially appearing to be accessible.
We would stress that only those properties that matched up to the criteria on the form in every aspect have been included in the *Smooth Ride Guide to Australia and New Zealand*, except where there are specific notes on certain aspects of the property. In these cases owners or managers had expressed a deep interest in catering for guests in wheelchairs, and their facilities almost met the stringent criteria.
We fully acknowledge that we have relied on forms being completed truthfully, but however we do feel that our small selection of hotel accommodation is as definitive as is possible.
The telephone code from the UK to Australia is 010 61 and to New Zealand 010 64. These codes must be dialled before dialling the specific hotel number shown. Hotel rates are given in Australian/New Zealand dollars.
NOTE: These rates are approximate, and give an indication only.
Where the hotel belongs to a chain, the codes set out below indicate the UK central reservation number of that chain. All hotels listed have been approached individually and have completed a stringent criteria questionnaire. The following specifications have been applied to every hotel.
Most accessible approach: Specific area for parking for the physically impaired. Ground floor, with either no steps or ramp of slight gradient only.
Door width, both outer and in inner lobby, if applicable, at least 75cm wide.
Passageways: Passageway widths throughout property at least 120cm.
Reception area: Ground floor and flat, or first floor with lift access (see lifts

for details). Door width into area at least 75cm. Some sections of the reception desk no more than 80cm in height, or alternative approach to easy check-in for those in wheelchairs.

Lifts: Car halt must be flush with floor level. Approach must be flat without steps. Doors should be automatic. Call buttons should be less than 140cm above floor level, both inside and outside the lift. Lift car should be 80cm or more wide, and 120cm or more deep.

Lounge areas: Either on ground floor or accessible by lift with level approach into room, no steps. Door width at least 75cm.

Restaurant: Either on ground floor or accessible by lift with level approach into room, no steps. Door width at least 75cm.

Adapted bedrooms: Either on ground floor or accessible by lift with level access and no steps. Free space within bedroom

of at least 120cm x 120cm. Space adjacent to bed at least 80cm. Door handles and switches easily reachable. **Bathrooms:** Level access from bedroom with no steps. Free space of at least 70cm for sideways transfer into bath of 80cm. **Showers:** Level access from either bedroom or bathroom without steps. Support rails and shower seat required. Door handles, light switches and shower controls not more than 140cm above floor level.

WC facilities: Either in bathroom or, if separate, with level access and no steps. If separate, free space must be at least 70cm, with measurement clear of door swing. Door handles and light switches less than 140cm above floor level. Support rails beside WC. Space for sideways transfer to WC of at least 75cm. Rim of WC not more than 50cm above floor level.

HOTEL CODES

BW – BEST WESTERN
Tel: 081-541 0033 Fax: 081-546 1638

CHI – CHOICE HOTELS INTERNATIONAL (incl. QUALITY INNS)
Tel: 0800 444444 Fax: 071-928 4762

FL – FLAG INTERNATIONAL
Tel: 081-543 4400 Fax: 081-543 2224

HDI – HOLIDAY INN INTERNATIONAL
Tel: 0800 897119 Fax: 081-754 7551

HH – HILTON HOTELS
Tel: 0800 289303 Fax: 0923 218548

HYA – HYATT HOTELS
Tel: 0345 581666 Fax: 081-785 4572

LHW – LEADING HOTELS OF THE WORLD
Tel: 0800 181123 Fax: 071-353 1904

MAR – MARRIOTT HOTELS AND RESORTS
Tel: 071-581 9840 Fax: 071-591 1128

MELIA – MELIA/SOL HOTELS
Tel: 0800 282720 Fax: 071-916 3431

NH – NIKKO HOTELS
Tel: 0800 282502 Fax: 071-724 9180

NOV – NOVOTEL WORLDWIDE
Tel: 081-748 4580 Fax: 081-741 0672

PP – PAN PACIFIC HOTELS AND RESORTS
Tel: 071-491 3812 Fax: 071-323 1791

RAD – RADISSON HOTELS
Tel: 0800 191991 Fax: 081-759 8422

RAM – RAMADA INTERNATIONAL HOTELS AND RESORTS
Tel: 0800 181737 Fax: 0293 823923

SH – SHERATON HOTELS
Tel: 0800 353535 Fax: 071-731 0532

SPHC – SOUTHERN PACIFIC HOTEL CORPORATION
Tel: 071-240 1937 Fax: 071-240 2943

WH – WESTIN HOTELS
Tel: 071-408 0636 Fax: 071- 408 0268

30

The origin of the word "Pom" or "Pommie" is derived, so D H Lawrence tells us in his book Kangaroo, from the pomegranate, rhyming slang for immigrant, plus the fact that Brits who have just arrived turn as red in the sun as pomegranates.

AUSTRALIA

MAJOR UK TOURIST BOARD

AUSTRALIAN TOURIST COMMISSION
Gemini House
10-18 Putney Hill
London SW15 6AA
Tel: 081-780 2227 Fax: 081-780 1496

THRUWAY DOMESTIC TRANSPORTATION

AIRLINES

ANSETT AIRLINES
Head Office:
501 Swanston Street
Melbourne 3001
Victoria

UK Office:
4th Floor Heathcote House
20 Savile Row
London W1X 2AN
Tel: 071-434 4071 Fax: 071-434 4433

A brochure outlining facilities inflight and on the ground – *Being disabled should not make it any harder to fly* – is available. Ansett also offer a service called Ansacare, a requirement of membership being that at least one return flight or two single flights a year must be undertaken. Details of special travelling needs are held on a nationwide computer system so when booking your flight you quote your Ansacare number and all arrangements will be made. Ansacare passengers must check in 45 minutes prior to departure. Passengers are transferred to a customised wheelchair that allows for movement down the aircraft aisle. Facilities are available for clinical air pumps (12-volt dc supply only), Stoma masks and leg support bridges. An all-weather module for boarding assistance is used at terminals where aerobridges are not available. Boeing 767 aircraft include specially designed WCs with easy access, removable armrests and stretcher fittings.

G'DAY PASS
Ansett Australia Airlines, Eastwest and Ansett New Zealand have joined forces to promote this excellent pass when travelling around Australasia.
Valid in conjunction with any international carrier, each coupon is under £60, (excluding Perth and Hayman Island that cost £80), and you must buy a minimum of two. Children aged 2-11 inclusive pay 67 percent of the adult fare, and rates are guaranteed until end March 1994.
If travelling after that time, check the appropriate fare with your travel agent. It is necessary to book and pay for all internal flights prior to arrival and full refund is permitted prior to commencement of travel only.
Cities available on the G'Day Pass include: Australia – Adelaide, Alice Springs, Uluru (Ayers Rock), Brisbane, Cairns, Canberra, Coolangatta (Gold Coast), Darwin, Grove, Hamilton Island, Hobart, Launceston, Mackay, Melbourne, Perth, Rockhampton, Sydney, Townsville. New Zealand – Auckland, Blenheim, Christchurch, Dunedin, Invercargill, Nelson, Palmerston North, Queenstown, Rotorua, Wellington, Whangarei, Whakatane.

RAILWAYS

Steel plates are available at all major stations for improved access from platform to train. The corridors of most interstate trains are too narrow for the standard wheelchair, but collapsible chairs are available at all capital city rail stations. Special wheelchairs are available for use on Indian Pacific and The Ghan services. Meals are served in sleeping compartments if more practical.

The Ghan, overnight from Adelaide to Alice Springs, provides special wheelchairs on board.

UK rail booking agents
LONGHAUL LEISURAIL
PO Box 113
Peterborough PE1 1LE
Tel: 0733 51780 Fax: 0733 505451

Australian rail information
RAIL AUSTRALIA
1 Richmond Road
Keswick SA 5035
Tel: 08 217 4321 Fax: 08 217 4567

RAIL AUSTRALIA
c/o ATS Tours
Suite 3101, 100 N 1st Street
Burbank CA 91502
Tel: 818 841 1030

RAIL AUSTRALIA
c/o Goway Travel Ltd
Suite 409
402 W Pender Street
Vancouver BC V68 1T6

RAIL AUSTRALIA
Goway Travel Ltd
Suite 2001, 2300 Yonge Street
Toronto ON M4P 1E4
Tel: 416 322 1034

Trains
INDIAN PACIFIC
Three times a week from Sydney to Perth.
Journey time three days.

MELBOURNE SYDNEY EXPRESS
Overnight

THE GHAN
Adelaide to Alice Springs – overnight

OVERLAND
Melbourne to Adelaide – overnight

BRISBANE LIMITED EXPRESS
Brisbane to Sydney – overnight

CANBERRA MONARO EXPRESS AND XPT
Canberra to Sydney – five hours

SUNLANDER AND QUEENSLANDER
Brisbane to Cairns – one-and-a-half days

PROSPECTOR
Perth to Kalgorrlie – eight hours

VINELANDER
Melbourne to Mildura – overnight

SUNLINK
Melbourne to Mildura – daytime

THE SPIRIT OF CAPRICORN
Brisbane to Rockhampton – overnight

XPT
Sydney to Murwillumbah – overnight

COACHES
Major cities are linked by a good national coach system. All coach companies recommend that when making a reservation they are informed of any disability and specific requirements of the traveller. No coaches are fitted with lifts, and many are not suitable for carrying those with impaired mobility.

AUSTRALIAN COACHLINES
96 Victoria Street
Brisbane QLD 4101
Tel: 07 840 9300 Fax: 07 844 7017
Australian Coachlines operate Greyhound, Pioneer and Bus Australia and although not catering specifically for wheelchair passengers, the company advises they are ready, willing and able to assist in any way possible.

AUSTRALIAN COACHLINES
Austravel
51 East 42nd Street
New York

NY 10017
Tel: 800 633 3404
Austravel has branches in Chicago, Houston and San Francisco.

AUSTRALIAN COACHLINES
See Goway Travel, under Railways above.

GREYHOUND INTERNATIONAL AND PIONEER EXPRESS
Sussex House, London Road
East Grinstead
West Sussex RH19 1LD
Tel: 0342 317317 Fax: 0342 328519
We found Greyhound singularly unhelpful. It is essential that wheelchairs are collapsible as no assistance is given in getting on or off coaches. Some degree of mobility is necessary unless accompanied.

CAR HIRE
HERTZ RENT A CAR
44 O'Dea Avenue
Waterloo
Sydney NSW 2017
Tel: 02 318 8710 Fax: 02 662 2775

AVIS AUSTRALIA
110-112 Christie Street
St. Leonards
Sydney NSW 2065
Tel: 02 437 5755 Fax: 02 906 1624

BUDGET RENT-A-CAR
UK Office:
41 Marlowes
Hemel Hempstead
Herts HP1 1LD
Tel: 0800 181181 Fax: 0442 230757

All three companies offer some cars in Australian outlets equipped with hand controls. Advance reservations essential.

TAXIS
Full details under each state.
A fleet of wheelchair-accessible taxis is available in each city, with the exception of Hobart, Tasmania.
It is advisable to book 24 hours in advance and indicate that you are a visitor in a wheelchair.

AUSTRALIAN CAPITAL TERRITORY (NSW)

Australia's National Capital, located between Sydney and Melbourne. (See Canberra.)

Time zone
October-March: GMT + 11 hours
April-September: GMT + 10 hours

TOURIST BOARDS
AUSTRALIAN TOURIST COMMISSION
Gemini House
10-18 Putney Hill
London SW15
Tel: 081-780 2227 Fax: 081-780 1496

ACT TOURISM COMMISSION
Level 8, CBS Tower
Corner Akuna and Bunda Streets
Canberra ACT 2601
Tel: 06 205 0666 Fax: 06 205 0629

SUPPORT ORGANISATIONS
AUSTRALIAN COUNCIL FOR THE
REHABILITATION OF THE DISABLED (ACROD)
33 Thesiger Court
Deakin ACT 2600
Tel: 06 282 4333 Fax: 06 281 3488
A support organisation for those with disabilities in Australia that provides access to information sources and facilities.

PARAPLEGIC QUADRIPLEGIC ASSOCIATION
(KOOMARI)
Tel: 06 806 143

INDEPENDENT LIVING CENTRE
24 Parkinson Street
Weston ACT 2611
Tel: 06 205 1900 Fax: 06 205 1906
This is a community service of the ACT government that provides information on equipment and resources.

NICAN (National Organisations for People with Disabilities)
PO Box 407
Curtin ACT 2605
Tel: 06 285 3713 Fax: 06 285 3717
National directory of organisations providing sport and recreation activities. It includes travel agents and tour operators who can arrange accessible holidays.

Canberra – a capital setting.

ACT & REGIONAL DISABLED SPORT AND
RECREATION ASSOCIATION
Po Box 412
Dickson ACT 2602
Tel: 06 249 6965 Fax: 06 257 3018

CANBERRA TOURISM DEVELOPMENT CENTRE
Tel: 06 456 464 Fax: 06 473 228

AIRPORTS
CANBERRA HAS NO
INTERNATIONAL AIRPORT

CANBERRA DOMESTIC ONLY
Tel: 062 275 5411 (airport)
062 275 5518 (reservations)

Car parking
There is a designated space area reserved
for those in wheelchairs. Telephone
airline passenger and flight information
at the airport, transfer arrangements will
be made to take you to the terminal.

Facilities
Terminal: Access is from road level by
kerb crossovers onto the pavement and
through automatic doors. Accessible
cocktail and refreshment bars are
opposite the passenger lounge. Male and
female WCs are on the ground floor, each
side of the cocktail bar and snack bar.
First aid facilities are available, but there
are no telephones at the correct height,
so contact airline staff for assistance.
Oxygen is available from Ansett and
further supplies can be obtained from
the aircraft if it is on the tarmac. An
RAAF doctor can be in attendance within
ten minutes.

AIRLINE OFFICES
ANSETT
4 Mort Street
Canberra ACT
Tel: 06 245 1111

QUANTAS
Jolimont Centre
Northbourne Avenue
Canberra ACT
Tel: 06 268 3333

ACCESSIBLE TRANSPORT
AERIAL TAXIS
Tel: 06 285 9222
Two wheelchair-accessible taxis.

ACT MINIBUSES
Tel: 06 287 1676

WHERE TO GO, WHERE TO STAY

CANBERRA
Following the federation of the Australian
colonies in 1901, the National Capital was
situated between arch rivals Sydney and
Melbourne. The city is in a beautiful
setting, surrounded by hills. The first
Parliament was convened in the ACT in
1927, but the depression and World War
II slowed development until the 1950s.
This orderly and neat city, centre of the
country's administration, is more lively
than its reputation suggests with a young
population taking advantage of its many
restaurants and clubs. Derived from the
Aboriginal word Canberry, meaning a
meeting place, appropriately Canberra is
where politicians meet at the New
Parliament House. Delightfully designed
around Lake Barley Griffin, grand public
buildings include the High Court,
National Library and Gallery and National
Science Centre. The Carillon Bell Tower
and the Captain Cook Memorial Jet adorn
the lake. The National Botanic Gardens
sprawl over 90 hectares on the lower
slopes of Black Mountain. Nearby
Cockington Green's delightful miniature
British village set in beautifully
landscaped gardens is well worth
a visit.

HOTELS
CANBERRA CITY GATEWAY MOTEL (BW)
Corner of Northbourne Avenue and Mouat
Street, Lyneham
Tel: 06 247 2777 Fax: 06 247 4871
No. of hotel rooms: 270
No. of adapted rooms: 10
Facilities: restaurant; pool; sauna; spa
Two persons per night: 180.00
On Canberra's main street.

Canberra has developed into a beautiful city.

EMBASSY MOTEL (BW)
Adelaide Avenue and Hopetown Circus, Deakin
Tel: 06 281 1322 Fax: 06 281 1843
No. of hotel rooms: 130
No. of adapted rooms: 4
Facilities: restaurant; pool
Two persons per night: 85.00
2km from Parliament House.

OLIMS CANBERRA HOTEL (FL)
Corner of Ainslie and Limestone Avenues
Braddon
Canberra ACT 2601
Tel: 06 248 5511 Fax: 06 237 0864
No. of hotel rooms: 126

No. of adapted rooms: 3
Facilities: 2 restaurants; bars; cocktail bar
and beer garden.
Two persons per night: 180.00
1km from city centre. Nostalgic building
with modern elegance. Heritage-listed
with landscaped garden courtyard.

ACCESSIBLE ATTRACTIONS
AUSTRALIAN NATIONAL GALLERY
King Edward Terrace
Parkes ACT 2600
Tel: 06 271 2502
Ramps where access is by steps.
Wheelchairs are available.

Sydney Opera House – an international icon.

AUSTRALIAN WAR MEMORIAL
Limestone Avenue
Campbell ACT 2600
Tel: 06 243 4211
Wheelchairs are available.

BLACK MOUNTAIN TOWER
Black Mountain
Acton ACT 2601
Tel: 06 248 1911
Designated parking facilities, but no accessible WC.

COCKINGTON GREEN
Gold Creek Road
Gungahlin ACT 2600
Tel: 06 230 2273

HIGH COURT OF AUSTRALIA
Parkes Place
Parkes ACT 2600
Tel: 06 270 6811
Accessible WCs, but no designated parking spaces.

LANYON HOMESTEAD
Tharwa Drive (off Monaro Highway)
Tharwa ACT 2600
Tel: 06 237 5136
Accessible WCs, but no designated parking spaces.

NEW PARLIAMENT HOUSE
Capital Hill
Parkes ACT 2600
Tel: 06 277 5399

OLD PARLIAMENT HOUSE
King George Terrace
Parliamentary Triangle
Parkes ACT 2600
Tel: 06 273 2104
Accessible WCs, but no designated parking spaces.

ROYAL AUSTRALIAN MINT
Denison Street
Deakin ACT 2600
Tel: 06 202 6999
Accessible WCs, but no designated parking spaces.

NEW SOUTH WALES

Popularly credited with Australia's original discovery, this was Captain Cook's first landing place in 1770 and was the site of the first permanent settlement. NSW is now Australia's most populous state and boasts over 60 national parks with the most varied scenery of all the states; the landscapes range from snow-capped mountains to long sandy beaches and from the emptiness of the Outback to the urban vitality of the state capital. The south coast of the state offers fishing villages, craggy coastlines, gentle hills and inlets in the Illawarra area from Wollongon through Ulladulla, Batemans Bay, Bega and Eden.

The southwest has busy ski resorts at Thredbo, Charlotte Pass and Perisher Valley and good fishing in the Kosciusko National Park during spring and summer. 120km south west of Sydney are the Southern Highlands centering on the townships of Mittagong, Bowral, Moss Vale, Berrima, Bundanoon and Robertson, where shops, tearooms and antique shops abound, surrounded by national park and bushland areas. To the west are the Blue Mountains (104km from Sydney), a spectacular range with a number of resorts and small villages set in national park lands. The main centre is at Katoomba.

Time zone
October-March: GMT + 11 hours
April-September: GMT + 10 hours
except Broken Hill area that keeps GMT + 9.5 hours from October-March

BRITISH CONSULATE-GENERAL
Level 16, The Gateway
1 MacQuarie Place
Sydney Cove
Sydney NSW 2000
Tel: 02 247 7521 Fax: 02 233 1826

TOURIST BOARDS
NEW SOUTH WALES TOURISM COMMISSION
Gemini House
10-18 Putney Hill

London SW15 6AA
Tel: 081-789 1020 Fax: 081-780 1496

TRAVEL CENTRE OF NSW
19 Castlereagh Street
Sydney NSW 2000
Tel: 02 231 4444 Fax: 02 232 6080

NEW SOUTH WALES TOURISM COMMISSION
5th and 6th Floors
140 George Street
Sydney NSW 2000
Tel: 02 931 1111 Fax: 02 931 1424

SUPPORT ORGANISATIONS
PARAPLEGIC & QUADRIPLEGIC ASSOCIATION OF NSW
33-35 Burlington Road
Homebush
NSW 2140
Tel: 02 764 4166 Fax: 02 764 2391
A charitable organisation providing information and services.

INDEPENDENT LIVING CENTRE
600 Victoria Road
Ryde
NSW 2112
Tel: 02 808 2233 Fax: 02 809 7132
Information and advisory service enabling people to achieve independence in all aspects of life, including leisure activities.

ACROD NSW
55 Charles Street
Ryde
NSW 2112
Tel: 02 809 4488 Fax: 02 809 6517

WHEELCHAIR SPORTS ASSOCIATION OF NSW
PO Box 628
Ryde
NSW 2112
Tel: 02 809 5260 Fax: 02 809 5638

DEPARTMENT OF SPORT AND RECREATION
Tel: 02 923 4234

DEPARTMENT FOR THE ARTS
Tel: 02 361 9111

NATIONAL ROADS AND MOTORISTS ASSOCIATION
151 Clarence Street
Sydney NSW 2000
Tel: 02 260 9222 Fax: 02 260 8472
Produces a comprehensive accommodation directory indicating accessible properties.

NSW NATIONAL PARKS AND WILDLIFE SERVICE
PO Box 1967
Hurstville
NSW 2220
Tel: 02 585 6444

AIRPORT
SYDNEY AIRPORT
Tel: 02 216 1922 (airport)
02 667 9111 (information)
02 237 8541 (reservations)

Car parking
International Terminal; no reserved spaces for wheelchairs, but access to terminals. A telephone call to the Assistant Terminal Manager will secure special arrangements to assist you in getting to the terminal.
On arriving flights, whoever is meeting you should park in the car park and having met you, collect the car and bring it to the pick-up point.
TAA Terminal; similar arrangements through the Assistant Terminal Manager, as there are no specific parking spaces for disabled persons.
Ansett Terminal; There are spaces reserved adjacent to the terminal.

Facilities
International Terminal; access to the terminal is from the ground level car park and first floor roadway by kerb crossovers onto the pavement and through automatic doors. Wheelchair-accessible facilities include shops, bars, restaurants, lifts, toilets and telephones. Department of Health doctors or sisters and doctors on the Qantas medical staff will assist.

TAA Terminal; wheelchair-accessible facilities include cocktail/refreshment bars on both ground and first floor levels. One accessible WC is on each level. Lifts and telephones are accessible. A Qantas sister is available to attend as required whilst on duty. Oxygen, a stretcher and general first aid are available through the terminal office.
Ansett Terminal; access to the terminal building is from road level by a kerb crossover onto the pavement and through automatic doors. Wheelchair-accessible facilities include cocktail/refreshment bars on the first floor, a snack bar on the ground floor and lifts and telephones. Two wheelchair-accessible WCs – male and female – are located adjacent to the snack bar and there is another on the first floor. A Qantas sister is available through the terminal office, together with oxygen, a stretcher and general first aid.

INTERNATIONAL AIRLINES
AIR NEW ZEALAND
5 Elizabeth Street
Sydney
Tel: 02 223 4666

BRITISH AIRWAYS
64 Castlereagh Street, Sydney
Tel: 02 258 3300

CANADIAN AIRLINES
30 Clarence Street, Sydney
Tel: 02 299 7843
Toll-free: 008 251 321

GARUDA INDONESIA
175 Clarence Street
Sydney
Tel: 02 334 9900

QANTAS
Qantas International Centre
Jamison Street
Sydney
Tel: 02 691 3636

SINGAPORE AIRLINES
17 Bridge Street
Sydney
Tel: 02 236 0111

DOMESTIC AIRLINES
EASTWEST AIRLINES (ANSETT)
UK Office:
4th Floor, Heathcote House
20 Savile Row
London W1X 2AN
Tel: 071-434 4071

EastWest is now part of the Ansett
Australia group and applies the Ansett
Ansacare policy on all flights.

KENDALL AIRLINES
Head Office:
43 Thompson Street
Wagga Wagga, NSW 2650
Fax: 09 220 116

Kendall uses Ansett facilities. Forklifts
are used where there are no aerobridges.
Currently (late 1993) offering a 50 percent
discount on an escort's fare, if one is
considered essential.

AIR NEW SOUTH WALES
Bookable through Qantas Airlines

TRANSPORT WITHIN NSW
COUNTRY LINK RAIL
02 217 8812

Wheelchairs can be provided at Sydney
terminal by calling 02 219 1777.
Portable ramps can also be obtained.
A Stairmate is available on request at
most stations and special seats can be
made available also.

Stations served (all within NSW unless
otherwise stated) include: Aberdeen,
Albury, Bathurst, Benalla (VIC), Blayney,
Bowral, Brisbane, Broadmeadow, Broken
Hill, Bromelton (Q), Bundanoon,
Bungendore, Byron Bay, Canberra,
Campbelltown, Casina, Coffs Harbour,
Condobolin, Cootamundra, Culcairn,
Dubbo, Dungog, Eungai, Geurie,
Glenreagh, Gloucester, Goulburn,
Gosford, Grafton City, Gunning, Harden,
Hornsby, Henty, Ivanhoe, Junee,
Katoomba, Kempsey, Kendall, Kyogle,
Lismore, Lithgow, Macksville, Maitland,
Melbourne (VIC), Menindee, Moss Vale,
Mullumbimby, Murrurundi,
Murwillumbah, Muswellbrook, Nambucca
Heads, Orange, Orange East Fork, Parks,

Parramatta, Penrith, Queanbeyan,
Wuirindi, Rydal, Sawtell, Scone,
Singleton, Stuart Town, Tamworth,
Tarago, Tarana, Taree, The Rock,
Urunga, Wagga Wagga, Wangaratta
(VIC), Wauchope, Wellington, Werris
Creek, Willowtree, Wingham, Wyong,
Yass Junction.

STATE RAIL AUTHORITY OF NSW
Tel: 02 219 8888

STATE TRANSIT AUTHORITY
Tel: 02 956 4777

WHEELCHAIR-ACCESSIBLE TAXIS
Tel: 02 339 0200

ABC RADIO TAXI CO-OP LTD
Tel: 02 897 4000

A mini-bus service, four vehicles have
hydraulic hoists.

SPECIALIST TOUR OPERATORS
TRAVEL ATTENDANT & COMPANION SERVICE INTERNATIONAL
PO Box 111
Byron Bay NSW 2481
Tel: 06 684 7589

MERYL BOLIN ENTERPRISES
PO Box 339
Avalon NSW 2107
Tel: 02 918 9770

Provides information on all aspects of
travel.

BARRIER-FREE TRAVEL
Suite 1-69A Station Road
Petersham NSW 2049
Tel: 02 569 9839

Information agency.

CROSSROADS TRAVEL
Suite 204, 2nd floor
Scots Church Assembly Building
44 Mahret Street
Sydney NSW 2000
Tel: 02 262 1811 Fax: 02 262 2452

Provides planned holiday and fully
escorted tours with accessible
accommodation.

CUMALONG TOURS
PO Box 224
Northbridge NSW 2063
Tel: 02 958 8379 Fax: 02 958 8950
Provides holiday tours and information on accessible accommodation and places of interest in both NSW and interstate.

ACCESSIBLE AIR SAFARI OPERATORS
AIR ROVER AUSTRALIA
501 Tower Road
Bankstown Airport
Moorebank NSW 2200
Tel: 02 771 3051 Fax: 02 771 5367
Accessible air tours, with proviso of collapsible wheelchairs.

AIRCRUISING AUSTRALIA
18 Ross Smith Avenue
Kingsford Smith Airport
Mascot NSW 2020
Tel: 02 693 2233 Fax: 02 669 6064
Toll free: 008 252 053
Using F27 aircraft, accessibility is restricted to those travelling with a companion for getting on and off via rear steps. The company suggests considering each client individually, and is happy to assist wherever possible.

WHERE TO GO, WHERE TO STAY

ARMIDALE
Armidale is at an altitude of approximately 1000 metres and is refreshingly cool in summer. It is an attractive university town known as the City of Education with some spectacular scenery and historical and cultural places of interest in its vicinity. The centre of town is a pedestrian precinct. South Hillgrove, 18 miles east, is a gold mining ghost town worth visiting.

TOURIST BOARD
NEW ENGLAND TOURISM
215 Beardy Street
Tel: 067 72 8155
Opening hours: Monday-Friday: 0900-1700

HOTEL
CATTLEMAN'S MOTOR INN (BW)
New England Highway
31 Marsh Street
Armidale NSW 2350
Tel: 067 72 7788 Fax: 067 71 1447
No. of hotel rooms: 54
No. of adapted rooms: 2
Facilities: 2 restaurants; pool; spa; sauna
Two persons per night: 120.00
Close to the shopping centre and the University of New England and ten minutes by car from the airport. Two blocks from the town centre with surrounding area sloping, but not hilly.

ACCESSIBLE ATTRACTION
ARMIDALE FOLK MUSEUM
Corner of Faulkner and Rusden Streets
Armidale NSW 2350
Museum has ramped entrance and accessible WC.

BATEMANS BAY
Fishing and diving resort at the mouth of the Clyde River. To the north is the Murramaranea National Park, and offshore, on the Tollgate Islands, is a penguin reserve. Wild life, eucalyptus forest and pebbly beach surround the town.

TOURIST BOARD
BATEMANS BAY VISITORS CENTRE
Corner of Princes Highway and Beach Road
Tel: 044 72 6900
Opening hours: daily 0900-1700

ACCESSIBLE ATTRACTION
BIRDLAND ANIMAL PARK
55 Beach Road
Batemans Bay NSW 2536
Accessible throughout, except WCs.

BATHURST
Australia's oldest inland city with many fine buildings and the country's best racing circuit at Mt. Panorama–the site of the Bathurst 1000km race for production cars. The town has a reconstruction of an old gold mining town.

TOURIST BOARD
TOURIST INFORMATION CENTRE
East Wing, Court House, Russell Street
Tel: 063 33 6288
Opening hours: Monday-Friday: 0900-1600
Saturday and Sunday: 1000-1600

ACCESSIBLE ATTRACTIONS
ABERCROMBIE CAVES
Goulburn Road, Trunkey Creek NSW 2795
Tel: 063 33 6288
There are special WCs but no designated parking spaces.

BEN CHIFLEY'S COTTAGE
10 Busby Street, Bathurst NSW 2795
Tel: 063 33 6288

BERRIMA
123km SW of Sydney with many well-preserved and restored buildings. The first woman hanged in Australia was executed in the town's Court House.

ACCESSIBLE ATTRACTION
COURT HOUSE
Wiltshire Street, Berrima NSW 2577
Tel: 048 77 1505
There are accessible WCs.

BOWRAL

ACCESSIBLE ATTRACTIONS
FITZROY FALLS
Moss Vale-Nowra Roads
Fitzroy Falls NSW 2577
Tel: 048 87 7270

BRADMAN MUSEUM
St. Jude Street
Bowral NSW 2576
Tel: 048 62 1247
Accessible WCs available.

BREWARRINA

ACCESSIBLE ATTRACTION
ABORIGINAL CULTURAL MUSEUM
Bathurst Street
Brewarrina NSW 2839
Tel: 068 39 2421
Accessible WCs available.

BROKEN HILL
Originally a company town where huge deposits of lead, zinc and silver spawned Australia's most powerful company, BH Proprietary. This guaranteed prosperity that was highly unusual in the Outback. Broken Hill has the richest silver/zinc/lead deposits in the world. It was the site of much bitter industrial strife and witnessed the death of many miners. The deepest mine is over a mile deep and at the seams the temperature is as high as 60 degrees centigrade, requiring a vast refrigeration plant. The old mines are now open to the public and despite its prosperity the town still clings to its Outback culture. Visit the Royal Flying Doctor Service, School of the Air, Afghans Mosque (a relic from camel train days), Mineral and Train Museum, Bond Store Museum and Whites Mineral Art Gallery and Mining Museum.

TOURIST BOARD
TOURIST INFORMATION CENTRE
Corner of Bromide and Blende Streets
Tel: 080 87 6077
Open daily 0830-1700

HOTEL
OVERLANDER MOTOR INN (BW)
142 Iodide Street
Broken Hill NSW 2880
Tel: 080 88 2566 Fax: 080 88 4377
No. of hotel rooms: 15
No. of adapted rooms: 1
Facilities: pool; spa; sauna; no restaurant but breakfast is served in guests rooms and several restaurants and takeaway outlets will deliver an evening meal.
Two persons per night: 75.00
Quiet, central location, 800m from the town centre. All rooms are on the ground floor. The surrounding area is flat.

ACCESSIBLE ATTRACTIONS
SCHOOL OF THE AIR
PO Box 405
Broken Hill NSW 2880
Tel: 080 87 3565
There is a ramp into the main building.

ROYAL FLYING DOCTOR SERVICE
PO Box 463
Broken Hill NSW 2880
Tel: 080 88 0777
Ramped access to the main screening room.

BYRON BAY
Backpackers' centre. Until 1992 conservation laws prohibited highrise development but now new complexes are being built. There is a relaxed and informal ambience.

TOURIST BOARD
VISITORS INFORMATION CENTRE
69 Jonson Street
Tel: 066 85 8050
Opening hours: daily 0900-1600

HOTELS
THE WHEEL RESORT
39-51 Broken Head Road
Byron Bay NSW 2481
Tel: 066 85 6139 Fax: 066 85 8754
No. of units: 6
No. of adapted units: 6
Facilities: restaurant—breakfast and dinner are available on request, either at the pool or in your unit; pool; whirlpool
THE WHOLE RESORT IS DESIGNED FOR THOSE IN WHEELCHAIRS, AND IS OWNED BY TWO PEOPLE IN WHEELCHAIRS.
Six luxury self-contained cabins set in natural bushland with screened in verandas with marvellous views. Fully equipped kitchens. 3km from the town with accessible taxi available. Visit the lighthouse and many fine beaches. The resort also provides transport from airports in either a station-wagon or small van with an hydraulic hoist. Discover bush wheeling/walking trails that start at the fully paved paths around the resort building. Vehicular access to the beach is permitted. Much additional equipment is available including shower chairs and a submersible pool-side wheelchair.

44

CABARITA BEACH

HOTEL
CABARITA GARDENS LAKE RESORT (FL)
Tamarind Avenue
Cabarita Beach
NSW 2488
Tel: 066 76 1103 Fax: 066 76 1108
No. of hotel rooms: 50
No. of adapted rooms: 1
Facilities: restaurant; pool; spa; sauna; award-winning gardens
Two persons per night: 90.00
On the banks of Cudgen Lake and 1km from the surf beach. The area is a total sanctuary abounding in native flora and fauna, 20km south of Gold Coast. Surrounding area is flat.

CABRAMURRA

ACCESSIBLE ATTRACTION
YARRANGOBILLY CAVES
Snowy Mountain Highway
via Cabramurra NSW 2630
Tel: 069 49 5334

CLARENCE

ACCESSIBLE ATTRACTION
ZIG-ZAG RAILWAY
PO Box 33
Woodford
Clarence NSW 2790
Tel: 047 57 3061
Accessible WCs available.

COBAR
Situated in the Outback where copper was first discovered in 1869, Cobar is a modern copper-mining complex with some old miners' dwellings nearby. Among them is the 1882 court house.

TOURIST BOARD
TOURIST OFFICE
Cobar Regional Museum
Tel: 068 36 2448
Opening hours:
Monday-Friday 0800-1700

ACCESSIBLE ATTRACTION
MT. GREENFELL ABORIGINAL CAVE PAINTINGS
Barrier Highway
Cobar NSW 2835
Tel: 068 36 2692

COFFS HARBOUR
The prominent feature here is the vibrant coastal landscape with the mountains of the Great Dividing Range falling into the South Pacific. There are wonderful sandy beaches stretching from Boambee and Jetty Beach to the northern reaches of Emerald. The climate here is sub-tropical and there are flourishing banana plantations.

TOURIST BOARD
VISITOR INFORMATION CENTRE
Grafton Street/High Street
Urara Park
Coffs Harbour
Tel: 066 52 1522
Opening hours: daily 0900-1700

ACCESSIBLE ATTRACTIONS
PET PORPOISE POOL
Orlando Street
Coffs Harbour NSW 2450
Tel: 066 52 2164
Porpoises and Australian seals are on view plus a small aquarium with sharks and marine animals and a reef tank. There are ramps and accessible seating and staff are willing to assist where necessary.

BIG BANANA
Pacific Highway
Coffs Harbour NSW 2450
Tel: 066 52 4355
This is an enormous, brightly coloured concrete banana, 3km north of the town, where the milk bar serves numerous variations of banana preparations. Accessible WCs, but no designated parking.

COONABARABRAN
The Warrambungles, an ancient mountain range, are the great attraction here.

ACCESSIBLE ATTRACTIONS
WARRAMBUNGLE NATIONAL PARK

PO Box 39
Coonabarabran NSW 2357
Tel: 068 25 4364
Accessible WCs but no designated parking.

SIDING SPRING OBSERVATORY
Coonabarabran NSW 2357
Tel: 068 42 6262

COWRA

ACCESSIBLE ATTRACTION
JAPANESE GARDEN AND CULTURAL CENTRE
Bellevue Road, Binnie Creek Road
Cowra NSW 2794

DENILIQUIN

ACCESSIBLE ATTRACTION
ISLAND SANCTUARY
Cressy Street
Deniliquin NSW 2710
Tel: 058 81 2878

DORRIGO
An old settlement on the rim of the New England Plateau. The National Park has some remarkable waterfalls.

ACCESSIBLE ATTRACTION
DORRIGO NATIONAL PARK
A highland subtropical rainforest with a sealed car park and two wide, designated bays. Separate accessible WCs. A skywalk leads from the Infocentre through the forest canopy terminating at a lookout, from where the Bellinger Valley can be seen. The skywalk is a flat gradient and wide. Timber walkways have been constructed through the rainforest between the Infocentre and The Glade picnic area. They are quite wide, but have very steep gradients near the Infocentre, and best access is via The Glade. The Infocentre has a bookshop, cafe and rainforest displays that are accessible.

DUBBO
An agricultural, sheep and cattle town on the Macquarie River and a gateway to the Outback. Many wide streets and some fine old buildings, with the museum and old

gaol with gallows of special interest. The main attraction is the Western Plains Zoo just outside town, a premier open-range zoo home to more than 800 animals.

TOURIST BOARD
DUBBO TOURISM
Corner of Erskine and Darling Streets
Tel: 068 84 1445
Opening hours: daily 0900-1700.

HOTEL
ASHWOOD COUNTRY CLUB MOTEL (FL)
Corner of Whyland and East Streets
Tel: 068 81 8700 Fax: 068 81 8930
No. of hotel rooms: 39
No. of adapted rooms: 1
Facilities: restaurant; pool; spa
Two persons per night: 85.00
Two acres of sub tropical plants.

ACCESSIBLE ATTRACTIONS
OLD DUBBO GAOL
Eddie Meek Place
(Macquarie Street)
Dubbo NSW 2830
Tel: 068 82 8122
There is accessible seating.

WESTERN PLAINS ZOO
Obley Road
Dubbo NSW 2830
Tel: 068 82 5888
Opening hours: daily 0900-1700
Accessible WCs, but no designated parking. Australia's premier open-range zoo set in 300 hectares of natural bushland. Home to more than 800 animals from five continental zones.

EDEN
Old whaling town on Twofold Bay with whaling museum. The first whaling station was established here in 1818.

TOURIST BOARD
EDEN INFORMATION CENTRE
Princes Highway
Eden NSW
Tel: 064 96 1953
Opening hours: Monday-Friday: 0900-1600
Saturday and Sunday: 0900-1200

ACCESSIBLE ATTRACTION
KILLER WHALE MUSEUM
94 Imlay Street
Eden NSW 2551
Tel: 064 96 2094

ERINA

ACCESSIBLE ATTRACTION
FRAGRANT GARDEN
Portsmouth Road
Erina NSW 2250
Tel: 043 67 7322
Accessible WCs available.

FAULCONBRIDGE

ACCESSIBLE ATTRACTION
NORMAN LINDSAY GALLERY
14 Norman Lindsay Crescent
via Chapman Parade
Faulconbridge NSW 2776
Tel: 047 51 1067

GOSFORD
The centre for visiting the Brisbane Waters National Park with its many Aboriginal rock engravings.
The main attraction in the area is Old Sydney Town, a major reconstruction of early Sydney. Replicas of shops and non-stop street theatre includes re-enacting duels, floggings and hangings sprinkled liberally with fast food.

TOURIST BOARD
GOSFORD TOURIST OFFICE
200 Mann Street
Tel: 043 25 2835

HOTEL
GOSFORD MOTOR INN (BW)
613 Pacific Highway
Tel: 043 23 1333
Fax: 043 23 3030
No. of hotel rooms: 37
No. of adapted rooms: 1
Facilities: pool
Two persons per night: 80.00
Overlooking the lake, the hotel is 800 metres from the town centre. The surrounding area is HILLY.

ACCESSIBLE ATTRACTIONS
OLD SYDNEY TOWN
Pacific Highway
Somersby NSW 2250
Tel: 043 40 1104
Recreation of the original Sydney Cove
settlements. Accessible WCs, but no
designated parking.

ERIC WARRELL'S AUSTRALIAN REPTILE PARK
Pacific Highway
Gosford North
NSW 2250
Tel: 043 28 4311
There are ramps in place.

GOULBURN
An old sheep town dating back to 1833
with several historic houses.

HOTEL
**GOULBURN HERITAGE
MOTOR LODGE (FL)**
1 Lagoon Street
Hume Highway
Tel: 048 21 9377 Fax: 048 21 5991
No. of hotel rooms: 42
No. of adapted rooms: 1
Facilities: restaurant
Two persons per night: 90.00
Family-owned and operated, this hotel is
central to both the beach and cities. It
takes three hours to reach Sydney and
about one hour to Canberra.
The centre of Goulburn is 3km away and
the surrounding area is flat.

ACCESSIBLE ATTRACTION
BIG MERINO
Hume Highway, Goulburn NSW 2580
Tel: 048 218 800
Accessible WCs, but no designated parking.

GRIFFITH

ACCESSIBLE ATTRACTIONS
GRIFFITH WINERIES
Rosetto's Road, Griffith NSW 2680
Tel: 069 63 5214
MIRANDA WINES
Jondaryan Avenue, Griffith NSW 2680
Tel: 069 62 4033

HAY
Hay is half way between Sydney and
Adelaide and is a major Merino sheep-
breeding centre.

HOTEL
BISHOP'S LODGE MOTEL (FL)
35 Sturt Highway
Hay NSW 2711
Tel: 069 93 3003 Fax: 069 93 1147
No. of hotel rooms: 35
No. of adapted rooms: 1
Facilities: restaurant; pool; spa
On Hay Plains next to an historic
homestead. The town centre is 1.3km
away and the surrounding area is flat.

HELENSBURG

ACCESSIBLE ATTRACTION
SYMBIO KOALA GARDENS
Lawrence Hargrave Drive
Stanwell Tops NSW 2508
Tel: 042 94 1244
There is parking and an accessible WC.

JENOLAN CAVES
Amazing limestone formations with
stalactites and stalagmites forming
extraordinay shapes. Located in the Blue
Mountains.

ACCESSIBLE ATTRACTION
JENOLAN CAVES
Jenolan Caves Road NSW 2790
Tel: 063 59 3311
Accessible WCs, but no designated parking.

JINDABYNE
On a man-made lake and an accessible
point for ski resorts. The town is quite new,
being relocated when the Snowy Mountains
Scheme dammed the Snowy River and the
first town was submerged.

TOURIST BOARD
SNOWY RIVER INFORMATION CENTRE
Petamin Plaza
Jindabyne NSW
Tel: 064 56 2444
Opening hours: daily 0900-1700

The spectacular Three Sisters epitomise Blue Mountain country around Katoomba.

ACCESSIBLE ATTRACTION
GARDEN TROUT HATCHERY
Kosciusko Road
Jindabyne NSW 2627
Tel: 064 56 1133
Accessible WCs but no designated parking.

KATOOMBA
The largest Blue Mountain town from where one can view the rocky points of The Three Sisters. There are also sweeping views of the bushland and valleys, waterfalls and rock formations.

ACCESSIBLE ATTRACTIONS
SCENIC RAILWAY AND SKYWAY
1 Violet Street
Katoomba NSW 2780
Tel: 047 82 2699
The railway steals steeply down a gorge, but sadly only the souvenir shop is accessible.

THREE SISTERS
Echo Point (off Great Western Highway)
Katoomba NSW 2780
There is good access to the lookout.

KEMPSEY
Home of the Akubra hat and the Macleay River Historical Museum and Cultural Centre.

LIGHTNING RIDGE
The only place in the world where the valuable black opal is found, a fact heavily promoted by local opal galleries. Otherwise, there is little to recommend in this town miles from anywhere.

TOURIST BOARD
VISITORS INFORMATION
Angledool Heights
Lightning Ridge NSW
Tel: 068 29 0565

ACCESSIBLE ATTRACTION
DRIVE-IN MINE
13 Gem Street
(PO Box 41)
Lightning Ridge NSW 2834
Tel: 068 29 0287

MAITLAND
Situated in Hunter Valley, heart of the wine-making region, the town was settled by convicts in 1818. It was once a coal-mining centre and now contains museums, craft shops and an old jail in King Street.

MERIMBULA
There are fine views of the south coast with Lake Merimbula and the mountains forming a spectacular background. Excellent beaches and even temperatures.

TOURIST BOARD
TOURIST INFORMATION CENTRE
Beach Street
Tel: 064 95 1129
Opening hours: Monday-Friday 0900-1600
Saturday and Sunday 0900-1200

MOREE

ACCESSIBLE ATTRACTION
ARTESIAN SPA BATHS
Corner of Anne and Gosport Streets
Moree NSW 2400
Tel: 067 52 9554

MUDGEE
A pleasant town with many fine old buildings. Well known for its wineries and Colonial Inn Museum.

ACCESSIBLE ATTRACTION
CRAIGMOOR WINERY
Graigmoor Road
Mudgee NSW 2850
Tel: 063 72 2208
Accessible WCs, but no designated parking.

NAMBUCCA HEADS
A restful small resort halfway between Perth and Sydney. One of the nicest spots on the NSW north coast with fine views from the headland across the river mouth. There is a well known surfing beach. Visit the Historical Museum.

TOURIST BOARD
TOURIST INFORMATION CENTRE
Ridge Street
Tel: 065 68 6954

ACCESSIBLE ATTRACTION
HISTORICAL MUSEUM
The Headland
Nambucca Heads NSW 2448
The museum is accessible and has a suitable WC.

NARRANDERA
In the Murrumbidgee Irrigation Area and the centre of the fruit and food processing industry. South is the town of Jerilderie where the notorious bush-ranger Ned Kelly held up the whole town for two days in 1879, locking up the police in their own jail.

NEWCASTLE
NSW's second largest city and a major industrial and commercial centre. It was originally named Coal River and was built for the worst of Sydney's convicts. The port still exports coal, its breakwaters stretching out to Nobbys Head.
Despite its industrial base, the city has wide leafy streets and surf beaches a short distance away.
The centre of the town is on a peninsula with the ocean on one side and the Hunter River on the other. Visit the Art Gallery, Regional Museum and the Maritime and Military Museum. Restaurants and entertainment in abundance.

TOURIST BOARD
NEWCASTLE TOURIST OFFICE
Queens Wharf
150 Wharf Road
Tel: 049 29 9297
Opening hours: Monday-Friday 0900-1700
Saturday and Sunday 0930-1500

HOTELS
BIMET LODGE (SPHC)
121 Union Street
Tel: 049 29 6677 Fax: 0949 29 4502
No. of hotel rooms: 30
No. of adapted rooms: 2
Facilities: restaurant
Hunter Valley, Port Stephens and Lake Macquarie are close by.

ACCESSIBLE ATTRACTIONS
NEWCASTLE REGIONAL ART GALLERY
Laman Street
Newcastle NSW 2300
Accessible seating and staff assistance.
Accessible WC and lifts.

NEWCASTLE REGIONAL MUSEUM
787 Hunter Street
Newcastle
Accessible WCs, ramped front, entrance
and inside display rooms.

FORT SCRATCHLEY MILITARY MUSEUM
Fort Drive
Newcastle 2300
There are no special facilities, but most
areas are accessible and ramps are
provided where necessary.
There is also accessible seating and the
staff are very happy to assist.

ORANGE
Considered as a site for the federal
capital before Canberra was chosen and
home to the poet Banjo Paterson, who
wrote the words of *Waltzing Matilda.*
Orange is the centre of one of Australia's
richest fruit farming areas, producing
mainly soft fruit and apples (despite its
obvious name).
It is home to the extinct volcano Mt.
Canobalas, the Banjo Paterson Park, an
art gallery and museum.
To the north at Ophir is the site of
Australia's first gold rush.

ACCESSIBLE ATTRACTIONS
BANJO PATERSON MEMORIAL PARK
Ophir Road
Orange NSW 2800
Mostly flat, accessible ground but no
accessible WC.

ORANGE REGIONAL GALLERY
Civic Square
Byng Street
Orange NSW 2800
The gallery is wheelchair-accessible.

PARRAMATTA
A suburb of Sydney, originally an

agricultural area and site of the second
European settlement. Several historic
buildings remain, plus the home of the
powerful Macarthur family who engineered
the removal of several governors.

TOURIST BOARD
TOURIST INFORMATION CENTRE
Market Street
Tel: 047 630 3703

ACCESSIBLE ATTRACTION
OLD GOVERNMENT HOUSE
Parramatta Park NSW 2150
Both the House and WCs are accessible.

PARKES
1860s gold town, with motor museum and
pioneer park museum. North of the town is
Kelly Reserve and a radio telescope (23km).

ACCESSIBLE ATTRACTION
PARKES RADIO TELESCOPE
Newell Highway
Parkes NSW 2870
Accessible WCs, but no designated parking.

PENRITH
At the edge of Sydney's urban sprawl on
the way to the Blue Mountains.
We are unsure of accessibility to the
paddlesteamers that cruise along the
Nepean River.

POKOLBIN
Famous for outstanding wines.
Traditional wineries open to the public.

ACCESSIBLE ATTRACTION
HUNGERFORD HILL WINES PTY LTD
Broke Road, Pokolbin NSW 2321
Tel: 049 98 7666
Accessible WCs, but no designated parking.

LAKES FOLLY WINERY
There is a lift and accessible seating here.

OAKVALE VINEYARD
Tasting and scales areas are accessible.

TULLOCHS GLEN ELGIN VINEYARD
Fully accessible.

TYRELLS VINEYARD
Ramps where necessary, accessible seating, and access to tasting rooms.

VINEYARD POTTERY AND CAFE
Fully accessible.

PORT MACQUARIE
Once a convict settlement, now a large coastal resort with a wide variety of entertainment. There are many beautiful beaches. Visit Roto in the nature reserve. 29km west of town along Oxley Highway is Timbertown, a re-creation of a working and living village of the 1880s.

TOURIST BOARD
TOURIST INFORMATION OFFICE
Horton Street
Tel: 065 83 1293
Opening hours: Monday-Friday 0830-1700
Saturday-Sunday 0900-1630

ACCESSIBLE ATTRACTION
SEA ACRES RAINFOREST CENTRE
Pacific Drive
Port Macquarie, NSW 2444
Tel: 065 82 3355
Accessible WCs, but no designated parking.

PORT STEPHENS
A favourite holiday destination with a giant bay, wide beaches and a major fishing and boating centre. Myall Lakes National Park, just to the north, is well worth a visit and is accessible.

TOURIST BOARD
VISITORS CENTRE
Victoria Parade
Nelson Street
Tel: 049 81 1579
Opening hours: Monday-Friday 0900-1700
Saturday and Sunday 0900-1630

Take off for the exciting Power House Museum near Darling Harbour.

SYDNEY

The oldest and largest city in Australia, split by Port Jackson Harbour and joined by the Harbour Bridge, known as "the old coat hanger". The Rocks area at the south end of the bridge is historic and has been much restored. The first European settlers came here, and many of the original buildings were constructed by convicts. Sydney is a cosmopolitan city, arcades, shops and businesses reflect its energetic ambience and the University proclaims academic achievement.

The Sydney Opera House, built on the site of a train depot, was completed in 1973. It took 14 years to build and is now an international icon. It is best viewed from a ferry available at the Circular Quay or Darling Harbour.

There are two good markets, both easily accessible – Rocks and Paddy's Markets. The music scene revolves around the many pubs in the Kings Cross and Oxford Street areas.

For outdoor pursuits Sydney is renowned for Bondi and Manly Beaches and the principal shopping area is George Street. Other places to visit and things to see are; Sydney Aquarium, with its underwater viewing; Maritime Museum; Powerhouse Museum; Museum of Contemporary Art; Royal Botanical Gardens; Centennial Park; Art Gallery of NSW; Australian Museum; State Library of NSW and the Taronga Zoo and Koala Park.

180km north of Sydney is the Hunter valley, Australia's oldest commercial wine-producing area. 65km west of town is Gledswood Homestead and Farm, an authentic colonial homestead with demonstrations of sheep shearing and sheepdog mustering.

HOTELS

AIRPORT INTERNATIONAL MOTOR INN (FL)
35 Levey Street
Arncliffe
Tel: 02 556 1555 Fax: 02 567 1309
No. of hotel rooms: 50
No. of adapted rooms: 3
Facilities: restaurant; bar
Two persons per night: 105.00

All-suite hotel 300m from the International Terminal with free transport. Town centre is 7km away and the surrounding area is flat.

HOLIDAY INN COOGEE BEACH (HDI)
242 Arden Street
Tel: 02 315 7600 Fax: 02 315 9100
No. of hotel rooms: 207
No. of adapted rooms: 3
Facilities: restaurant

Directly opposite the beach where the area is flat. Surroundings away from the beach are hilly. The town centre is 7km away and the international airport 6km.

NIKKO HOTEL (NH)
161 Sussex Street
Sydney NSW 2000
Tel: 02 299 1231 Fax: 02 299 3340
No. of hotel rooms: 645
No. of adapted rooms: 6
Facilities: 2 restaurants, one Japanese; pool; spa

Located on the Darling Harbour waterfront development, the hotel is incorporated into the architecture of the old stone Corn Exchange.

NOVOTEL ON DARLING HARBOUR (NOV)
100 Murray Street
Pyrmont NSW 2009
Tel: 02 934 0000 Fax: 02 934 0099
No. of hotel rooms: 527
No. of adapted rooms: 6
Facilities: restaurant; pool; sauna
Two persons per night: 190.00

Adjacent harbour, Maritime Museum, Aquarium, Chinatown.

OLD SYDNEY PARKROYAL (SPHC)
55 George Street
Sydney NSW 2097
Tel: 02 252 0524 Fax: 02 251 2093
No. of hotel rooms: 174
No. of adapted rooms: 2
Facilities: restaurant; pool; sauna ; spa

Quality hotel in historic Rocks area, ten minutes from harbour, Opera House and central shopping district. The surrounding area is hilly and flat.

PARKROYAL AT DARLING HARBOUR (SPHC)
150 Day Street
Sydney NSW 2000
Tel: 02 261 4444 Fax: 02 261 8766
No. of hotel rooms: 295
No. of adapted rooms: 3
Facilities: 2 restaurants

Flanked by historic Chinatown and some of the city's most impressive new architecture, Darling Harbour is a cosmopolitan crossroads. The hotel is located on the city side of the harbour, close to the commercial and entertainment areas and the new National Maritime Museum.
The beach is 15 minutes' drive away, and the surrounding area is relatively flat.

RADISSON CENTURY HOTEL (RAD)
203-219 Victoria Street
Tel: 02 368 4000 Fax: 02 267 4119
No. of hotel rooms: 291
No. of adapted rooms: 3
Facilities: restaurant; Harbour View Lounge
Two persons per night: 140.00

Located in the Kings Cross entertainment and restaurant district and five minutes from Sydney Harbour and Opera House.

REGENT HOTEL (LHW)
199 George Street
Sydney 2000
Tel: 02 238 0000 Fax: 02 251 2851
No. of hotel rooms: 594
No. of adapted rooms: 4
Facilities: 3 restaurants; pool; sauna
Two persons per night: 300.00 upwards

Luxurious hotel in historic Rocks area, harbour views, large rooms. One of Australia's best hotels. 7km from the nearest beach. The surrounding area is flat.

THE HILLS LODGE MOTOR INN (BW) CASTLE HILL
Corner of Windsor and Salisbury Roads
Tel: 02 680 3800 Fax: 02 899 1182
No. of hotel rooms: 69
No. of adapted rooms: 1
Facilities: restaurant; pool; spa

Tudor style in garden setting. 5km from the city centre, 15 minutes from business centre and 30 minutes from the Blue Mountains. Hills Centre for the Performing Arts, one of Australia's most versatile theatres, is a few minutes from the Lodge.

ACCESSIBLE ATTRACTIONS
ART GALLERY OF NSW
Art Gallery Road
The Domain
Sydney NSW 2000
Tel: 02 225 1700
Opening hours: Monday-Saturday 1000-1700

Permanent exhibition of Australian, European, Asian and primitive art.

AUSTRALIAN WILDLIFE PARK and WONDERLAND
Wallgrove Road
Eastern Creek NSW 2766
Tel: 02 957 4655
Open daily 0900-1700

There are no steps and WCs are available. Cuddle a koala, feed a kangaroo, most native species are represented here in a variety of habitats ranging from red desert to swamp and rainforest.

BENTS BASIN STATE RECREATION AREA
off Wolstenhome Avenue
Bents Basin NSW 2750
Tel: 04 774 8662

Accessible WCs available.

CENTENNIAL PARK
Oxford Street
Paddington NSW 2021
Tel: 02 331 5056

Accessible WCs available. Opened in 1888 to commemorate Australia's first century, the park covers about 528 acres. Ten minutes from the city centre.

CHINATOWN
Dixon Street
Haymarket NSW 2000
Tel: 02 281 1018

Dixon Street, between Hay and Goulburn Streets, is now a pedestrian area with exotic shops and restaurants. The courtyard is accessible.

53

DARLING HARBOUR
Sydney NSW 2000
Tel: 02 286 0100
There are designated parking spaces and the harbour is accessible. Once a run-down railway goods yard, the harbour has been redeveloped to house convention facilities and exhibition centres, restaurants, the National Maritime and the Power House Museums and Sydney Aquarium.

ELIZABETH BAY HOUSE
7 Onslow Avenue
Elizabeth Bay NSW 2011
Tel: 02 356 3022
Built in 1835 the house is a fine example of colonial architecture. It is now a museum displaying Australian life in colonial days. Accessible seating inside. Entrance is by the back door.

FEATHERDALE WILDLIFE PARK
217-229 Kildare Road
Doonside NSW 2767
Tel: 02 622 1644
Open seven days a week 0900-1700
Accessible WCs available. The park holds the country's largest collection of native fauna, plus koalas, emus, wallabies and exotic animals.

GLEDSWOOD WINERY
Camden Valley Way
Catherine Field NSW 2171
Tel: 02 606 5111
The winery is totally accessible with a suitable WC facility.
Wheelchairs are for hire if required and there is special seating.

KOALA PARK
Castle Hill Road
West Pennant Hills
NSW 2120
Tel: 02 484 3141
Open daily 0900-1700
This is a compact and popular zoo specialising in Australian indigenous species.
It was the first private koala sanctuary when it opened in 1930. Wheelchairs are available and ramps are provided where and when necessary.

LUNA PARK (opening mid-1994)
Olympic Drive
(under Harbour Bridge)
Milsons Point NSW 2061
Tel: 02 954 1899
Accessible WCs available.

54

The Royal Botanic Gardens – a tropical centre, palm grove and rose garden beautifully set in 30 hectares.

MANLY OCEANWORLD
West Esplanade
Manly NSW 2095
Tel: 02 949 2644
Accessible WCs available.

MOORE PARK
Oxford Street
Paddington NSW 2021
Tel: 02 331 5056
Cafes and WCs accessible.

PADDY'S MARKET
Garden Street off Henderson Road
(Adjacent Redfern Railway Station)
Sydney NSW 2016
Tel: 02 325 6200
On the edge of Chinatown opposite the Hay Street end of Dixon Street, the market is open at weekends, selling everything including kangaroo belts. A good place to watch the natives, the ground level is accessible.

PARLIAMENT HOUSE
Macquarie Street
Sydney NSW 2000
Tel: 02 230 2111
Open daily Monday-Friday
Georgian and colonnaded, Parliament House includes a wing from one of the earliest colonial buildings in the country. Once part of the notorious Rum Hospital of 1811. It is wheelchair accessible.

POWER HOUSE MUSEUM
500 Harris Street
Ultimo NSW 2007
Tel: 02 217 0111
Open daily 1000-1700
Ramps where necessary, wheelchairs and accessible WCs are available.
The museum has been cleverly created from the shell of a former power station. There are over 25 exhibitions on human achievement, science and technology, decorative arts and everyday life in Australia.

QUARANTINE STATION
Sydney Harbour National Park
PO Box 703

Manly NSW 2095
Tel: 02 977 6229
Accessible WCs available.

QUEEN VICTORIA BUILDING
455 George Street
Sydney NSW 2000
Tel: 02 264 9209
Accessible parking, lifts and WCs available. Originally designed as an enormous fruit and vegetable market in 1893, the building was re-vamped in 1985 and returned to its former Romanesque-Byzantine glory replete with a great copper dome.

ROYAL BOTANIC GARDENS
Mrs. Macquarie's Road
Sydney NSW 2000
Tel: 02 231 8111
Open daily 0630-1830
Accessible WCs available. Located on the foreshores of the harbour, the gardens cover 30 hectares and include a tropical centre, palm grove and rose garden.

SYDNEY AQUARIUM
Pier 26
Darling Harbour-Eastside
Sydney NSW 2009
Tel: 02 262 2300
Open daily 0930-2100
Designated parking and accessible WCs available. All exhibits can be seen daily from 0930-2100, except the seals who go to bed at 1700! One of the largest and most spectacular aquariums in the world, with a fine shark exhibition and the new Eastwest Marine Mammal Sanctuary. Viewed through either outdoor floating oceanarium or underwater viewing chamber. A must, not to be missed.

SYDNEY ENTERTAINMENT CENTRE
Harbour Street
Haymarket NSW 2000
Tel: 02 211 2222
Open daily 0900-1600
Accessible WCs available.

SYDNEY OPERA HOUSE
Bennelong Point
NSW 2000
Tel: 02 250 7111
Designated parking and accessible WCs available. Frequently called the eighth wonder of the world, the Opera House was opened by Queen Elizabeth in 1973. It was 20 years in the planning and building from a design by Dane Joern Utzon. Geometric shells representing the sails of many sailboats are set on a perfect sphere. Each shell is covered with Swedish tiles to create a luminous effect. There are four restaurants and daily guided tours.

SYDNEY TOWER
Corner of Pitt and Market Streets
Sydney NSW 2000
Tel: 02 229 7444
Opening hours: Sunday-Friday 0930-2130
Saturday 0930-2330
The enclosed observation deck offers an amazing 360-degree view of the city and its outlying suburbs. On a good day even the Blue Mountains in the west are visible. There is an escalator from the street level up four floors to the ticket booth and high-speed elevators shoot up to the highest man-made peak in Australia.

TARONGA ZOO
Bradleys Head Road
Mossman NSW 2088
Tel: 02 969 2777
Open daily from 0900
On the shores of the harbour the zoo is home to Sydney's only platypus exhibit. Also on view are Tasmanian devils, giraffes, chimps, snow leopards and other species.

THE AUSTRALIAN MUSEUM
6-8 College Street
Sydney NSW 2000
Tel: 02 339 8111
Opening hours: Monday 1200-1700
Tuesday-Sunday 1000-1700
Accessible WC facilities.
Natural history museum with Australian and Pacific exhibits.

THE HYDE PARK BARRACKS
Queens Square, Macquarie Street
Sydney NSW 2000
Tel: 02 223 8922
Opening hours: daily 1000-1700 except Tuesday from 1200 to 1700
Designed by convict Francis Greenway for Governor Lachlan Macquarie, the barracks are built in a Georgian architectural style.

VAUCLEUSE HOUSE
Wentworth Road
Vaucleuse NSW 2030
Tel: 02 388 7922
Open Tuesday-Sunday 1000-1630.
Closed Monday
Accessible WCs available.
This is an historic colonial house that was built between 1829 and 1847 and owned for a time by William Charles Wentworth, father of the Australian constitution. This delightful building has recently undergone expert restoration and refurbishment to represent a mid-19th century home.

TAMWORTH
Australia's answer to Nashville, Tamworth is the undisputed Country and Western capital of Australia.
There are numerous craft workshops and galleries in the vicinity that are well worth a visit.

TOURIST BOARD
TAMWORTH INFORMATION CENTRE
Corner of Kable Avenue and Bridge Street
Tel: 067 68 4461
Opening hours: Monday-Friday 0830-1600
Saturday and Sunday 0900-1500

ACCESSIBLE ATTRACTION
COUNTRY COLLECTIONS
Quartpot Lane
New England Highway
Tamworth NSW 2340
Tel: 06 765 2688

TAREE
This is the main town in the Manning River District with good forest drives in picnic areas.

TOURIST BOARD
MANNING VALLEY TOURIST OFFICE
Pacific Highway
Taree North
Tel: 06 552 1900

ACCESSIBLE ATTRACTION
ELLENBOROUGH FALLS
Comboyne Plateau (via Elands)
Taree NSW 2429
Tel: 06 583 7100
No designated parking or accessible WC.

THIRLMERE

ACCESSIBLE ATTRACTION
THIRLMERE RAILWAY MUSEUM
Barbour Road
Thirlmere NSW 2572
Tel: 04 681 8001
Mostly accessible.

TWEED HEADS
There is an 18 metre-high monument to Captain Cook at Point Danger, where his ship *Endeavour* almost went down. On top of the mountain there is a laser lighthouse that can be seen 35km out to sea. Boating, river cruises, oyster farming and Australia's finest gambling clubs also available.

TOURIST BOARD
TWEED TOURIST INFORMATION CENTRE
4 Wharf Street
Tel: 07 536 4244
Open daily 0900-1700

ULLADULLA
Fishing town with a splendid beach in an area of beautiful lakes, lagoons and beaches. No designated parking or accessible WC.

WAGGA WAGGA
A major city on the Murrimbidgee River with a busy farming centre, botanical gardens, a zoo and historic buildings.

ACCESSIBLE ATTRACTION
BOTANICAL GARDENS
Williams Hill, Macleay Street
Wagga Wagga NSW 2650
Ramps to all facilities are provided.

WELLINGTON

ACCESSIBLE ATTRACTION
WELLINGTON CAVES
Caves Road, Wellington NSW 2820
Tel: 06 845 1418
Accessible WCs available.

WEST WYALONG
An old mining town, whose Historical Museum in Main Street includes a model gold mine.

WOLLONGONG
NSW's third largest city, an industrial centre with the largest steelworks in the country. An attractive city set between superb surf beaches and the hills of the Illawarra Escarpment. There is an interesting harbour cut from solid rock and a lighthouse of 1872. Parks situated all along the shoreline make the city particularly pleasant. The museum includes a reconstruction of the 1902 Mt. Kembla village mining disaster.

HOTELS
NOVOTEL NORTHBEACH (NOV)
2-14 Cliff Road
North Wollongong NSW 2500
Tel: 04 226 3555 Fax: 04 229 1705
No. of hotel rooms: 203
No. of adapted rooms: 3
Facilities: 2 restaurants; lobby bar; beach bistro; pool; sauna; spa
With a beachfront location, the hotel is situated about 5km from the town centre. The surrounding area is slightly hilly.

ACCESSIBLE ATTRACTIONS
MOUNT KEIRA LOOKOUT
Queen Elizabeth Drive
Mount Keira NSW 2500
Tel: 04 229 3294
Accessible WCs available.

SUBLIME POINT LOOKOUT
Princes Highway
(CPO Box 22, Thirroul, NSW 2515)
Bulli NSW 2516
Tel: 04 267 1211
Accessible WCs available.

NORTHERN TERRITORY

The least populated and most barren area of Australia, Northern Territory has always been associated with Uluru (Ayers Rock), rising from the red centre of Australia. It is the world's biggest monolith and an Aboriginal sacred site. But there is a great deal more to the territory than Uluru.

Alice Springs is located in the heart of the striking Macdonnell Ranges, along with Simpson's Gap and the ancient Standley Chasm. At noon the cliff faces change colour as the sun reaches the bottom of the gorge. 323km west of Alice is Kings Canyon, a mighty canyon of pastel-coloured walls, and 152km southwest is the tropical Palm Valley and Kakadu National Park is now becoming increasingly well known.

At the northern end of the Territory, the Top End as it is known locally, is Darwin, surrounded by crocodile-inhabited swamps. The area has a tropical climate with a distinct wet season from November to April.

There is great mineral wealth and agricultural potential in Northern Territory and when this was first realised at the beginning of the 20th century, trade routes were established with the southern states. The discovery of gold in the Outback region around Katherine, led to rapid development.

Although Alice Springs and Darwin are now examples of urban life, beyond them is the wilderness that remains unchanged.

Time zone
October-March: GMT+ 10.5 hours
April-September: GMT + 9.5 hours

TOURIST BOARDS
NORTHERN TERRITORY TOURIST COMMISSION
612 Kingston Road
London SW20 8DN
Tel: 081-544 9845 Fax: 081-544 9843

The impressive Olgas have Uluru as a close neighbour.

AUSTRALIAN TOURIST BOARD
NORTHERN TERRITORY TOURIST COMMISSION
PO Box 2532
67 Stuart Highway
Alice Springs NT 0870
Tel: 089 518 555

NORTHERN TERRITORY TOURIST COMMISSION
1st Floor, Old Supreme Court Building
Mitchell Street
Darwin NT 0800
Tel: 089 893 900 Fax: 089 811 539

GOVERNMENT TOURIST BUREAU
31 Smith Street Mall
Darwin NT 0800
Tel: 089 814 300 Fax: 089 817 346

NORTHERN TERRITORY TOURIST COMMISSION
Suite 1230, 12th Floor

2121 Avenue of the Stars
Los Angeles CA 90067
Tel: 213 277 7877 Fax: 213 277 3061

SUPPORT ORGANISATIONS
ACCESS ADVISORY COMMITTEE – DARWIN
Tel: 089 822 560 Fax: 089 410 849
Information on transport, accommodation and arts venues.

ACROD – NT
PO Box 37363
Winnellie NT 0821
Tel: 089 470 681 Fax: 089 844 586
Support organisation providing information and access to resources and facilities.

DISABLED PERSONS BUREAU ALICE SPRINGS
Tel: 089 514 882

DISABLED PERSONS BUREAU DARWIN
Tel: 089 203 213

STEPOUT – KATHERINE
Tel: 089 710 689

KATHERINE TOWN HALL
Tel: 089 721 322

TENNANT CREEK TOWN HALL
Tel: 089 622 401

YULARA (AYERS ROCK) COMMUNITY RESOURCE CENTRE
Tel: 089 562 420

MOBILITY AND ACCESS COMMITTEE DARWIN CITY CO.
Tel: 089 822 511

AUTOMOBILE ASSOCIATION OF NT
MLC Building, 79-81 Smith Street
Darwin NT 0800
Tel: 089 813 387 Fax: 089 412 965
Provides accommodation guide to properties with accessible facilities.

NT WHEELCHAIR SPORTS
PO Box 40194
Casuarina NT 0810
Tel: 089 844 794 Fax: 089 844 794

OFFICE OF SPORT AND RECREATION
DARWIN
Tel: 089 811 877

OFFICE OF THE ARTS DARWIN
Tel: 089 897 376

AIRPORTS
ALICE SPRINGS
Tel: 089 521 211 Fax: 089 530 258

Car Parking
No spaces reserved for wheelchair users,
but telephone the Duty Traffic Officer to
arrange transfer from the car park to the
terminal.

Facilities
Terminal: Access to the terminal building
is from road level by raised kerb onto the
pavement and through automatic doors.
The refreshment bar is accessible and is
adjacent to the passenger lounge. There
is one WC adjacent to the courtyard and
there are telephones and medical and
first aid facilities.

DARWIN
Tel: 089 453 333 (airport)
089 891 274 (information)
089 802 710 (reservations)

Car Parking
Spaces are reserved for those in wheelchairs.

Facilities
Terminal: The terminal is for both
international and domestic flights and
access is from road level directly into the
terminal. There are no roadside doors.
Wheelchair-accessible facilities include a
kiosk on the ground floor of the domestic
departure hall; a WC is located adjacent
to domestic arrivals on the ground floor
and there are telephones and first aid
facilities. Some airline staff and federal
policemen are holders of first aid

certificates and oxygen is available from
the doctor's room in the international
arrivals hall.

AIRLINE OFFICES
ANSETT AIRLINES
Tel: 089 504 100

QANTAS
Tel: 089 505 222

WHERE TO GO, WHERE TO STAY

ALICE SPRINGS
Alice Springs is at the geographical heart
of Australia's "Red Centre" and offers
sightseers plenty of variety.
The town was originally founded as a
staging point for the telegraph system,
and built near a permanent water hole in
the bed of the dry River Todd.
"The Alice" is now a pleasant, modern
town with good shops and restaurants.
Chambers Pillar Historical Reserve,
149km south of Alice Springs on the Old
South Road, is a sandstone formation
rising 50m above the surrounding plain.
A symbolic site in the Aboriginal
Dreamtime, it was also a prominent
landmark in early central Australian
history.

HOTEL CODES: THE CODE *AS1428* APPLIES TO
ALL PROPERTIES THAT CONFORM TO THE
AUSTRALIAN STANDARD, WITH ACCESS TO
CAR-PARKING, ROOMS, BATHROOMS AND WC
FACILITIES.

HOTELS
ALICE MOTOR INN (FL) *AS1428*
27 Undoolya Road
Tel: 089 522 322 Fax: 089 532 309
No. of hotel rooms: 20
No. of adapted rooms: 1
Facilities: restaurant - 200 metres; pool
Two persons per night: 85.00
The city is 1km away and local shops 500m.

ALICE SPRINGS PACIFIC RESORT (FL) *AS1428*
34 Stott Terrace
Tel: 089 526 699 Fax: 089 530 995

No. of hotel rooms: 108
No. of adapted rooms: 5
Facilities: restaurant; pool
Two persons per night: 125.00
A tree-studied and lawned hotel on the bank of the Todd River and just 500m from the town centre.

MELIA ALICE SPRINGS (SOL)
Barrett Drive
Alice Springs NT 0870
Tel: 089 528 000 Fax: 089 523 822
No. of hotel rooms: 235
No. of adapted rooms: 12
Facilities: 2 restaurants; pool; sauna; spa
Located 2km from the town centre and 15km from the airport. The surrounding area is flat.

OASIS FRONTIER RESORT (BW) *AS1428*
10 Gap Road
Tel: 089 521 444 Fax: 089 523 776
No. of hotel rooms: 102
No. of adapted rooms: 5
Facilities: restaurant; 2 pools; sauna; spa
The hotel overlooks the Todd River and is set in spacious gardens.

VISTA HOTEL ALICE SPRINGS *AS1428*
Stephens Road
Tel: 089 526 100 Fax: 089 526 234
No. of hotel rooms: 140
No. of adapted rooms: 3
Facilities: restaurant; accessible outdoor dining area and barbecue; pool
Two persons per night: 115.00
2km from the centre of town, the surrounding area is hilly.

ACCESSIBLE TRANSPORT
ALICE SPRINGS AIR CHARTER
PO Box 2987
Alice Springs
NT 0871
Tel: 089 521 250 Fax: 089 530 055
Air Charter runs a one-day Uluru (Ayers Rock) Air Adventure Tour which is accessible. If your wheelchair is small and collapsible it will fit comfortably into the luggage locker of the aircraft. If not, a loan chair can be made available at Uluru (Ayers Rock) for a small fee.

ANSETT INTERNATIONAL TRAVEL
Todd Mall
Tel: 089 504 100

CATA
Todd Street
Tel: 089 525 266

CHARTER COACHES
Tel: 089 531 775

DELUXE COACHLINES
Ford Plaza
Hartley Street
Tel: 089 524 444

PIONEER TRAILWAYS
Todd Mall
Tel: 089 522 422

RED CENTRE TRAVEL
Todd Street
Tel: 089 525 477

ACCESSIBLE ATTRACTIONS
ADELAIDE HOUSE MUSEUM
48 Todd Mall
Alice Springs NT 0871
Tel: 089 521 856
Open Saturdays and public holidays
Closed December, January and February
Exhibit of the work of "Flynn of the Inland". First hospital. Early radio. There is no designated parking.

ANZAC HILL MEMORIAL AND LOOK OUT
It is necessary to drive to the top parking bay before proceeding up the side ramp to the summit. No designated parking.

ARALUEN ART CENTRE
Laparinta Drive
Alice Springs NT 0870
Tel: 089 525 022 Fax: 089 520 259
Open daily
Two art galleries of local art and craft and five hectares of gardens. There is designated parking.

AVIATION MUSEUM
Tel: 089 524 241
There is designated parking.

Uluru – the world's best known rock.

GHAN PRESERVATION SOCIETY
Norris Bell Avenue
Alice Springs NT 0870
Tel: 089 555 047 Fax: 089 555 220
Open daily
This includes the Old Ghan Train Museum and working sheds. There is no designated parking.

MECCA DATE GARDENS
Palm Circuit
Alice Springs NT 0870
Tel: 089 522 425 Fax: 089 522 425
Open daily
This was the first date farm in Australia and tasting is permitted! There is no designated parking.

STUART TOWN GAOL
Parsons Street
Alice Springs NT 0870
Tel: 089 524 516 Fax: 089 522 185
Open daily
Constructed from stone quarried locally from the range near Heavitree Gap. There is no designated parking.

ULURU (AYERS ROCK)
The world's best known rock, 3.6km long by 348m high, that changes colour as the day goes by, red to grey and back again. The area has deep cultural significance to the Aborigines who own the surrounding national park. Maggie Springs, at the base of the rock, form a permanent water hole. 32km away, a collection of smaller rocks, called the Olgas, are equally impressive.

HOTELS
DESERT GARDENS
PO Box 121, Yulara Drive Yulara
Tel: 089 562 100 Fax: 089 562 156
No. of hotel rooms: 100
No. of adapted rooms: 6
Facilities: 2 restaurants; pool
Two persons per night: 230.00
500m from the town centre, with all the adapted rooms having a view of the Rock. The surrounding area is flat.

OUTBACK PIONEER HOTEL
Yulara Drive
Yulara NT 0872

Tel: 089 562 170 Fax: 089 562 320
No. of hotel rooms: 125
No. of adapted rooms: 1
Facilities: 3 restaurants; pool
The town centre is 1.5km away along a flat path and the surrounding area is HILLY.

SAILS IN THE DESERT HOTEL
PO Box 21
Yulara Drive
Yulara NT 0872
Tel: 089 562 200 Fax: 089 562 018
No. of hotel rooms: 236
No. of adapted rooms: 10
Facilities: 3 restaurants; pool; spa; art gallery
Near Uluru (Ayers Rock), the Olgas, Mt. Connor, Lake Amadeus, Valley of the Wings, Curtain Springs Outback Station and Uluru National Park.

ACCESSIBLE TRANSPORT AND TOURS
ULURU EXPERIENCE
PO Box 254, Kooringal
New South Wales 2650
Tel: 069 218 170 Fax: 069 218 346
Edible Desert, Spirit of Uluru and Uluru Experience Champagne Sunset Tours are confirmed as suitable, and the Olgas and Dunes tour also if travelling with a companion. The vehicles are not equipped with loading/lifting facilities but guides are very willing to help. Disability of visitor is matched to the tours.

DELUXE COACHES
Yulara Resort
Tel: 089 562 171

AYERS ROCK TOURING CO
Yulara Resort
Tel: 089 562 066

VIP CHAUFFEUR HIRE CARS
Yulara Resort
Tel: 089 562 283

AVIS RENT A CAR
Tel: 089 562 066

BUDGET RENT A CAR
Tel: 089 562 075/093

CHEAPA RENT A CAR
Tel: 089 562 229

CENTRAL AUSTRALIAN HELICOPTERS PTY
Tel: 089 562 093/114

Note that the Australian National Parks and Wildlife Service has provided a dirt, sandy track around the base of Uluru (Ayers Rock) suitable for wheelchairs with thick wheels.

Uluru has deep Aboriginal cultural significance.

BATHURST

Bathurst and Melville Islands, 80km north of Darwin, have been home to the Tiwi Aborigines for thousands of years. Take a tour from Darwin to visit the Aboriginal community, learn about their culture and join in activities.

There is wonderful Tiwi fabric to buy from their co-operative craft and fabric workshops.

DARWIN

Capital city of Northern Australia, Darwin is located on the shores of one of the continent's largest harbours. It is a warm and relaxed city, but isolated. Named after Charles Darwin by whom the area was discovered on a visit by HMS Beagle in 1839, it is now a cosmopolitan and racially mixed city with much evidence of new building after Hurricane Tracy flattened much of it in 1974.

The city was founded in 1869 after several abortive attempts by the British to settle in the area. Its purpose was to exclude the French and the Dutch. The growth of the city was accelerated by the discovery of gold at Pine Creek in 1871.

World War II put Darwin on the map when it became an important Allied base in the war against the Japanese.

The centre of the town is at the end of a peninsula and the main shopping area is located around Smith Street. The suburbs spread from 12 to 15km towards the north and east.

Few of the colonial buildings survived the cyclone, but some of historic interest, such as the Commonwealth Bank, remain. The tropical climate often can be debilitating for some visitors from the northern hemisphere.

Darwin does have beaches, although even outside the GREEN season (November to April) crocodiles can be seen and there is also the deadly Box Jellyfish.

TOURIST BOARD

DARWIN REGION TOURISM ASSOCIATION
PO Box 4392
Darwin NT 0801
Tel: 089 814 300 Fax: 089 817 346

AIRLINE OFFICES

ANSETT
46 Smith Street Mall
Tel: 089 803 333

GARUDA INDONESIA
Tel: 089 811 103

ACCESSIBLE TRANSPORT

TAXIS
ACCESS CAB
Tel: 089 818 777 Darwin

HANDIBUS
Tel: 089 263 0675

HOTEL

MELIA DARWIN (SOL)
32 Mitchell Street
Darwin NT 0800
Tel: 089 820 000 Fax: 089 811 765
No. of hotel rooms: 233
No. of adapted rooms: 5
Facilities: 2 restaurants; 2 bars; pool; spa
In the heart of Darwin's central business district, looking northwards over the Timor Sea. The airport is 20 minutes' drive away. This is an elegant hotel close to the shopping malls. The surrounding area is flat.

ACCESSIBLE ATTRACTIONS

DARWIN CROCODILE FARM
On Stuart Highway, south of the Arnheim Highway turnoff, 40 km from Darwin, Noonamah, Darwin NT 0837
Tel: 089 881 450 Fax: 089 882 001
Open daily 0900-1700
Salt- and freshwater crocodiles fed at 1400.

FANNIE BAY GAOL MUSEUM
East Point Road, Fannie Bay NT 0820
Tel: 089 410 341 Fax: 089 411 258
Open daily 1000-1700
Contains the gallows constructed for the last execution in the territory in 1952 plus display on Cyclone Tracy.

INDO PACIFIC MARINE
Stokes Hill Wharf
Darwin NT 0801
Tel: 089 811 294 Fax: 089 815 176

Open daily 0900-1700
Exhibition of living coral reefs from the Darwin area.

MUSEUM OF ARTS AND SCIENCES
Conacher Street, Fannie Bay
Darwin NT 0820
Tel: 089 824 211, Fax: 089 411 258
Opening hours: Monday-Friday 0900-1700
Saturday and Sunday 1000-1600
A fine art collection plus Northern Territory and military history, Aboriginal art, natural science and maritime.

NORTHERN TERRITORY WILDLIFE PARK
Cox Peninsula Road
Berry Springs NT 0837
Tel: 089 886 000 Fax: 089 886 210
Open daily 0830-1800
Located 50 minutes from Darwin, the park displays all native wildlife in natural habitats set in 400 hectares of natural bushland. The park actively promotes its welcome to people in wheelchairs, admission staff going to cars to greet them. The car park has designated parking bays as close as possible to the main terminal. All paths are smooth. All trains have a hydraulic platform at the rear, lowered for easy access. All exhibits, kiosks and souvenir shops have wide doors and all three large WCs blocks have accessible WCs.

KAKADU
200km east of Darwin, Kakadu National Park covers the floodplains of the Wildman and Alligator Rivers and the spectacular waterfalls of Jim Jim and Twin Falls. At Ubirr there are galleries of Aboriginal rock paintings thought to be 60,000 years old. Many birds make the wetlands here their home.
There are several Aboriginal settlements contained within the National Park plus three uranium mining leases in the east. Extensive wildlife abounds, some of which may have their eyes on you! So take heed of the crocodile warning signs. KAKADU NATIONAL PARK IS ACCESSIBLE IN SOME PARTS. THE MAIN ATTRACTIONS OF NOURLANGIE ROCK, UBIRR, YELLOW WATERS AND JABIRU ARE ACCESSIBLE IN RESTRICTED AREAS ONLY.
There are good facilities at Muirella camping area, with accessible parking and WC facilities at Nourlangie and Ubirr and wheelchair tracks to rock art sites. There is a boardwalk at Yellow Waters but no facilities. An early morning boat cruise is accessible with helpful crews.

Aboriginal drawing at Nourlangie.

TOURIST BOARD
KAKADU PARK HQ AND VISITORS' CENTRE
Near the junction of Arnhem and Kakadu
Highways
Tel: 089 792 101
Open daily 0800-1700

ACCESSIBLE TRANSPORT
OUTBACK NT AIR SAFARIS
KAKADU AIR SERVICES
Air Terminal
PO Box 95
Jabiru
NT 0886
Tel: 089 792 411 Fax: 089 792 303
This company offers half-hour and one-
hour scenic flights over Kakadu and
Arnhemland for those in wheelchairs.
Also available is a tour of the Ranger
Uranium Mine.

KATHERINE
Katherine Gorge is one of Australia's
greatest natural wonders. South of the
town are the Cutta Cutta Caves that
house a colony of rare bats and
Mataranka thermal pools. A busy little
town, where the Victoria Highway
branches off to the Kimberleys and
Western Australia.

TOURIST BOARD
KATHERINE REGION TOURIST ASSOCIATION
PO Box 555
Katherine
NT 0851
Tel: 089 722 650 Fax: 089 722 969
Opening hours: Monday-Friday 0845-1700
Saturday 0845-1200

HOTEL
PINE TREE MOTEL
3 Third Street
Tel: 089 722 533 Fax: 089 722 920
No. of motel units: 50
No. of adapted units: 2
Facilities: restaurant; pool
Two persons per night: 90.00
In central business district within a
tropical garden. All units have
refrigerator and television.

ACCESSIBLE ATTRACTIONS
MATARANKA THERMAL POOLS
The pools are accessible only by a dirt
pathway so a companion is advised.
There is no designated parking.

KINGS CANYON
Dubbed Australia's Grand Canyon, there
is a spectacular gorge with natural
outcrops called the Lost City. Also lush
palms in a beautiful, idyllic narrow gorge
called the Garden of Eden. The walls of
the canyon soar upwards over 200m, but
this Garden of Eden is not accessible.

TENNANT CREEK
Word has it that Tennant Creek was first
settled when a wagon carrying a load of
beer broke down here sometime during
the 1930s. Incidentally, there was a small
gold rush at the same time. An important
mining centre since the early 1930s, the
Eldorado Mine, the largest of the early
diggings, closed in 1958 after yielding
175,000 grams of fine gold.
Tennant Creek is now a modern Outback
town with wide tree-lined streets. The
surrounding district has a fascination all
of its own, offering the chance to find
gold around the old diggings or to
discover the mystical majesty of the
Devils Marbles, on the road to Alice
Springs

TOURIST BOARD
TENNANT CREEK REGIONAL TOURIST
ASSOCIATION
PO Box 601
Tennant Creek NT 0861
Tel: 089 623 337/388 Fax: 089 622 509

HOTELS
BLUESTONE MOTOR INN
1 Paterson Street
Tel: 089 622 617 Fax: 089 622 883
No. of hotel rooms: 65
No. of adapted rooms: 2
Facilities: restaurant; pool
Two persons per night: 80.00
On the Stuart Highway with 65 self-
contained units. The town is 1km away
and the surrounding area is flat.

QUEENSLAND

Geographically more tropical in the northern part of the state, Queensland's booming tourist trade on its coastal strip offers beaches, bays, islands and the Great Barrier Reef. There are also many sugar cane fields and rain forests.

The whole state offers a relaxed lifestyle and Brisbane, the state capital, sits astride the meandering Brisbane river. Just an hour's drive north of Brisbane is the beautiful Sunshine Coast, and an hour to the south, the beach resorts of the Gold Coast.

Mountains of the Great Dividing Range run west of Brisbane down through NSW to Victoria. West across the Range through the long-established rural centre there is the vastness of Queensland's rich pastoral regions. 45km west of the Gold Coast is Lamington National Park, a region of rugged mountains and jungle-like rainforest, with many walking tracks, 500 waterfalls, abundant wildlife and ancient beech trees.

Time zone
October-March: GMT + 11 hours
April-September: GMT + 10 hours

TOURIST BOARDS

QUEENSLAND TOURIST AND TRAVEL CORPORATION
Queensland House
392 Strand
London WC2R 0LZ
Tel: 071-836 7242 Fax: 071-836 5881

QUEENSLAND TOURIST AND TRAVEL CORPORATION
36th Floor, Riverside Court
123 Eagle Street
Brisbane QLD 4000
Tel: 07 833 5400 Fax: 07 833 5436

BRITISH CONSULATE-GENERAL
BP House
193 North Quay
Brisbane QLD 4000
Tel: 07 236 2575/7 Fax: 07 236 2576

UNITED STATES TOURIST BOARD
Queensland Tourist and Travel Corporation
Suite 330, Third Floor
Northrop Plaza
1800 Century Park East
Los Angeles CA 90067
Tel: 213 788 0997 Fax: 213 788 0128

Natural attractions at Bunya Park.

SUPPORT ORGANISATIONS

QUEENSLAND DEPARTMENT OF HEALTH
Queensland Health Building
147-163 Charlotte Street
Brisbane QLD 4000
Tel: 010 617 234 0111
Fax: 010 617 221 0951

QUEENSLAND DEPARTMENT OF TRANSPORT
Capital Hill, 85 George Street
Brisbane QLD 4001
Tel: 010 617 237 9650
Fax: 010 617 237 9670

PARAPLEGIC AND QUADRIPLEGIC ASSOCIATION OF QUEENSLAND
28 Horan Street, West End
Brisbane QLD 4101
Tel: 07 844 7311 Fax: 07 846 1184
Toll free in Australia: 008 810 513
A charitable organisation providing information and services.

INDEPENDENT LIVING CENTRE OF QUEENSLAND
c/o Repatriation General Hospital
Newdegate Street, Greenslopes
QLD 4120
Tel: 07 394 7471 Fax: 07 394 1013
Information and advisory service about equipment, sources of supply for both hire and purchase.

DISABLED PERSONS' SERVICE
Tel: 07 224 2111 Fax: 07 221 2728

ACROD Tel: 07 395 3095

DISABILITY SERVICES CO-ORD. BRISBANE CITY COUNCIL
GPO Box 1434, Brisbane QLD 4001
Tel: 07 225 4416 Fax: 07 225 5230
Produces *Access Brisbane* – a guide for people with disabilities that is invaluable.

SPORTING WHEELIES & DISABLED SPORT AND RECREATION ASSOCIATION OF QUEENSLAND
24 Ross Street, Newstead QLD 4006
Tel: 07 252 5244 Fax: 07 252 7552

ROYAL AUTOMOBILE CLUB OF QUEENSLAND
300 St Pauls Terrace, Fortitude Valley

Brisbane QLD 4001
Tel: 07 361 2444 Fax: 07 849 0610
Produces an accommodation directory with accessible properties.

QUEENSLAND DEPARTMENT OF ENVIRONMENT AND HERITAGE
PO Box 155, North Quay
Brisbane QLD 4002
Tel: 07 227 7111
The department does not produce specific access publications but will help with advice and information about Queensland's national parks.

AIRPORTS

BRISBANE
Tel: 07 268 6666 (airport)
07 268 9511 (information)
07 234 3833 (reservations)

Car Parking
There are no spaces reserved for wheelchair users in any of the three terminal car parks, but telephone the airport manager of the airline with which you are travelling to make arrangements for transfer to the terminal buildings.

Facilities
International Terminal: Access is from road level by kerb crossovers onto the pavement and through automatic doors. Wheelchair-accessible facilities include cocktail/refreshment bars situated adjacent to the departures hall.
There are three accessible WCs adjacent to the departures hall and gate lounges. Telephones and medical and first aid facilities are accessible. There is a casualty centre open 0830-1630 Monday to Friday and a registered nursing sister is available during these hours. At other times first aid facilities are available within the terminal. Domestic Terminal: Wheelchair-accessible facilities include cocktail/refreshment bars on ground floor, one WC located off the public concourse, telephones, medical and first aid facilities. TAA Terminal: Access is from road level by kerb crossovers onto the pavement and through automatic

doors. Cocktail and refreshment bars are situated near the public lounge and are accessible. The first floor restaurant is not accessible.

One wheelchair-accessible WC is located off the public concourse. Telephones are at the correct height for wheelchair users. The casualty centre is available – see International Terminal.

Ansett Terminal: Access from road level by kerb crossovers onto the pavement and through automatic doors. Wheelchair-accessible facilities include cocktail/refreshment bars adjacent to the public lounge. One WC near bistro, telephones, medical and first aid facilities. The casualty centre is available – see International Terminal.

CAIRNS
Tel: 070 504 150 (airport)
008 177 767 (reservations)

Car Parking
Spaces are reserved for those in wheelchairs, the car park serving the single terminal for both international and domestic flights.

Facilities
Terminal: Access is from road level by kerb crossovers onto the pavement and through automatic doors. The aerobridge to aircraft is accessible by ramp. Wheelchair-accessible WCs are adjacent to all WC blocks. Telephones and drinking fountains are at an accessible height. Department of Health doctors can attend whilst on duty. There is a first aid room and counter staff should be contacted if the room is required. Oxygen is available if the aircraft is parked on the tarmac.

AIRLINES
ANSETT AUSTRALIA AIRLINES
Corner of George and Queen Streets
Tel: 07 854 2828
FLIGHT WEST AIRLINES
PO Box 10096, 333 Adelaide Street
Brisbane 4000
Tel: 07 229 1177 Fax: 07 221 7487
Toll-free: 008 77 7879

PO Box 517
Garbutt 4817 Townsville
Tel: 07 725 3855 Fax: 07 779 0007

PO Box 107
Cairns Mail Centre
Cairns 4870
Tel: 07 035 9511 Fax: 07 035 9858

PO Box 13
Horn Island Torres Straits 4875
Tel: 07 069 1543 Fax: 07 069 1361

PO Box 1808
Mount Isa 4825
Tel: 07 743 9333 Fax: 07 743 6191

SUNSTATE AIRLINES
Brisbane Airport
Box 256 Hamilton Central
Queensland 4007
Tel: 07 860 4577 Fax: 07 860 4578

AIRLINE OFFICES
AIR NEW ZEALAND
288 Edward Street
Brisbane
Tel: 07 229 2799 (administration)
Tel: 07 229 3044 (reservations)

AUSSIE AIRWAYS
PO Box 100
Manunda 4870
Tel: 070 53 3980 Fax: 070 53 6315
Toll-free 008 620 022

BRITISH AIRWAYS
243 Edward Street
Brisbane
Tel: 07 223 3123

QANTAS
214 Adelaide Street
Brisbane
Tel: 07 234 3833 (administration)
Tel: 07 234 3747 (reservations)

SINGAPORE AIRLINES
100 Eagle Street
Brisbane
Tel: 07 237 7777

ACCESSIBLE TRANSPORT
RAILWAYS
Contact Queensland Railways
Tel: 07 235 2222
There is wheelchair access at the
following stations:
NORTH COAST LINE; Caboolture, Nambour,
Gympie North, Maryborough West,
Bundaberg, Gladstone, Rockhampton,
Mackay, Proserpine, Bowen, Ayr,
Townsville, Tully, Innisfail, Cairns.
INLANDER; Townsville, Charters Towers,
Hughenden, Richmond, Julia Creek,
Colncurry, Mt. Isa.
MIDLANDER; Rockhampton, Emerald,
Alpha, Jericho, Barcaldine, Ilfracombe,
Longreach, Winton.
WESTLANDER; Ipswich, Toowoomba,
Dalby, Chinchilla, Roma, Charleville,
Cunnamulla, Qulipie, Warwick,
Inglewood, Goondiwindi, Thallon,
Dirrimbandi.

TAXIS
B & W CABS
Tel: 07 238 1000

YELLOW CABS
Tel: 07 391 0191

WHEELCHAIR-ACCESSIBLE VEHICLES
ARE PROVIDED BY CAB COMPANIES AT
THE FOLLOWING CENTRES:
Bundaberg, Cairns, Gladstone, Gold
Coast, Hervey Bay, Ipswich, Mackay,
Maryboro, Redcliffe, Rockhampton,
Townsville and Yeppoon.

SPECIALIST TOUR OPERATORS
SPECIAL CARE TRAVEL
PO Box 109
Mooloolaba QLD 4557
Tel: 07 143 7511 Fax: 07 143 7208
This operator provides fully escorted
holiday tours.

HANDI HOLIDAYS
11 Telina Drive
Mackay QLD 4740
Tel: 07 942 4513
Provides suitable tours in the Mackay
region.

WHERE TO GO, WHERE TO STAY

BRIBIE ISLAND (see SUNSHINE COAST)

BRISBANE
Once home to Sydney's criminal class,
"free" settlers arrived in 1842, but were
required to labour in expanding mining
and agricultural industries.
Now the third largest city and sunniest
capital in Australia, Brisbane is situated
on the River Brisbane with an exciting
Manhattan-style skyline, good restaurants
and shopping malls, (particularly in
Queen Street Mall, Edward and George
Streets). It is surrounded by hills and
offers numerous squares and stilt houses
with wide verandas. Host to Expo '88
where much use was made of the
Brisbane River. Brisbane is seen as the
gateway to the Sunshine and Gold Coasts,
each an hour's drive away.
Brisbane somehow manages to combine
the friendly atmosphere of a large
country town with the vitality of a
modern city. Morton Island is 50km
north east of Brisbane, a large sand mass
with 40km of beaches. The extensive
national park area is rich in flora and
fauna and includes the world's highest
sand dune.

SUPPORT ORGANISATION
DISABILITY SERVICES SECTION
Brisbane City Council
GPO Box 1434
Brisbane QLD 4001
Tel: 07 225 4416 Fax: 07 225 5230

ACCESSIBLE TRANSPORT
TAXIS
ACCESS CABS
Tel: 07 391 1000

CAR RENTAL WITH HAND CONTROLS
AVIS AUSTRALIA
Tel: 07 252 7111

BUDGET RENT-A-CAR
Tel: 07 252 0151

70

Brisbane – Manhattan style in Australia's sunniest capital.

HOTELS

BRISBANE CITY TRAVELODGE (SPHC)
Roma Street
Tel: 07 238 2222 Fax: 07 238 2288
No. of hotel rooms: 191
No. of adapted rooms: 1
Facilities: 2 restaurants; pool; sauna; spa
Adjacent to Brisbane Transit Centre in the city centre. The surrounding area is both hilly and flat.

GREGORY TERRACE MOTOR INN (FL)
297 Gregory Terrace
Spring Hill
Bisbane QLD 4000
Tel: 07 832 1769 Fax: 07 832 2640
No. of hotel rooms: 36
No. of adapted rooms: 1
Facilities: restaurant; pool
Two persons per night: 90.00
In Spring Hill, 1km from Brisbane city centre. Panoramic views of Brisbane. The surrounding area is HILLY.

HILTON INTERNATIONAL (HH)
190 Elizabeth Street
Brisbane QLD 4000
Tel: 07 231 3131 Fax: 07 231 3199
No. of hotel rooms: 321
No. of adapted rooms: 2
Facilities: 3 restaurants; pool; sauna; spa
A premier hotel in the city centre on Queen

Street Mall in the heart of the business district. The best shops and restaurants are accessible by a covered walkway from the lobby. A striking feature is the atrium, soaring 25 floors above the grand lobby. The surrounding area is flat.

QUALITY HOTEL RIVER PLAZA (CHI)
South Brisbane, 21 Dock Street
South Brisbane QLD 4101
Tel: 07 844 4455 Fax: 07 844 9254
No. of hotel rooms: 141
No. of adapted rooms: 1
Facilities: restaurant; pool
Two persons per night: 240.00
Set on the south bank of the Brisbane River with stunning views of the city skyline, Botanical Gardens and mountains beyond. Close by are the Queensland Cultural Centre and South Bank Parklands. Set on a slight slope but fairly flat.

RADISSON NORTH QUAY HOTEL (RAD)
293 North Quay
Tel: 07 236 1440 Fax: 07 236 1582
No. of hotel rooms: 120 suites, 19 rooms
No. of adapted rooms: 2 suites (1 queen, 1 twin)
Facilities: pool; spa
Two persons per night: 130.00
On the north bank of the Brisbane River, 7 minutes' walk from the central business district and Queen Street Shopping Mall. Adjacent to Brisbane Transit Centre with superb views.

SHERATON BRISBANE HOTEL AND TOWERS (SH)
249 Turbot Street
Tel: 07 835 3535 Fax: 07 835 4960
No. of hotel rooms: 410
No. of adapted rooms: 8
Facilities: restaurant; pool; sauna
Near Kookuburra Queen Riverboat and Riverside attractions. 16km to Botanical Gardens and Lone Pine Koala Sanctuary.

ACCESSIBLE TRANSPORT
RAILWAYS
BRISBANE CITYTRAIN
Tel: 07 235 1632
There are many accessible stations within Cityrail. A map is available from Citytrain.

ACCESSIBLE ATTRACTIONS
ALMA PARK ZOO
Alma Road
Kallangur
Tel: 07 204 6566
There is public parking only and no accessible WC facility.

AUSTRALIAN WOOLSHED
148 Samford Road
Ferny Grove
Tel: 07 351 5366
There is public parking only and no accessible WC facility, but most areas are accessible.

BOARDWALK AT BREAKFAST CREEK
Breakfast Creek Road
Newstead
Tel: 07 252 7140
There is designated parking and accessible WC facilities for both sexes.

BUNYA PARK WILDLIFE SANCTUARY
Bunya Park Drive
Eatons Hill
Tel: 07 264 1200
Public parking only and no accessible WC available, but most areas are accessible.

CITY BOTANIC GARDENS
Alice Street
Brisbane
Tel: 07 221 4528
Designated parking is available and both male and female accessible WC facilities.

EARLYSTREET HISTORICAL VILLAGE
75 Mcilwraith Avenue
Norman Park
Tel: 07 398 6866
This is partly accessible, although no suitable WC facility is on site.

EXPO 88 now SOUTH BANK PARKLANDS
Stanley Street Plaza
South Brisbane
Tel: 07 867 2051
Good, designated parking bays accessed through Merivale Street, and whole site is reasonably accessible. Three unisex and two separate male/female accessible WCs

located throughout the 16 hectare site. Attractions such as the Butterfly House and Gondwana Rainforest Sanctuary are at least partly accessible.

LONE PINE KOALA SANCTUARY
Jesmond Road
Fig Tree Pocket
Tel: 07 378 1366
Spacious designated parking and accessible male and female WC facility. Two wheelchairs available free of charge.

MARITIME MUSEUM
Stanley Street
South Brisbane
Tel: 07 844 5361
Mostly accessible with male/female accessible WCs. Limited parking with no designated bays.

MT COOT-tha-BOTANIC GARDENS
Mt Coot-tha Road
Toowong
Tel: 07 377 8893
Designated parking and accessible male and female WC accessible at the Tropical Dome and also near the lookout.

PIER AT WATERFRONT PLACE
1 Eagle Street
Brisbane
There is only public parking here, and accessible unisex WC facility.
The pub, restaurant, shops and Sunday craft market are accessible.

QUEENSLAND CULTURAL CENTRE
Stanley Street
South Brisbane
A large complex housing the following:

QUEENSLAND ART GALLERY
Tel: 07 840 7333

QUEENSLAND MUSEUM
Tel: 07 840 7555
Designated parking and accessible male and female WC facilities for both buildings. Ask the parking attendant for directions to the museum lift or Art Gallery lift.

QUEENSLAND MUSEUM SCIENCENTRE
Willam Street
Brisbane
Tel: 07 224 6003
No designated parking, but accessible male and female WC facilities and an accessible lift into this technological exhibit with light and sound shows.

RIVERSIDE MARKETS
Riverside Centre, 123 Eagle Street
Brisbane
Designated parking, accessible male and female WC facility and accessible lift for this Sunday craft market.

SIR THOMAS BRISBANE PLANETARIUM
Mt Coot-tha Road
Toowong
Tel: 07 377 8896
Designated parking and accessible male and female WC facility. In Mt Coot-tha Gardens there is seating for guests in wheelchairs.

ACCESSIBLE NATIONAL AND ENVIRONMENTAL PARKS IN BRISBANE AREA
WALKABOUT CREEK
Brisbane Forest Headquarters Park
Mt Nebo Road
The Gap
Tel: 07 300 4855
Public parking only, but accessible male and female WC facility. There is a wheelchair access ramp, gradient 1:11, to the freshwater aquaria and terraria. Please phone for permission to park near this access ramp.

BRISBANE FOREST PARK
Mt Nebo Road
Upper Kedron
This is a tall open forest, with a sealed car park with designated bays and separate accessible WCs. There is an accessible picnic area and an old gold mine in the eucalyptus forest.

BRISBANE FOREST PARK
North Brook Parkway
Dry open forest with sealed car

park without designated bays.
There is an accessible unisex WC. There is also a sealed path to the Wivenhoe Outlook with good views of the Brisbane Valley and Wivenhoe Dam

DOWNFALL CREEK BUSHLAND CENTRE
851 Rode Road
Chermside West

A dry open forest, freshwater swamp and creekside closed forest. There is a sealed car park but no designated bays.
Separate accessible WCs.
Wheelchair-accessible tables and shelters.
The Senses Trail Walkway has a less than 1:14 gradient, is wide and has kerbs and seats on both sides. Bushland Infocentre is staffed and accessible.

HAY'S LANDING
off Wivenhoe-Somerset Road
Wivenhoe Dam

Parkland, dry open forest, grassland and wetland here with an unsealed car park and no designated parking.
There is an accessible unisex WC facility and accessible shelters and BBQs at reasonable height. Good views of dam and surrounding ranges.

MANGROVE FOREST BOARDWALK
Granada Street
Wynnum North

A mangrove forest with a large unsealed car park and one designated bay. Separate accessible WCs located in Elanora Park. The walkway is a single boardwalk through the forest and to preserve the character, tree trunks and limbs have not been cut. Overhanging mangrove trunks and boughs allow trees to be felt. Birdwatching and listening is good.

BUNYAVILLE STATE FOREST
Old Northern Road
Bunya

Public parking only in unsealed car park without designated bays.
The picnic area is in a clearing in dry open forest. A circuit drive through the forest is two-wheel-drive accessible.

DAISY HILL STATE FOREST
Daisy Hill Road
Daisy Hill

Public parking only in unsealed car park without designated bays. The picnic area is a clearing in the eucalyptus forest and a circuit drive through is two-wheel-drive accessible.

HARMONY GARDENS
Gladstone Road
Dutton Park

Public parking, accessible male/female WCs.

IRONBARK GULLY AND LOMANDRA
Samford Road
Ferny Grove

Public parking and accessible male/female WCs available.
This is a dry, open forest with three accessible shelters and a picnic area amongst the eucalyptus. Busy at weekends, but not so during the week.

JOLLYS LOOKOUT
Mt Nebo Drive
Jollys Lookout

Designated parking and accessible male/female WCs available.

GREY GUM PARK AND MT COOT-tha LOOKOUT
Sir Samuel Griffith Drive
Mt Coot-tha

Public parking and accessible male/female WCs available.

MAIALA NATIONAL PARK
Mt Glorious Road
Mt Glorious

Public parking and accessible male/female WCs available.

There are a number of areas along Mt Nebo Road with public parking, but no accessible WCs.

BROAD BEACH (see GOLD COAST)

BUNDABERG

At the north end of Hervey Bay, the main product here is sugar. It is the birthplace of Bert Hinkler who made the first solo flight from England to Australia in 1928. From November to January, turtles lay their eggs at Mon Repos. There is a large sandstone slab, 25 million years old with 35 mystery craters in it on the Gin Gin road.

TOURIST BOARD
BUNDABERG TOURIST OFFICE
Corner of Bourbon and Mulgrave Streets
Tel: 07 152 2333
Open daily 0900-1700

BUNDABERG RUM DISTILLERY
Some areas accessible.

HISTORICAL MUSEUM
Fully accessible with adapted restaurant.

REPTILE RESERVE
Assistance required from car park where ground is steep. Reserve itself accessible, but no WC facility.

CAIRNS
One of the country's top tourist destinations, Cairns has a relaxed ambience, many tourist entertainments – cinemas, art galleries, zoos, pubs, watersports – and a picturesque waterfront. Cairns is very flat and ideal for wheelchairs. The town began life as the terminus of the railway to the tableland, following the "tin rush" in 1880. There are mangrove swamps both to the north and the south where many varieties of water bird can be seen at low tide.
The Esplanade is worth the trip with views over the estuary to the rainforest mountains beyond. There is easy access to the Barrier Reef.
All around Cairns there are green mountains, white beaches and blue water filled with technicolor fish. Rainforests run down to the sea and islands pepper the coast. 100km west of town is the unique Atherton Tableland of rolling hills, lush rainforests, waterfalls and crater lakes dotted with small villages. North of Cairns is Cape York Peninsula, the most northerly point on the mainland and one of the wildest, least populated areas of Australia. The best time to visit is between June and September.

TOURIST BOARD
36-38 Aplin Street
Tel: 07 031 3588
Opening hours: Monday-Friday 0900-1600
and 99 Esplanade Tel: 07 031 3588
Opening hours: Monday-Friday 0900-1600

AIRLINE OFFICES
AIR NEW ZEALAND
Cairns Airport
Tel: 07 051 4177

ANSETT
84 Lake Street
Tel: 07 050 2211

QANTAS
Corner of Lake and Shield Streets
Tel: 07 050 3711

FLIGHT WEST
Corner of Grafton and Spence Streets
Tel: 07 051 0718

ACCESSIBLE TRANSPORT
BUDGET RENT A CAR
Lake Street

AJAX RENT A CAR
141 Lake Street

JOLLY FROG
101 The Esplanade

HOTELS
HOLIDAY INN (HDI)
Corner of Esplanade and Florence Streets
Tel: 07 031 3757 Fax: 07 031 3770
No. of hotel rooms: 232
No. of adapted rooms: 2
Facilities: restaurant; pool; spa
The hotel is located right on the Esplanade overlooking Trinity Bay, the centre of town is 500 metres away. The surrounding area is flat.

RADISSON PLAZA HOTEL at the PIER (RAD)
Pierpoint Road
Tel: 07 031 1411 Fax: 07 031 3226
No. of hotel rooms: 220
No. of adapted rooms: 2
Facilities: restaurant; pool; sauna; spa

Two persons per night: 220.00
Water frontage on Trinity Bay in central
Cairns. Surrounding area is flat. Adjacent
to Marlin Marina, the main terminal for
Gt. Barrier Reef Cruises.
The hotel adjoins the Pier Marketplace, a
speciality retail complex, and has over an
acre of tropical gardens.

ACCESSIBLE ATTRACTIONS
HARTLEYS CREEK CROCODILE FARM
Cook Highway, Wangetti
40km north of Cairns
Open daily 0800-1700
Hundreds of crocodiles are on display and
can be seen in action at feeding time. The
farm's tropical setting is a backdrop to
the cassowary bird and native snakes.

ROYAL FLYING DOCTOR VISITORS CENTRE
1 Junction Street
Edgehill
7km north of Cairns
Open daily 0830-1630
An integral part of Australia's history.
The visitors centre features a 15-minute
talk on how the service evolved and a
short video that gives an insight into a
Day in the Life of a Flying Doctor. There
is also an extensive collection of
memorabilia on display.

ACCESSIBLE PARKING
Aplin Street, Lake Street, Grafton Street,
Spence Street, Abbott Street, The Pier
(Pierpoint Road)

ACCESSIBLE WC FACILITIES
City Place, Cairns City Library, (123 Lake
Street), Trinity Wharf (Wharf Street), The
Pier (Pierpoint Road)

COOKTOWN
158km north of Cairns. An historic town
on the banks of the Endeavour River that
served as a port for the nearby gold fields
in the 1870s. An abundance of rare native
flora flourishes here. Nearby, the
Endeavour National Park has excellent
examples of Aboriginal rock art.

COOLANGATTA (see GOLD COAST)

DAINTREE
126km north of Cairns, Daintree is a
small unspoiled township in the heart of
a tropical rainforest. There is a butterfly
farm in Daintree village and one can cruise
up the Daintree River to view mangrove and
rainforest scenery and wildlife.

DAISY HILL (BRISBANE)
A suburb 28km south of Brisbane.

HOTEL
LOGAN CITY MOTOR INN (FL)
3725 Pacific Highway
Daisy Hill QLD 4127
Tel: 07 209 7925 Fax: 07 209 7607
No. of hotel rooms: 20
No. of adapted rooms: 1
Facilities: restaurant; pool; spa; sauna
Two persons per night: 75.00
25 minutes from the Gold Coast and 30
minutes from the centre of Brisbane.

DALBY

TOURIST BOARD
TOURIST INFORMATION CENTRE
Thomas Jack Park
Dalby QLD 4405
Tel: 07 662 1066
Visit the Rock and Mineral Museum,
Pioneer Park Museum and Lake
Broadwater Environment Park. All are
accessible.

DUNK ISLAND (see GREAT BARRIER REEF)

GLADSTONE
Access to Heron, Masthead and Wilson
Islands that are on the Reef itself.
Gladstone boasts unspoiled beaches and
stunning views.
The port is very busy and is also home to
the mudcrab and sizeable fishing fleets.

GOLD COAST
This is a strip of beaches that runs from
the NSW border northwards for 35km
ending in the high rise of Surfers Paradise.
Obtain a copy of "Wheelchair Access to
Recreation" a marvellous guide to the
Gold and Sunshine Coasts. Contact

School of Applied Science,
University College of South Queensland,
Toowoomba 4350, Queensland.

GOLD COAST (BROAD BEACH)

HOTEL
PAN PACIFIC HOTEL (PP)
81 Surf Parade
Broadbeach QLD 4218
Tel: 07 592 2250 Fax: 07 592 3747
No. of hotel rooms: 298
No. of adapted rooms: 1
Facilities; 2 restaurants; pool; sauna; spa
Two persons per night: 180.00
Direct access to Kurrawa Beach, this
hotel towers above it. Adjoins a 190-store
shopping resort. Surrounding area is flat.

ACCESSIBLE ATTRACTION
HOTEL CONRAD-JUPITER CASINO
Broadbeach Island
Tel: 07 592 1133
Wide-designated parking and accessible
lifts. Male and female WC accessible.
There is a casino, restaurants, nightclub
and monorail to Oasis Shopping Resort.

GOLD COAST (COOLANGATTA)

TOURIST BOARD
TOURIST INFORMATION CENTRE
Beach House
Marine Parade
Tel: 07 536 7765
Opening hours: Monday-Friday 0830-1600

HOTELS
ALL SEASONS GREENMOUNT BEACH RESORT (FL)
Eden Avenue, PO Box 3 QLD 4225
Tel: 07 536 1222 Fax: 07 536 1102
No. of hotel rooms: 151
No. of adapted rooms: 1
Facilities: restaurant; pool
Two persons per night: 105.00
Overlooking the beach near the
Queensland/New South Wales border.
Located at the bottom of Greenmount
Hill but the surrounding area is flat.
500m to the town centre.

GOLD COAST (COOMERA)

ACCESSIBLE ATTRACTIONS
DREAMWORLD
Dreamworld Parkway
Tel: 07 573 1133
Public parking and unisex WCs
accessible. Most areas are practical for
wheelchairs. There is a theme park, live
entertainment, wildlife sanctuary and
restaurant, all accessible.

KOALA TOWN
Pacific Highway
Tel: 07 573 2166
Public parking and unisex-accessible WCs.

GOLD COAST (HOPE ISLAND)
A rural area at northern end of coast with
Sanctuary Cove at its centre.

ACCESSIBLE ATTRACTION
SANCTUARY COVE MARINE VILLAGE
Casey Road
Tel: 07 530 8400
Designated parking and wheelchairs
available. There are male/female WCs, but
assistance is needed.

GOLD COAST (LABRADOR)

HOTELS
LABRADOR HOLIDAY UNITS
9 McWilliam Close
Labrador GC. QLD 4215
Tel: 07 537 4766 Fax: 07 254 1291
No. of units: 6, two extensively adapted for
maximum independence
Located near Surfers Paradise. Units
specifically for people with disabilities.

GOLD COAST (MAIN BEACH)
Main Beach, just offshore on a spit, is the
biggest marine park in the southern
hemisphere. The strip stretches south.

HOTELS
SEA WORLD NARA RESORT
Sea World Drive, PO Box 690
Southport QLD 4215
Tel: 07 591 0000 Fax: 07 591 2375
No. of hotel rooms: 403

No. of adapted rooms: 3
Facilities: restaurant; pool; spa
Two persons per night: 250.00
On the site of a calm beach, 300 metres
from the hotel. The nearest town,
Southport, is 4km away. The surrounding
area is flat.

ACCESSIBLE ATTRACTIONS
MARINA MIRAGE
74 Sea World Drive
Tel: 07 557 0088
Designated parking and accessible
male/female WCs and lift. There is one
step at the entrance.

SEA WORLD
Sea World Drive
Tel: 07 588 2222
Designated parking and accessible
male/female WC facilities.

GOLD COAST (SURFERS PARADISE)
An extension of Main Beach, this is a very
popular lively resort with beautiful beaches.
Its Aboriginal name was Oomby Goomby,
meaning place beside the sea. Very
developed, swimming can be dangerous.

TOURIST BOARD
TOURIST INFORMATION CENTRE
Cavill Avenue
Tel: 07 538 4491
Opening hours: Monday-Friday 0800-1130,
1200-1645. Saturday 0900-1130, 1200-1630.
Sunday 0900-1130, 1200-1600

HOTELS
MARRIOTT SURFERS PARADISE RESORT (MAR)
158 Ferny Avenue
Tel: 07 592 9800 Fax: 07 592 9888
No. of hotel rooms: 330
No. of adapted rooms: 2
Facilities: 2 restaurants; pool; sauna; spa
Two persons per night: 175.00
Quality hotel located on Nearing River.
Close to beaches and shopping. 3km from
town centre, the surrounding area is flat.

SURFERS PARADISE LODGE (SPHC)
807 Gold Coast Highway
PO Box 730 QLD 4217

Tel: 07 592 9900 Fax: 07 592 1519
No. of hotel rooms: 265
No. of adapted rooms: 1
Facilities: 3 restaurants; pool; sauna;
whirlpool; kiddies' club
Close to shops and the beach. Surfers
Mall is 3km away and the beach 500m.
The surrounding area is flat.

ACCESSIBLE ATTRACTION
GRUNDY'S at SURFERS PARADISE
Cavill Avenue
Tel: 07 538 9011
Spacious designated parking and accessible
male/female WC facilities and accessible lift
in the Paradise Centre, level one.

GOLD COAST (TWEED HEADS)

ACCESSIBLE ATTRACTION
MINJUNGBAL ABORIGINAL CULTURAL CENTRE
Kirkwood Road
at the corner of Duffy Street
South Tweed Heads
Tel: 07 554 2275
This town is actually within the State of
New South Wales, but is listed here
because of Tweed Heads.
This is a dry, open forest with mangroves
and some vine thickets; an Aboriginal
cultural centre and bora ring.
Sealed car park without designated bays.
A sealed forest walk and mangrove
boardwalk are level and negotiable and
have signs illustrating plants used for
food and other resources.

ACCESSIBLE NATIONAL AND ENVIRONMENTAL PARKS – GOLD COAST AND HINTERLAND AREA
PINE RIDGE ENVIRONMENTAL PARK
Oxley Drive
Hollywell
A dry open forest, wet heath and
an unsealed car park without designated
bays. A sealed walkway leads to a
boardwalk that goes through wetter areas
of the reserve. The boardwalk terminates
at an unsealed path proceeding over a
sand ridge. Koalas can be seen in scribbly
gums and wild flowers are wonderful in
spring.

MARY CAIRNCROSS PARK
Mountain View Road
Maleny

Highland subtropical rainforest with sealed car park without designated bays. WCs are not accessible. There is an easily accessible lookout near the main entrance with spectacular views of Glass House Mountains.

The walkway is unsealed, level and easily accessible at first, becoming steeper and rougher after the path forks at about 100m.

MT TIBROGARGAN NATIONAL PARK
Barrs Road
Glass House Mountains

A dry open forest with an unsealed car park without designated bays, There is an accessible picnic area in the eucalyptus forest at the foot of Tibrogargan.

HOLT'S HILL LOOKOUT
Beerburrum Forest Drive
Glass House Mountains

A dry open forest with sealed car park without designated bays. Good lookout gives views of surrounding volcanic plugs, state forests, the ocean and sand islands.

THE KNOLL NATIONAL PARK
Knoll Road
Mt Tambourine

Tall and open eucalyptus forest with a sealed car park without designated bays. The lookout is easily accessed and gives good views to the north and west. There is a picnic area in tall open forest.

GOONDIWINDI

Goondiwindi is the Aboriginal name for "Resting Place of the Birds". On the Queensland/NSW border and the banks of Macintyre River; it is a major centre for wool, beef, cotton and grain.

HOTEL
TOWN HOUSE MOTOR INN AND LICENSED RESTAURANT
110 Marshall Street
Tel: 07 671 1855

This property has not been contacted direct but we are informed through an independent Queensland assessor that many ACCOMPANIED wheelchair users use the motel.

Assistance is needed but is available. There is one step into the office; no space on the sides of WCs; back-door access to the restaurant; one step into the adapted unit; hub in shower; sturdy plastic chair; but no shower rails or hose.

ACCESSIBLE ATTRACTIONS
HISTORIC CUSTOMS HOUSE
McLean Street
Opening hours: every day except Wednesday 1000-1600.

The last house on the right before bridge, it was used as the border crossing before there was free trade between the states.

WAR MEMORIAL PARK
Soldier memorial with record of Australians killed in WW1, WW11 and Vietnam.

FALCON COURT ROSE FARM
Leichhardt Highway

GUNSYND "GOONDIWINDI GREY"
Statue in Apex Park on the bank of Macintyre River, that forms the border between Queensland and NSW. There is a picnic area beside the bridge.

GREAT BARRIER REEF
The Reef runs 1,800km north-south off the coast, from Gladstone to just south of Papua New Guinea. It is the largest structure in the world made from living organisms. Near the coast in the north, it is almost 300km from the mainland in the southern part. The coral in places is over 500m thick and is a fascinating haven for many fish and sea creatures, including turtles, scorpions and sharks. Tours are available from coastal towns.

DUNK ISLAND (GBR)
Named by Captain Cook in 1770, the island is one of only three tropical rainforests on the reef with many varieties of bird, butterfly and wild orchid. Bananas and palm trees shade

79

trails from Brammo Bay to the summit. The first inhabitants called the island "Coonanglebah," meaning island of peace and plenty.

Air access is via Townsville or Cairns where assistance is provided, as it is on Dunk Island. There is a daily launch from Clump Point and a water taxi from Mission Beach.

HOTEL
DUNK ISLAND RESORT (FL)
PMB 28
Townsville
Tel: 07 068 8199 Fax: 07 068 8528
No. of hotel rooms: 148
No. of adapted rooms: 1
Facilities: 2 restaurants; pool; spa
Two persons per night: 300.00

The Resort is situated right on the beach front. There is a wide range of activities with special emphasis on groups and on interaction in the local tropical environment.

GYMPIE (see SUNSHINE COAST)

HAYMAN ISLAND (GBR)

A beautiful resort, this is the most northerly of the Whitsunday Islands and the closest to the Outer Barrier Reef. The island is owned by Ansett Airlines. Take the water taxi from Abel Point.

HOTEL
HAYMAN ISLAND HOTEL (LHW)
North Queensland 4801
Tel: 07 946 9100 Fax: 07 946 9410
No. of hotel rooms: 214
No. of adapted rooms: 69
Facilities: 4 restaurants; 3 pools (one far larger than Olympic size); sauna; spa
Two persons per night: 450.00

World-class resort hotel in lush tropical gardens, right on the beach and furnished with antiques and Australian art. The library is ideal for chess and other games. The surrounding area is hilly and flat. THERE ARE TWO UNRAMPED STEPS INTO THE LOUNGE. THE LIFT IS OPERATED MANUALLY. THERE IS NO SHOWER SEAT BUT

ONE CAN BE SUPPLIED. SPACE FOR LATERAL TRANSFER TO WC IS 70cm, NOT 80cm.

WHITSUNDAY (GBR REGION)

This is the largest in a group of 74 islands. Although not on the reef, the islands are ringed with coral formations.

HOTELS
CLUB CROCODILE RESORT
South Sea Island
Shute Harbour Road
Airlie Beach QLD 4802

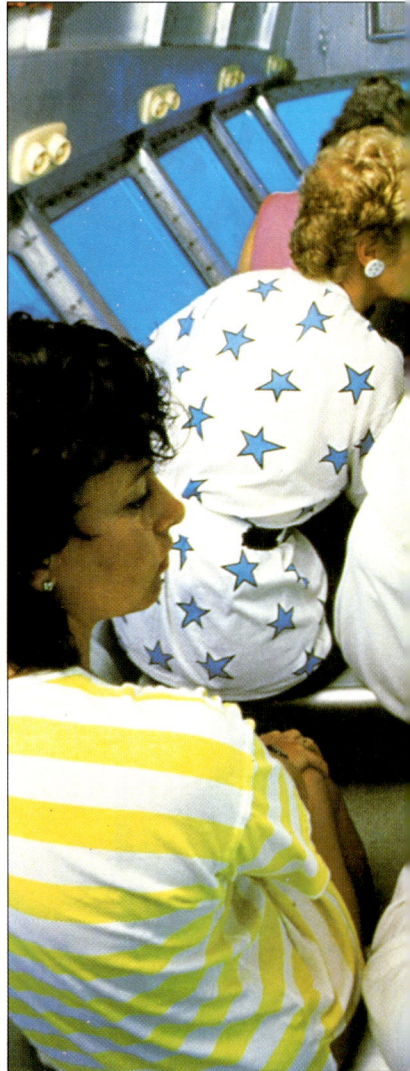

Tel: 07 946 7155 Fax: 07 946 6007
No. of hotel rooms: 160
No. of adapted rooms: 1
Facilities: 2 restaurants; pool; spa
Two persons per night: 125.00
Resort with Outback oasis ambience.
Unspoilt views across Whitsunday Islands.
NOTE THAT LIFT BUTTON INSIDE
CAR IS 150CM ABOVE FLOOR LEVEL.

DAYDREAM ISLAND TRAVELODGE RESORT (SPHC)
Daydream Island
Tel: 07 948 8488 Fax: 07 948 8499
No. of hotel rooms: 303

No. of adapted rooms: 3
Facilities: restaurant; pool; spa
Covering just 41 acres, the southern end
of Daydream Island contains the Beach
Club, coffee shop, boutiques and heated
swimming pool. At the northern end is
the main resort. There is a regular water
taxi to the mainland.

KANGAROO POINT

Inner suburb of Brisbane, 3km east.

*Semi-submersibles allow visitors to enjoy the
wonders of the Great Barrier Reef in comfort.*

HOTEL
STORY BRIDGE MOTOR INN (BW)
321 Main Street, Kangaroo Point
Tel: 07 393 1433 Fax: 07 891 1192
No. of hotel rooms: 49
No. of adapted rooms: 1
Facilities: restaurant; pool (THERE ARE FIVE
STEPS DOWN TO THE POOL)
Two persons per night: 75.00
Overlooking river and city centre from
the south. Chinatown is just over the
bridge. Town centre is 1km away and the
motel property on level ground, although
some of the surrounding area is HILLY.

KURANDA
24km north of Cairns, a picturesque
village set in lush forest on the edge of
the Atherton Tablelands. This is an area of
lush World Heritage rainforests, sparkling
mountain streams and waterfalls, at the
home of a major proportion of Australia's
plant and animal species. There are tree-
climbing kangaroos in these wet tropics;
in the upland rainforests from Atherton
south, the Lumholtz Tree Kangaroo is
seen in the treetops feeding on the leaves
of sarsaparilla and celery top. Farther
north around the Daintree region is the
Bennetts Tree Kangaroo.

HOTEL
KOAH BED AND BREAKFAST
Lot 4, Koah Road
MSI 1039
Kuranda, QLD 4872
Tel: 07 093 7074 Fax: 07 093 7629
No. of hotel rooms: 2
No. of adapted rooms: 2
Facilities: restaurant
Close to Kuranda, this is a special home,
the owner being in a wheelchair himself.
Situated on 10 acres of open bushland at
Koah, which is renowned for its tropical
fruits, it is only a 20-minute drive from
Mareeba, one of the largest Tableland
towns, and a tobacco and cattle area.
There are two vehicles with hand controls
for hire from the owners and you can be
met at Cairns Airport for immediate self-
drive or shuttle service between the
airport and their home.

ACCESSIBLE ATTRACTIONS
GREAT ADVENTURES
Wharf Street
Cairns QLD
Tel: 07 051 0455 Fax: 07 031 3753
UK Office: Sprint Australia
Paramount House, 71/75 Uxbridge Road
Ealing Broadway
London W5 5SL
Tel: 081-579 8648 Fax: 081-579 8281
Cruises on the Great Barrier Reef and
Islands. The big catamarans have every
convenience, including an accessible WC
and we are advised that the crew are
familiar with assisting people in chairs.
The crew will also assist wheelchair users
in and out of the semi-submersible for
those who do not wish to get wet. Diving
and snorkelling are also available.

DAINTREE RAINFOREST RIVER TRAINS
PO Box 448
Mossman, QLD 4873
Tel: 07 090 7676 Fax: 07 090 7660
This Kuranda train trip is also a must. It
winds through World Heritage forest up
the mountains to Kuranda. The
wheelchair carriage is fitted with
lockdowns and is accessible at both
stations. The Daintree river train cruises
the river spotting crocodiles and other
wildlife and is fully accessible.

LABRADOR (see GOLD COAST)

LONGREACH
Prosperous Outback town, with the sheep
population outnumbering the humans.
Visit the Australian Stockman's Hall of
Fame – there was a bicentennial project
here to honour the stockmen of Outback
Australia – which is accessible.

TOURIST BOARD
TOURIST OFFICE
Corner of Eagle and Duck Streets
Tel: 07 658 2133

MACKAY
The sugar capital of Australia , the
world's largest bulk sugar terminal is at
Port Mackay. Situated on the banks of the

Pioneer River with a picturesque hinterland and island-studded coastline. Fine man-made harbour.

TOURIST OFFICE
TOURIST INFORMATION CENTRE
320 Nebo Road
(The office is 3km outside town)
Tel: 07 952 2677

HOTELS
ALL SEASONS DOLPHIN HEADS RESORT (FL)
Beach Road
Dolphin Heads QLD 4740
Tel: 07 954 6666 Fax: 07 954 8341
No. of hotel rooms: 84
No. of adapted rooms: 42
Facilities: restaurant; pool; spa
Two persons per night: 188.00
Absolute beach-front location overlooking Barrier Reef islands. No high rise, no roads to cross and Queensland's largest national park close by. All facilities, apart from some adapted bedrooms, are on the ground floor.

ACCESSIBLE ATTRACTIONS
BOTANIC GARDENS
No accessible WC.

MARITIME MUSEUM
No accessible WC.

MAIN BEACH (see GOLD COAST)

MISSION BEACH
Palm-fringed beach resort, a three- to four-hour drive from Townsville and Cairns (88km). This is an area of outstanding beauty, stretching along 14km of clean white beach, fringed by lush tropical rainforest. The beach overlooks a string of reef islands, including Dunk Island.

HOTELS
CASTAWAYS BEACH RESORT
Corner Pacific Parade and Seaview Street
Tel: 07 068 7444 Fax: 07 068 7429
No. of hotel rooms: 54
No. of adapted rooms: 1
Facilities: restaurant; pool; spa

Two persons per night: 110.00
Beach resort right on the Coral Sea overlooking Dunk and Bedarra Islands.

MOSSMAN
90km north of Cairns. The largest virgin rainforest area in Australia stretches from Mossman to Cooktown. Mossman is Australia's most northerly sugar-milling town and the gateway to Mossman River Gorge in Daintree National Park.

NOOSA HEADS (see SUNSHINE COAST)

PORT DOUGLAS
A tourist resort with a quiet, elegant character. A tropical beachside village between the Great Barrier Reef and Daintree Forest. A lovely drive 70km to the north of Cairns.

HOTELS
RADISSON ROYAL PALMS RESORT (RAD)
Port Douglas Road
Port Douglas QLD 4871
Tel: 07 099 5577 Fax: 07 099 5559
No. of hotel rooms: 301
No. of adapted rooms: 2
Facilities: 2 restaurants; pool; spa; nightly in-house entertainment
Two persons per night: 140.00
Similar to a deluxe country club with many facilities. Close to Four Mile Beach and five minutes' drive to Marina Mirage for Great Barrier Reef cruises.

SHERATON MIRAGE HOTEL (SH)
Davidson Street
Tel: 07 099 5888 Fax: 07 098 5885
No. of hotel rooms: 210
No. of adapted rooms: 7
Facilities: restaurant; pool
Beach-front location with grounds that offer five acres of swimmable saltwater lagoons. Close to Marina Mirage, Daintree Rainforest and shops.

ACCESSIBLE ATTRACTION
RAINFOREST HABITAT
Easy parking, accessible designated WC, ramps and restaurant. Our independent wheelchair reporter recommends a visit.

BENN CROPP'S SHIPWRECK MUSEUM
6 Dixie Street
Port Douglas
Open daily 0900-1700
Visit one of the largest maritime shipwreck displays in Australia.

ROCKHAMPTON

Australia's beef capital on the banks of the Fitzroy River. First settled in 1855 after a gold rush. There are many fine old buildings on Quay Street. Visit the Botanic Gardens that are accessible.

TOURIST BOARDS
CAPRICORN INFORMATION CENTRE
Tropic Marker
Bruce Highway
Tel: 07 927 2055
Open daily 0900-1700

RIVERSIDE INFORMATION CENTRE
Quay Street
Tel: 07 922 5339
Open daily 0900-1700

SUNSHINE COAST (BRIBIE ISLAND)

Connected to the mainland by a bridge across Pumicestone Passage, a scenic waterway 25km east of Caboolture. 40 minutes from Brisbane Airport via Bruce Highway from Brisbane.
Visit the Botanic Reserve wildflowers, at their peak in late winter-early spring. Bribie Island is in the centre of the world's largest marine park.

HOTEL
BRIBIE WATERWAYS RESORT
155 Welsby Parade
Bongaree
Tel: 07 408 3000 Fax: 07 408 3076
No. of hotel rooms: 27
No. of adapted rooms:1
Facilities; restaurant; pool; coffee shop; resort shop; private jetty
Two persons per night: 95.00
On the waterfront and the beach, 800m from the Bongaree Jetty. The island is all sand and totally flat.

ACCESSIBLE NATURE WALK
BOTANIC RESERVE
Sunderland Drive, Bribie Island
Public parking only. Turn in at the Telecom micro-wave tower. Information Centre, heath and wildflower walk are accessible. There is a sealed car park without designated bays. WCs are accessible and picnic table sets are designed for those in wheelchairs. A sealed walkway through dry, open forest ends at the rainforest grove with an almost nil gradient. Sit near the beach front at Bellara or Banksia and watch the sun go down behind the Glass House Mountains across Pumicestone Passage.

OCEAN BEACH
There is an accessible path and paved lookout with fine views, with no need to leave the car. At the first car park past 5th Avenue, on North Street, there is a bitumen wheelchair ramp to the beach. Boyd Street car park is also bitumen with a great view of the ocean, Moreton Bay and Island are visible from the car.

SUNSHINE COAST (GYMPIE)

Scene of a gold rush in 1867, now the centre of a rich agricultural district. Visit the Historical Mining Museum, Wood Works Forestry and Timber Museum and Mothar Mountain State Forest Park. All accessible.

SUNSHINE COAST (NAMBOUR)

ACCESSIBLE ATTRACTION
SUNSHINE PLANTATION
Bruce Highway
Tel: 07 442 1333
Designated parking and accessible male/female WC facilities. Mostly accessible.

SUNSHINE COAST (NOOSA HEADS)

The most chic Australian resort with smart restaurants and beautiful beaches and the gateway to Noosa National Park.

TOURIST BOARD
NOOSA JUNCTION TOURIST CENTRE
Sunshine Beach Road
Tel: 07 447 3755

HOTEL
SHERATON NOOSA RESORT (SH)
Hastings Street
Noosa Heads QLD 4567
Tel: 07 449 4888 Fax: 07 449 2230
No. of hotel rooms: 169
No. of adapted rooms: 2
Facilities; 3 restaurants; pool; sauna; whirlpool
On the beach and close to Fraser Island, Noosa National Park and Sunshine Plantation. The surrounding area is flat.

SURFERS PARADISE (see GOLD COAST)

TOOWOOMBA
A delightful city with parks and streets lined with trees, 130km inland from Brisbane and the centre of the rich agricultural area of Darling Downs.

TOURIST BOARD
TOOWOOMBA AND GOLDEN WEST TOURIST ASSOCIATION
541 Ruthven Street
Box 3037 Toowoomba QLD 4350
Tel: 07 632 1988

QUEENSLAND RECREATION COUNCIL
142 Margaret Street, Toowoomba
Tel: 07 632 4944

ACCESSIBLE TRANSPORT
GARDEN CITY CABS LTD
Tel: 07 635 5599
Van with rear access for wheelchairs.

YELLOW CABS
Tel: 07 632 3344
Stretch taxi for wheelchairs, book 24 hrs ahead if possible.

FRIENDLY SOCIETIES DISPENSARY
8 Mylne Street
Tel: 07 632 3866
Hire out wheelchairs and aids.

HOTEL
GRAMMAR VIEW MOTOR INN (FL)
39 Margaret Street
Toowoomba QLD 4350
Tel: 07 638 3366 Fax: 07 638 1976
No. of hotel rooms: 25

No. of adapted rooms: 1
Facilities: restaurant; pool
Two persons per night: 80.00
1.5km from town, surrounding area is flat.

ACCESSIBLE ATTRACTIONS
WILLOW SPRINGS ADVENTURE PARK
Spring Street, between West and Ruthven Streets. Tel: 07 635 8613
Opening hours: summer 0900-2100; winter 1000-1730
Access through the side gate beside the main entrance kiosk. Accessible food outlet, WCs and solar-heated swimming pool, picnic areas, kiosk and shelters.

WATERBIRD HABITAT
Alderley and Mackenzie Streets
There are wide, concrete paths and accessible picnic areas in this 7.6 hectare site. Deep and shallow lakes, mudbanks, islands and grassy weeds provide feeding, roosting and nesting spots. Concrete paths run for several kilometres to Lake Annand (barbecues and ducks); Kitchener Street (willows); East Creek Park (war memorials) to Margaret Street. Continue through Queens Park to the Botanical Gardens. Accessible WCs in the habitat and in Queens Park, opposite Arthur Street.

WAR MEMORIALS, EAST CREEK PARK
Parking and entrance are accessible. Bricks forming the wall at Margaret Street were handmade in 1862-64 to build the walls of the gaol closed in 1904 and purchased by the Austral Society to become the Austral Memorial Hall, dedicated to local gentlemen who served in the Boer War. Demolished in 1917, all that remains is a fragment of the walls from which the bricks were recovered.

JU RAKU EN
Adjacent to University College of Southern Queensland on West and Baker Streets
Ju Raku En means "Long life and happiness in a public garden". Wheelchair entrance is from Regent Street, via Wuth Street, off West Street. Waterfall, lakes, ring of hills, gazebo, flowering trees and shrubs are all found in this four-hectare garden.

PICNIC POINT CHAINSAW SCULPTURE
This 18m-high sculpture, transformed from a giant pine tree, was struck by lightning in 1988. Tallest of its kind in Australia, it depicts Aboriginal faces and indigenous animals.

CLASSIC STAINED GLASS
37 Raff Street
Tel: 07 638 2597
Glass blowing, glassware and stained glass windows observable from a viewing platform via main front entrance. Wider access at the rear entrance from the car park where there is accessible parking.

TOWNSVILLE
The town was founded in 1864, and is the largest coastal town north of Brisbane. The port handles mining and agricultural exports for Northern Australia. Attractions include interesting buildings, good shopping, gambling, boats to the Reef, and the Reef Wonderland. Townsville is a relaxed and graceful coastal city, keeping pace with the times, but retaining much of its 19th century elegance. 28km north is Paulma, a tiny town set high in the rainforest. There are art and craft shops here and just beyond are the awe-inspiring eucalyptus forests of Hidden Valley. 135km south west, in the heart of savannah country is Charters Towers, a colonial town that once boasted a stock exchange, over 100 hotels and thousands of eager gold miners. Its heyday over, the town is now a beautifully preserved example of fine colonial architecture, many of the buildings still maintained for their original purpose. Driving from Townsville will give a glimpse of Outback Queensland.

HOTEL
SHERATON BREAKWATER CASINO HOTEL (SH)
Sir Leslie Thiess Drive
Tel: 07 722 2333 Fax: 07 772 4741
No. of hotel rooms: 193
No. of adapted rooms: 9
Facilities; 3 restaurants; pool; sauna; spa
Overlooking Cleveland Bay and close to Reef Wonderland and Magnetic Island.

The surrounding area is flat, the town centre is 1km away, the beach 800m, with easy access to both.

ACCESSIBLE ATTRACTIONS
GBR WONDERLAND
Flinders Street East
Tel: 07 772 4249
Fully accessible with nearby public parking, but with no designated bays. Accessible WCs but not listed as unisex or separate sex.

PERC TUCKER ART GALLERY
Flinders Mall
Tel: 07 772 2560
Accessible from the street, with street parking only.
There are no accessible WC facilities.

TOWNSVILLE MUSEUM
Flinders Street East
Tel: 07 772 5725
Fully accessible, with street parking only. Accessible WC but not designated unisex or separate sex.

TOWNSVILLE TOWN COMMON
Heatley's Parade
Rowes Bay
Townsville
Tropical wetlands, grasslands, woodlands and rock and scree slopes. Several scattered unsealed car parks without designated bays. There are two walkways, both unsealed, but gradients are mostly acceptable. Waster birds and wildlife can be observed from cars at special stops or as you drive through the park.

MT SPEC NATIONAL PARK
Paluma (75km north of Townsville). Clearly signposted on Bruce Highway. Highland tropical forest and tall open forest. Car parking is sealed without designated bays.
Walkway from car park to lookout has a steep initial slope of about 5m, and there is a similar slope from lookout to picnic area. Elsewhere the gradients are small.

WHITSUNDAY (see GREAT BARRIER REEF)

SOUTH AUSTRALIA

South Australia stretches through surreal desert landscapes where the finest opals are found to rolling green vineyards where 60 percent of Australia's wine is produced. Adelaide, the state capital, is one of the country's most beautiful and well-planned cities. Every two years the city hosts the famous Adelaide Arts Festival and by contrast goes wild each year when it is turned into a formula-one race circuit in November as part of the World Grand Prix series. The Flinders Ranges change colour every spring across their plunging gorges and folding hills. Wildflowers and the hues of the escarpments in the interior are always amazing.

Time zone
October-March: GMT + 10.5 hours
April-September: GMT + 9.5 hours

TOURIST BOARDS
UK TOURIST BOARD
SOUTH AUSTRALIAN PROMOTION
South Australia House
50 Strand
London WC2N 5LW
Tel: 071-930 7471 Fax: 071-930 1660

AUSTRALIAN TOURIST BOARD
TOURISM SOUTH AUSTRALIA
Head Office, 7th and 8th Floors
Terrace Towers Building
170-178 North Terrace
Adelaide 5000
Tel: 08 303 2222 Fax: 08 212 4251

Adelaide Travel Centre
Ground and 8th Floors
AMP Building, 1 King William Street
Adelaide SA 5000
Tel: 08 212 1505 Fax: 08 303 2249

UNITED STATES TOURIST BOARD
SOUTH AUSTRALIA DEPT. OF TOURISM
Suite 1210
2121 Avenue of the Stars
Los Angeles CA 90067
Tel: 310 552 2821 Fax: 310 557 0322

SUPPORT ORGANISATIONS
ACROD
PO Box 196
Greenacres SA 5086
Fax: 08 266 3310

The Adelaide Arts Festival in full swing.

DISABILITY INFORMATION AND RESOURCE CENTRE
195 Giles Avenue
Adelaide SA 5000
Tel: 08 223 7522 Fax: 08 223 5082
Opening hours: Monday to Friday 0900-1700
The centre has a car park at the rear with flat entrances and automatic doors. Six unisex WCs are accessible, easily located and well signed. Information is provided on accessible accommodation, tourist attractions and general enquiries.

INDEPENDENT LIVING CENTRE
180 Daws Road
Daw Park SA 5041
Tel: 08 276 3455
Toll-free within Australia: 008 800 523
Fax: 08 276 7417
Information on aids and equipment.

PARAPLEGIC AND QUADRIPLEGIC ASSOCIATION OF SA
PO Box 283
Kilkenny SA 5009
Tel: 08 347 4199 Fax: 08 347 0063

WHEELCHAIR SPORTS ASSOCIATION OF SA
PO Box 144
Greenacres SA 5086
Tel: 08 349 6366 Fax: 08 349 6223

DEPARTMENT OF SPORT AND RECREATION
Tel: 08 226 7300

DEPARTMENT OF WOODS AND FORESTS
Tel: 08 226 9900

RECREATION ASSOCIATION FOR PEOPLE WITH DISABILITIES (RADSA)
Tel: 08 332 5171

ROYAL AUTOMOBILE ASSOCIATION OF SOUTH AUSTRALIA
41 Hindmarsh Square
Adelaide SA 5000
Tel: 08 202 4500 Fax: 08 202 4521
Publishes an accommodation guide with accessible properties.

SA NATIONAL PARKS AND WILDLIFE SERVICE
GPO Box 1782
Adelaide SA 5000
Tel: 08 207 2000 Fax: 08 207 2235
No specific access publications but advice and information about the state's national parks.

AIRPORTS
ADELAIDE
Tel: 08 216 1911 (airport)
08 234 4484 (information)

Car parking
Spaces are reserved for those in wheelchairs for both the domestic and international terminals in the public car park and also in the authorised car parks adjacent to the terminals. If you telephone the Duty Traffic Officer arrangements will be made for transfer to either terminal.

Facilities
Domestic Terminal: Access if from road level by kerb crossovers onto the pavement and through automatic doors. Light refreshments available on ground floor are accessible. The cocktail bar and bistro on the first floor are accessible by lift. Wheelchair-accessible male and female WCs are located adjacent to the gate lounges. Telephones are at the correct height.
Airlines have first aid attendants on duty and oxygen supplies are available if the aircraft is on the tarmac.
International Terminal: Access as above. Wheelchair-accessible facilities include an aerobridge to the aircraft accessible by lift; WCs and telephones; Medical and first aid facilities are also available.

AIRLINE OFFICES
QANTAS
14 King William Street
Adelaide
Tel: 08 217 3333 (domestic)
Tel: 08 237 8541 (international)

SINGAPORE AIRLINES
Tel: 08 238 2700

ANSETT AIRLINES
142 North Terrace
Tel: 08 233 3322
Ansett Airlines also sells tickets for
Kendall Airlines

KENDALL AIRLINES
43 Thompson Street
Wagga Wagga NSW 2650
Contact: John McArdell
Federal Airport Corporation Fax: 08 281 5006
Kendall uses facilities available through
Ansett at Adelaide Airport. Both Adelaide
and Parafield international and domestic
terminals are within the Australian
Standard for Disabled Building Code.

ACCESSIBLE TRANSPORT
TAXIS
ACCESS CABS
Tel: 08 371 0033

TAXI COMBINED SERVICES
Tel: 08 223 3111

HANDI-BUS
15 Gordon Avenue
St. Agnes SA 5097
Tel: 08 263 0675 (no fax)

SPECIALIST TOUR OPERATORS
INDEPENDENT TRAVEL
41a Woodville Road
Woodville SA 5011
Fax: 08 347 3144

TARDIS TRAVEL 2000
Westfield Shopping Centre
Arndale
Torrens Road
Kilkenny SA 5009
Tel: 08 268 4466 Fax: 08 243 1033

USEFUL STATE AUTHORITIES
STATE TRANSPORT AUTHORITY
136 North Terrace
Adelaide SA 5000
Tel: 08 218 2200 Fax: 08 211 7614
Domestic aerodromes within the state
should be contacted for details of the
standards they incorporate for people
with disabilities.

COUNCILS FOR ASSISTANCE
CEDUNA
District Council of Murat Bay
PO Box 175
Ceduna SA 5690

COOBER PEDY
District Council of Coober Pedy
PO Box 265
Coober Pedy SA 5723

KINGSCOTE
District Council of Kingscote
PO Box 121
SA 5223

MOUNT GAMBIER
District Council of Mount Gambier
PO Box 724
SA 5290

PORT AUGUSTA
Corporation of City of Port Augusta
PO Box 1704
Port Augusta SA 5700

PORT LINCOLN
District Council of Eyre Peninsula
PO Box 41
Cummins SA 5631

RENMARK
Corporation of Town of Renmark
PO Box 730
Renmark SA 5341

WHYALLA
Corporation of City of Whyalla
PO Box 5600
Whyalla SA 5600

WHERE TO GO, WHERE TO STAY

ADELAIDE
There is a discrepancy over the origin of
the name Adelaide – some say the city
was named in memory of the wife of
William Light who announced the area as
British in 1836, and others claim it was
named after the wife of William IV. A
civilised and conservative city, built on old

money, the centre is laid out as a grid, encompassing several squares and set in parkland. There is a range of hills around the city.

HOTELS
THE TERRACE INTER-CONTINENTAL ADELAIDE (LHW)
150 North Terrace
Adelaide SA 5000
Tel: 08 217 7552 Fax: 08 231 7572
No. of hotel rooms: 334
No. of adapted rooms: 18
Facilities: 4 restaurants; lobby bar; nightclub; pool; sauna; whirlpool
Top hotel in the heart of the city on North Terrace's cultural boulevard. Close to the Festival Theatre, Art Gallery and State Museum.

WEST END ALL SUITE HOTEL (FL)
255 Hindley Street
Adelaide SA 5000
Tel: 08 231 8333 Fax: 08 231 4741
No. of suites: 144
No. of adapted suites: 8
Suites are one- or two-bedded, fully adapted with separate lounge/dining room and kitchen/bathroom.
Facilities: restaurant; pool; spa
Two persons per night: 120.00
In CBD town centre with 5km of flat road, beach 6km. Surrounding area is flat.

ADELAIDE SUBURBS
HOTELS
MORPHETVILLE MOTOR INN (BW)
CAMDEN PARK
444 Anzac Way
Camden Park SA 5038
Tel: 08 294 8166 Fax: 08 376 1280
No. of motel units: 29
No. of adapted units: 1
Facilities: restaurant; pool; spa
6km from Adelaide centre and adjacent to Morphetville Racecourse. Glenelg Beach is 3km away. The surrounding area is flat.

OLD ADELAIDE INN (FL)
NORTH ADELAIDE
160 O'Connell Street
North Adelaide SA 5006

Tel: 08 267 5066 Fax: 08 267 2946
No. of hotel rooms: 64
No. of adapted rooms: 3
Facilities: restaurant; sauna; spa; resident manager on site at all times; 24-hour reception; refrigerators, minibars and complimentary tea/coffee in rooms.
Comfortable hotel, 2km north of city. Shopping and restaurants virtually at the front door. The nearest beach is 10km away and the surrounding area is flat.

ACCESSIBLE ATTRACTIONS
PARLIAMENT HOUSE
North Terrace
Adelaide
Tel: 08 237 9100
Tours at 1000 and 1400 when Parliament is not sitting.
Access is via the western entrance, through the front veranda of the Constitutional Museum then through a secured door on the western side of Parliament House.
Passengers may be set down and picked up at the front of the building. Car parking at Festival Centre car park or King's car park. There is a unisex accessible WC on the ground floor, signposted on walls throughout the floor.

PILGRIM CHURCH
Tel: 08 212 3295
Opening hours: Monday-Friday 1000-1500
Built 1867, a fine example of the gothic revival style.

MIGRATION MUSEUM
82 Kintore Avenue
Adelaide
Tel: 08 207 7570
Opening hours: Monday-Friday 1000-1700
Saturday and Sunday 1300-1700
Learn the story of SA's migrants.
There is off-street parking in Kintore Avenue. A wide, gentle ramp leads to the doorway and automatic doors. Male and female accessible WCs are situated in the airlock of WCs in the courtyard. Despite being signed they are hard to find, rather small and difficult to use.

OLD PARLIAMENT HOUSE
Constitutional Museum
North Terrace
Adelaide
Tel: 08 212 6881
Opening hours: Monday-Friday 1000-1700
Saturday and Sunday 1200-1700

Built in 1855 and well restored with a fine museum. A space may be reserved at the front of the museum for Access Cabs or private vehicles to set down or pick up. Nearest accessible parking is in King's car park. There is a gentle ramp to the entrance, with a heavy, hinged door. Reception is close to the door and staff will assist. Male and female accessible WCs in airlock of WCs on the ground floor outside.

SOUTH AUSTRALIAN MUSEUM
Tel: 08 223 8911
Open daily 1000-1700

Recognised for its indigenous tribal collections.

ADELAIDE FESTIVAL CENTRE
Tel: 08 216 8670
Guided tours Monday-Saturday 1100 and 1400

Major venue for performing arts. An interesting feature is the 1.2 hectares of open plaza and terrace surrounding the complex.

ART GALLERY OF SOUTH AUSTRALIA
North Terrace
Adelaide
Tel: 08 207 7000
Open daily 1000-1700

Four-section collection of Australian, European and Asian decorative arts and prints and drawings.
There is a safe setdown area in the laneway between the Art Gallery and Adelaide University. Use John Martin's car park. The entrance, stepped and ramped, leads to an automatic glass sliding door. Male and female accessible WCs on the ground floor off the front foyer. Position of door to WC makes independent access difficult.

TANDANYA ABORIGINAL CULTURAL INSTITUTE
253 Grenfell Street
Adelaide
Tel: 08 223 2467
Opening hours: Monday-Friday 1030-1700
Saturday and Sunday 1200-1700

First major Aboriginal cultural facility and the only multi-arts complex in Australia. Park in Wilson car park or Union Street Harris Scarfe car park. There is a gentle ramp at the entrance. Unisex designated accessible WCs are on the ground floor. Large wheelchairs need to reverse into the WC through sliding door.

AYERS HOUSE (NATIONAL TRUST BUILDING)
288 North Terrace
Adelaide
Tel: 08 223 1655
Opening hours: Tuesday-Friday 1000-1600

Use car park 251 or John Martin's as there is no designated parking on the site car park. Passenger set down is at the front entrance. The western entrance has a portable ramp, but advance notice is required. Conventional WC only.

UNION GALLERY
Level 6, Adelaide University
North Terrace
Adelaide
Tel: 08 228 5013
Opening hours: Monday-Friday 1000-1700

Within the grounds of Adelaide University with exhibitions of modern jewellery, craftwork and ceramics. Park either on the street or in the University car park with a permit. There is designated accessible car parking at Victoria Street car park, at the rear of the campus and in John Martin's car park. A flat entrance is through Union Building that also houses the nearest accessible WC.

ADELAIDE BOTANIC GARDENS
North Terrace
Adelaide
Tel: 08 228 2311
Opening hours: Monday-Friday 0700-1700
Saturday and Sunday 1900-1700

The Conservatory, Adelaide.

There are parking meters and street parking. Enter through the northern entrance via the Botanic Park on Plain Tree Drive. Paths around the gardens are mainly bitumen and wide. Kiosk and cafe have three 153mm (6") steps above the pathway. The glasshouses, seed museum and the WCs are inaccessible.

BICENTENNIAL CONSERVATORY
Plane Tree Drive, off Hackney Road
Adelaide
Tel: 08 228 2345
Open daily 1000-1600

Largest glasshouse in the southern hemisphere with a tropical rainforest. The main entrance is off Plane Tree Drive on the northern side, with off-street parking available on Plane Tree Drive. The entrance has a gentle slope.

ADELAIDE HIMEJI GARDEN
Tel: 08 203 7296
Opening hours: Monday-Friday 0730-1600
Saturday and Sunday 0800 until sunset
Traditional Japanese garden built to commemorate friendship between Adelaide and the Himeji Region of Japan

ZOOLOGICAL GARDENS
Frome Road
Adelaide
Tel: 08 267 3255
Open daily 0930-1700
Conservation, education and research with a special emphasis on breeding rare species. Park on the street and use the Botanic Park Entrance. The ground surface is asphalt, where there are steps ramps are provided. Accessible WCs are adjacent to the ladies' WC near the kiosk.

CONSTITUTIONAL MUSEUM TRUST
North Terrace
Adelaide
Tel: 08 212 6066
Park in the Festival Theatre car park and enter through the main entrance that has a ramp. There is an accessible lift to the audio visual programme and a stair aid for access to other areas. Accessible WCs are via a long outside ramp.

CORKWOOD GALLERIES
Southern Cross Arcade
Adelaide
Tel: 08 231 5811
Opening hours Monday-Thursday 0900-1730
Friday 0900-2100 Saturday 0900-1600
There is no on-street parking nearby, so use David Jones or Harris Scarfe car parks. There are two ramps up to the entrance, the first, rather uneven, leads past the shop and the second slopes up into the shop with wide access.
No public WCs. The nearest designated accessible facilities are in James Place.

BUGLE GALLERIES
Bonython Road
Bugle Ranges
Tel: 08 391 0053
Opening hours: Sunday 1330-1730. Other days by appointment only.
45km from Adelaide. Specialists in Australian art from colonial days to the 1940s plus selected later artists.
There is a private car park and entry through the main entrance that is flat and leads to a wide doorway.

ACCESSIBLE SHOPPING CENTRES IN THE CITY
DAVID JONES PTY LTD
44 Rundle Mall
Adelaide
Tel: 08 213 8111
Opening hours: Monday-Thurday 0830-1730, Friday 0830-2130, Saturday 0830-1700
Major shop in large shopping mall. There is an on-site carpark with reserved accessible bays on the first floor in the corner nearest the lifts. Entry is flat at the front of the building.
Accessible female WCs are in the ladies' lounge on the second floor and male WCs in the men's lounge on the first floor.

MYER S.A. STORES LTD
36 Rundle Mall
Adelaide
Tel: 08 212 1200
There are two reserved spaces on the first floor in the Galer Place car park. Access to the store is via Little Rundle Arcade and Stephens Place.
Rundle Mall entrances are at street level. Lifts to all floors are on the eastern wall and accessible restaurants in the basement and on the fifth and eighth floors.
Unisex accessible WCs are on the third floor, and male only on the fourth floor.

ACCESSIBLE ATTRACTIONS IN THE ADELAIDE SUBURBS
CARRICK HILL
Springfield
Tel: 08 379 3886
Opening hours: house and gardens Wednesday-Sunday 1000-1700
One of the finest private art collections with 39 hectares of grounds developed as a sculpture park.

BELAIR RECREATION PARK
Old Goverment House, Upper Sturt Road
Belair
Tel: 08 278 5477
Opening hours: Park Gates 0800-sunset Government House Sundays and public holidays 1230-1600
The Old Government House was built in 1859 as a summer residence for Governor

93

MacDonnell and has been faithfully restored. Its mid-Victorian furnishings provide an insight into the lifestyle of South Australia's former gentry. There is a nursery full of colourful native species. Two accessible WCs, one near the Pines Oval and one near Old Government House. The gardens are accessible by wheelchair and a portable ramp aids entry. There is an information centre, also with a ramped entrance, near the main entrance.

OLD HIGHERCOMBE HOTEL FOLK MUSEUM
Tea Tree Gully
Tel: 08 264 1644
Opening hours: Saturdays, Sundays and public holidays 1400-1700
Built in 1853 the museum contains photographic records and artifacts from pioneer families. Each room looks as it would have done in early colonial days.

SOUTH AUSTRALIA MARITIME MUSEUM
Port Adelaide
Tel: 08 240 0200
Opening hours: Tuesday-Sunday 1000-1700
Living, working maritime museum on several sites.

ACCESSIBLE ATTRACTIONS IN ADELAIDE HILLS
PETALUMA'S BRIDGEWATER MILL
Bridgewater
Tel: 08 339 3422
Opening hours: Monday-Friday 0930-1700 Saturday and Sunday 1000-1700
Built 1860 in beautiful hills setting with water wheel and renovated mill buildings.

LOBETHAL HERITAGE FARM
Lobethal
Tel: 08 389 6549
Opening hours: Monday-Friday 1000-1700 Saturday1400-1700 Sunday 1000-1700
Fine early German Pioneer Farms.

PROSPECT HILL HISTORICAL MUSEUM
Tel: 08 536 6090
Opening hours: Sundays 1400-1700
Old furnished cottage of 1872. Includes original store, post office and shed with implements.

GOLDEN RAY GARDENS
Meadows
Tel: 08 388 3377
Open daily 1100-1700
Garden of glorious blooms, flowering bushes, waterways and fountains.

BAROSSA VALLEY
Originally settled by Germans escaping religious persecution in Prussia and Silesia, there is still a Germanic flavour to this region. This area of rolling countryside is one of the main vine-growing areas and produces 100 million litres of wine per year – 25 percent of the country's total wine output. Many vineries are open to the public.

CEDUNA
Surrounded by beaches, Ceduna is at the end of the Eyre Peninsula. Exhibits from the British Atomic Weapons programme at Maralinga are on display in the Old School House Museum.

TOURIST BOARD
INFORMATION CENTRE
Poynton Street
Tel: 08 625 2780

CLARE
This is yet another great place for wine and wineries. Nearby Mintaro has been named a heritage town and contains many interesting and unusual sights. The town was settled in 1842 and named after County Clare in Eire. It has continuing Irish connections.

TOURIST BOARD
TOURIST INFORMATION CENTRE
Town Hall
229 Main North Road
Tel: 08 842 2131
Open daily 1000-1600

COOBER PEDY
An opal mining town that has doubled in size since 1987 when many new areas were opened up for mining. Many houses and a church have been carved out of the rock underground.

GLENDAMBO

A new development with much traffic.

HOTEL

GLENDAMBO HOTEL-MOTEL (FL)
PMB 36, via Port Augusta
Glendambo SA 5710
Tel: 08 672 1030
Fax: 08 672 1039
No. of hotel units: 60
No. of adapted units: 4
Facilities: restaurant; pool
Two persons per night: 85.00

Designed to authenticate an Australian Outback woolshed. All accommodation is on the ground floor. There are no support rails in the showers or WCs. Glendambo welcomes wheelchair guests and advise that assistance is given where necessary.

GOOLWA

On Lake Alexandria. Departure point for river cruises up the Murray River. There are several buildings of historic interest.

TOURIST BOARD

TOURIST INFORMATION CENTRE
Railway Terrace
Tel: 08 555 1144
Open daily 1000-1600

HAWKER

Small town famous for sheep rearing.

KANGAROO ISLAND

113km south west of Adelaide and the third largest island off the Australian coast, Kangaroo Island is quiet and unspoilt with wonderful wildlife and flowers and good beaches. There is also a permanent breeding colony of sea lions.
There is an accessible ferry service on *Philanderer* and for vehicles and passengers departing Cape Jarvis it takes about an hour to reach Penneshaw on Kangaroo Island.

Sea lion cubs enjoy the unspoilt beaches of Kangaroo Island.

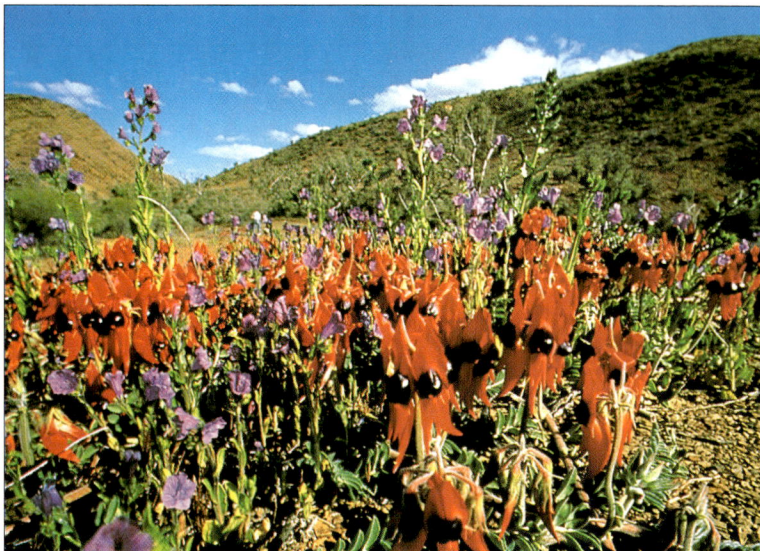

Wild flowers on Flinders Ranges.

TOURIST BOARD
TOURIST INFORMATION CENTRE
Dauncy Street
Kingscote
Tel: 08 482 2381
Opening hours: Monday-Friday 0845-1700

ACCESSIBLE ATTRACTIONS
SEAL BAY
The second largest breeding colony of
Australian sea lions, visible from the beach
lookout. Because of coastal conditions
about 50 percent of the area is accessible
to wheelchairs. Good unisex accessible WC
500m from the main parking area.

FLINDERS CHASE NATIONAL PARK
800sq km of the western end of the island,
a wilderness of dense vegetation and home
to many native animals. Kangaroos and
emus are especially friendly. Although
only accessible by car, for those in
wheelchairs there is an easy drive from the
Chase to the island's most south-westerly
tip where many famous features stand
including Cape du Couedic Lighthouse,
Weirs Cove and Admiral's Arch.
Flinders Chase is fully accessible and
suitable WC facilities are available within
the picnic grounds.

HOPE COTTAGE MUSEUM
Located in Kingscote and established by
the South Australia Company in 1836 a
few months before Adelaide, the museum
reflects the early pioneering days with
many original artefacts.
There is a small step at the rear of the
museum but otherwise it is accessible.
There are also accessible WCs. Contact the
National Parks and Wildlife Service at
Flinders Chase on 08 483 7235 or Hope
Cottage on 08 482 2140.

KIMBA
Visits to Lake Gilles and Gawler Ranges
are available from this town located near
the Outback.

KINGSTON
A fishing port with renowned seafood,
particularly rock lobster.

MILANG
Milang is the only town on the shores of
Lake Alexandria, the largest natural
freshwater lake in Australia.
First surveyed in 1853 the town has many
historic buildings reminiscent of days
when Port Milang was the major river
port of South Australia. Paddle steamers

unload their cargo to be transported overland to Port Adelaide first by bullock dray then by steam train.

HOTEL
MILANG HOTEL SAWASDEE
5 Daranda Terrace, Milang SA 5256
Tel: 08 537 0090 Fax: 08 537 0404
No. of hotel rooms: 12
No. of adapted rooms: 1
Facilities: all meals served in guest rooms, service available until 22.00
All accommodation is on the ground floor. The surrounding area is flat.

MT. GAMBIER
Built on a volcano and renowned for its four crater lakes particularly the blue lake that changes colour from dull grey to brilliant blue every November and reverts to grey at the end of the summer. Taste the local wines at Coonawarra. The main trade is timber and agriculture.

NARACOORTE
One of the oldest towns in South Australia, first settled in 1840.

NURIOOPTA
In the Barossa Valley, with many vineyards. The Barossa Vintage Festival every Easter includes street fairs, exhibitions and a procession between the town and Tanunda.

TOURIST BOARD
BAROSSA INFORMATION CENTRE
Coulthand House
Tel: 08 562 1866
Opening hours: Monday-Friday 0800-1700
Saturday and Sunday 0930-1330

PORT AUGUSTA
A busy port with several historical buildings and museums.

PORT LINCOLN
A popular resort and base for Australia's largest commercial fishing fleet. There are many safe swimming and excellent fishing spots.
One can take a day cruise to Dangerous Reef, a breeding ground for sea lions and home to the white pointer shark.

ROBE
Settled in 1845, Robe is a small historic port with a fine old customs house and a dignified ambience. It becomes very popular during the summer.

TOURIST BOARD
TOURIST INFORMATION CENTRE
The Library
Corner of Smiley and Victoria Streets
Opening hours: Monday-Friday 1000-1200, 1300-1700 Saturday 0830-1230

TANUNDA
The original settlers at Tanunda were German. There is a Lutheran Church dating from 1849 and some early cottages are still standing in the centre of the Barossa Valley. The town is surrounded by wineries.

VICTOR HARBOUR
Formerly a whaling station, Victor Harbour is now a holiday resort. There are steam train excursions and at nearby Urimbirra Wildlife Park you can cuddle a koala.

HOTEL
APOLLON MOTOR INN (FL)
Hindmarsh Road
Victor Harbour SA 5211
Tel: 08 552 2777 Fax: 08 552 2701
No. of hotel rooms: 32
No. of adapted rooms: 1
Facilities: restaurant; pool; spa
Two persons per night: 80.00
Although right in the city centre, it is a quiet location. 100m from beach and accessible by wheelchair. The surrounding area is flat.

WHYALLA
South Australia's second city – a steel town with historic and maritime museum.

TOURIST BOARD
Tel: 08 645 8900
Open daily 1000-1600

TASMANIA

Discovered in 1642 by the Dutch navigator Abel Tasman, Tasmania was not settled until the end of the 18th century and much evidence of its colonial past remains. Captain Cook and William Bligh landed in 1773, but it was not until 1798, when Lieutenant Flinders completed a circumnavigation of the island, that it was realised it was not part of the mainland. The island is 240 x 220 miles with a population of half a million. There is a nostalgic England-in-the-50s feel about Tasmania.

The landscape and climate are similar to the Lake District in the UK, with oak, ash and elm trees originally brought over by settlers. The landscape varies from mountain ranges, rain forests and wild river rapids to rolling pastures, lakes and sandy surf beaches. Tasmania is home to the original Granny Smith apple, and is famed for its apple production as well as seafood and high quality dairy products. The majority of the population live on the east and north coasts where the land is fertile and there are beautiful beaches,

whilst the west and southwest coasts are untouched. Cradle Mountain, rising to 5,000 feet, is a World Heritage site.

In November 1994, Hobart will host the World Congress on Adventure Travel and Eco Tourism and Tasmania is leading the promotion of the outdoor adventure holiday. The Lyell Highway heads west from Hobart passing through rural townships. Farther on are the World Heritage wilderness areas of Franklin and Gordon Rivers National Park and Cradle Mountain-Lake St. Clair National Park. Spectacular mountains, rainforests, high moorlands and calm lakes make this a fascinating area. On the east coast there are fishing and holiday villages such as St. Helens, Bicheno and Swansea, all worth visiting. Tasmania is closer to the equator than Rome, Chicago or the Azores.

It has the cleanest air in the world and its rainwater is so pure that it has even been shipped to Australian Olympic

Dove Lake overlooked by Cradle Mountain.

competitors overseas. Tasmania has the longest and deepest caves in Australia and Launceston's Cataract Gorge Chairlift is the longest single-span chairlift in the world. The Bush Inn in New Norfolk (1825) is the oldest continually licensed public house in Australia, and Tasmania has the oldest brewery, the Cascade Brewery in Hobart.

Time zone
October-March: GMT + 11 hours
April-September: GMT + 10 hours

TOURIST BOARDS
TOURISM TASMANIA
Gemini House
10-18 Putney Hill
London SW15 6AA
Tel: 081-789 7088 Fax: 081-780 1496

AUSTRALIAN TOURIST OFFICE
TOURISM TASMANIA HEAD OFFICE
1 Franklin Wharf
Hobart TAS 7000
Tel: 002 300 150 Fax: 002 312 175

US TOURIST BOARD
AUSTRALIA'S SOUTHERN TOURISM
PROMOTION
Suite 1270, 12th Floor
2121 Avenue of the Stars
Los Angeles CA 90067
Tel: 301 553 6352 Fax: 301 277 2883

SUPPORT ORGANISATIONS
ACROD TASMANIA
Tel: 002 236 086 Fax: 002 236 136
Provides information on facilities.

ROYAL AUTOMOBILE ASSOCIATION OF
TASMANIA
Corner Murray and Patrick Streets
Hobart TAS 7000
Tel: 002 382 200 Fax: 002 348 784
Produces an accommodation guide on accessible properties.

TASMANIAN WHEELCHAIR SPORTS
48 Bowden Road
Glenorchy TAS 7008
Tel: 002 732 399 Fax: 002 732 649

TASMANIAN DEPARTMENT OF PARKS,
WILDLIFE AND HERITAGE
134 Macquarie Street
Hobart TAS 7005
Tel: 002 306 285 Fax: 002 238 765
Produces a guide to Tasmania's National Parks and Reserves that indicates those areas with easy access and facilities for people with disabilities.

DOUGLAS PARKER REHABILITATION CENTRE
Tel: 002 381 801

AIRPORTS
HOBART INTERNATIONAL AIRPORT
Tel: 002 485 066 (airport)
002 485 014 (information)
008 112 121 (reservations)

Car Parking
Domestic Terminal:There are no designated parking spaces, but a call to the Airline Manager will secure transfer from the public car park to the terminal. International Terminal: There are designated parking spaces and a call to the Duty Traffic Officer will secure transfer to the terminal.

Facilities
Domestic Terminal: Access is from road level by kerb crossovers onto the pavement and through automatic doors. Cocktail and refreshment bars are situated off the public lounge and are accessible. Accessible WCs both male and female are also located off the public lounge. Telephones are accessible. First aid can be administered by trained airline hostesses, and oxygen is available from aircraft if on the tarmac. International Terminal: Access is from road level by kerb crossovers onto the pavement and through automatic doors. Cocktail and refreshment bars and accessible WCs, both male and female are located off the public lounge. Telephones are accessible. Oxygen is available from aircraft if on the tarmac and first aid administered by trained airline hostesses.

AIRLINE OFFICES
AIRLINES OF TASMANIA
Launceston Airport
Evandale TAS 7212
Tel: 003 918 755 Fax: 003 918 688

ACCESSIBLE TRANSPORT
DEPARTMENT OF ROADS AND TRANSPORT
Tel: 002 389 210
The Department of Transport and Works
in Hobart advises that the following
operators will provide transport services
for people with wheelchairs.

CITY CABS CO-OP SOC.
215 Harrington Street
Hobart TAS 7000
Tel: 002 343 633

HILDERS COACHES
33 Lennox
Moonah TAS 7009
Tel: 002 284 029

Mr & Mrs B. BAHRY
178 Pomona Road
South Riverside TAS 7005
Tel: 003 27 1764

Mr & Mrs R. COLGRAVE
20 South Street
George Town TAS 7253
Tel: 003 821 923

Mr & Mrs R. SAINTY
26A Ravenswood Road
Ravenswood TAS 7250

Hobart – one of the best deep-water harbours in the world.

WHERE TO STAY, WHAT TO SEE

BURNIE

Third largest city in Tasmania, situated on the shore of Emy Bay. The surrounding area is mainly farmland. There is a deepwater port for the export of minerals, timber and vegetables, and the town is renowned as a paper producer. Visit the Pioneer Village Museum and Burnie Park.

DELORAINE

A picturesque town with many restored Georgian and Victorian buildings, surrounded by lush countryside. Look for antiques. There are many waterfalls in this agricultural centre. The Bowerbank Mill Gallery built in 1853 is to the east and the nearby Tasmanian Wildlife Park is worth a visit.

HOTEL
MOUNTAIN VIEW HOTEL (BW)
144 Emu Bay Road
Tel: 003 622 633 Fax: 003 623 232
No. of hotel rooms: 23
No. of adapted rooms: 3
Facilities: restaurant
NB: THERE IS ONE STEP INTO THE RESTAURANT
Close to glow worm caves, a wildlife park, Cradle Mountain, Lakes wilderness areas and overlooking Gt Western Tiers.
All adapted rooms are on the ground floor.

DEVONPORT

Lively and interesting port. The town crosses the Mersey River and is a terminus for the Melbourne Ferry. There is a famous lighthouse, Bluff, built in 1889.

EAGLEHAWK NECK (Port Arthur)

A natural causeway leads to the Tasman Peninsula and the ruins of a former convict settlement. There are also some dramatic rock formations along the coast.

HOBART

Hobart is a delightful harbourside city, its nautical links typified by wharves, jetties and warehouses. It is one of the best deep-water harbours in the world. The historical sandstone buildings,

particularly along the waterfront of Salamanca Place, are set against the incredible backdrop of Mount Wellington. which is snow-capped for much of the year. 38km north of Hobart is New Norfolk, famous for its hop fields and turn-of-the-century architecture. The town was first settled in 1807 by convicts brought from Norfolk Island. Richmond, 26km north east of Hobart also retains much of its colonial past, including the oldest bridge, postal buildings and Catholic church in Australia. In the Huon Valley, 37km southwest, is the centre for Tasmania's apple growing industry. There is an Apple Museum at Grove (accessibility unknown).

TOURIST BOARD
TASMANIAN TRAVEL CENTRE
80 Elizabeth Street
Tel: 002 300 250

AIRLINE OFFICES
AIRLINES OF TASMANIA
Tel: 002 485 030

ANSETT AIRLINES
Tel: 002 380 800

HOTELS
SHERATON HOTEL (SH)
1 Davey Street
Tel: 002 354 535 Fax: 002 238 175
No. of hotel rooms: 234
No. of adapted rooms: 8
Facilities: 2 restaurants; pool; sauna
On the waterfront adjacent to the historic Victoria and Constitution docks. Restaurants, harbour area, historic Salamanca Place and markets are relatively easy to access from the hotel on flat surroundings. The immediate area around the hotel is reasonably flat.

WESTSIDE HOTEL (FL)
156 Bathhurst Road
Tel: 002 326 255 Fax: 002 347 884
No. of hotel rooms: 139
No. of adapted rooms: 2
Facilities: 2 restaurants
Two persons per night: 120.00
A modern hotel in the city centre with

access to all attractions. The surrounding area is SLOPING.

ACCESSIBLE ATTRACTIONS
ANTARCTIC RESEARCH HQ
Channel Highway Kingston
Opening hours: Monday-Friday: 0900-1700
View a video of the icy continents and some rare old photographs.

CASCADE BREWERY
Cascade Road
A historic stone building, set among mountain gullies, rich forests and sweeping lawns.

TASMANIAN MUSEUM AND ART GALLERY
40 Macquarie Street
Open daily 1000-1700
A fine collection of colonial art and exhibitions displaying the cultural and natural history of Tasmania.

LAUNCESTON
Originally settled in 1805, the town is set in a fertile valley formed by the Tamar and Esk Rivers. The city retains much Georgian flavour. The Penny Royal Gunpowder Mill and Cataract Gorge are worth a visit. Nearby is the historic town of Evandale. 50km north of Launceston is George Town, first settled in 1811, with historic buildings, a maritime museum and lighthouse. George Town is an important commercial centre with an extensive fruit-growing area. The ruins of Lefroy, a 19th century gold-mining town, are nearby.

TOURIST BOARD
TASMANIAN TRAVEL CENTRE
Corner of St. John and Paterson Streets
Tel: 003 373 111
Opening hours: Monday-Friday 0845-1700
Saturday 0900-1200

HOTEL
BALMORAL MOTOR INN (FL)
19 York Street
Launceston TAS 7250
Tel: 003 318 000 Fax: 003 341 870
No. of hotel rooms: 37
No. of adapted rooms: 1 plus 24 for guests with assistance.
Facilites: restaurant; pool
Two persons per night: 80.00
Central location, one block from city shopping mall, with fine city centre views. The adapted unit is on the ground floor. The surrounding area is HILLY

Port Arthur – Tasmania's greatest tourist attraction.

The beautiful setting of Penny Royal, Launceston.

COUNTRY CLUB CASINO (FL)
Country Club Avenue
Tel: 003 448 855 Fax: 003 431 880
No. of hotel rooms: 104
No. of adapted rooms: 1
Facilities: restaurant; pool
Two persons per night: 230.00
In city outskirts with many facilities.

NOVOTEL LAUNCESTON (NOV)
29 Cameron Street, Launceston TAS 7250
Tel: 003 343 434 Fax: 003 317 347
No. of hotel rooms: 165
No. of adapted rooms: 1
Facilities: restaurant
In the heart of the central business district, the hotel has an arcade with speciality shops. A short distance from Yorktown Square and spectacular Cataract Gorge and 30 minutes from the beach. The surrounding area is flat.

PORT ARTHUR

Situated on the Tasman Peninsula, this former convict settlement is the greatest tourist attraction in Tasmania. A place of isolated incarceration for more than 12,000 prisoners, the ruins still capture the atmosphere that must have prevailed 130 years ago. This prison town developed some fine industries including timber milling, shop building and shoe making. The Island of the Dead, in the middle of the bay, contains the bodies of many convicts. The lunatic asylum is now a museum reflecting the misery of the time.

HOTEL
FOX & HOUNDS RESORT (FL)
Port Arthur Highway
Tel: 002 502 217 Fax: 002 502 590
No. of hotel rooms: 28
No. of adapted rooms: 1
Facilities: restaurant; pool
Two persons per night: 90.00
NB: THERE IS A SMALL STEP INTO THE SHOWER
Old English Tudor villas with 28 acres of water frontage.

ACCESSIBLE ATTRACTION
CONVICT SETTLEMENT RUINS
Accessible, designated car parking and WC facilities. Access to only one building and the museum but well worth a visit.

QUEENSTOWN

Gateway to the wilderness – mountains, rivers, gorges and the rainforest. The copper mine on which the town depended is being gradually turned into a museum. The town's surroundings show much evidence of mining on a major scale.

TOURIST BOARD
RACT OFFICE
18 Orr Street
Opening hours: Monday-Friday 0900-1700

STRAHAN

A pretty little port on Macquarie Harbour and the only town on the west coast. Ocean Beach with enormous surf and high sand dunes is 6km away.

VICTORIA

Prior to the 19th century sealers and whalers had used the Victoria coast, but it wasn't until 1835 that the first permanent European settlement was founded at Melbourne by Bateman and Fawkner. In 1851 they separated from NSW and established their own territory. Gold was discovered and the population grew rapidly. Victoria is now the most densely populated state and Australia's major agricultural and industrial producer. It claims the title Garden State because of its position in the fertile south-east corner of the country, that is well watered by the Murray River system. Surrounded by a variegated landscape of mountains, rainforests, deserts, snowfields, tobacco plantations, vineyards, potato fields, wheatland and market gardens, much of the state is rolling farmland and sheep country. Inland is Victoria's high country with the Grampian Range rising to 3,500 feet.

Time zone
October-March: GMT + 11 hours
April-September: GMT + 10 hours

TOURIST BOARDS

The VICTORIAN TOURISM COMMISSION is closed. Enquiries should be directed to:

AUSTRALIAN TOURISM COMMISSION
Gemini House
10-18 Putney Hill
London SW15 6AA
Tel: 081-780 2227 Fax: 081-780 1496

AUSTRALIAN TOURIST OFFICE
TOURISM VICTORIA
55 Swanston Street
Melbourne VIC 3000
Tel: 03 653 9777 Fax: 03 653 9733

TOURISM COMMISSION
PO Box 279
World Trade Centre
Melbourne VIC 3005
Tel: 03 619 9444

BRITISH CONSULATE-GENERAL
17th Floor, 90 Collins Street
Melbourne VIC 3000
Tel: 03 650 4155 Fax: 03 650 2990

UNITED STATES TOURIST BOARD
AUSTRALIA'S SOUTHERN TOURISM
PROMOTION
Suite 1270, 12th Floor
2121 Avenue of the Stars
Los Angeles CA 90067
Tel: 301 553 6352 Fax: 301 277 2883

SUPPORT ORGANISATIONS

INDEPENDENT LIVING CENTRE
52 Thistlethwaite Street
South Melbourne VIC 3205
Tel: 03 690 9177 Fax: 03 696 1956

DISABLED PERSONS INFORMATION BUREAU
12th Floor, 555 Collins Street
Melbourne VIC 3001
Tel: 03 616 7704 Fax: 03 616 8142

DISABILITY RESOURCE CENTRE
381 Burnley Street
Richmond VIC 3121
Tel: 03 480 2877
Active on issues that affect people with disabilities.

DISABLED MOTORISTS' ASSOCIATION
Tel: 03 386 0413

PARAPLEGIC & QUADRIPLEGIC ASSOCIATION
OF VICTORIA
229 Burwood Road
Hawthorn VIC 3122
Tel: 03 819 4055 Fax: 03 818 2967

PARA QUAD ASSOCIATION
208 Wellington Street
Collingwood
Tel: 03 415 1200

ACROD VICTORIA
PO Box 210
Hampton VIC 3188
Tel: 03 597 0157 Fax: 03 598 4158

TRAVELLERS' AID SUPPORT CENTRE
2nd Floor, 169 Swanston Street
Melbourne VIC 3000
Tel: 03 654 7690 Fax: 03 650 1112
Provides a wide range of free services to
travellers with disabilities.

CITIZENS ADVICE BUREAU
37 Swanston Street
Melbourne VIC 3000
Tel: 03 650 1062
A referral service with a list of contacts
for similar services throughout Victoria.

MULTICARE
616 Riversdale Road
Camberwell VIC 3124
Tel: 03 882 0588 Fax: 03 882 8205
Provides a range of attendant care.

HOST FARMS ASSOCIATION
332 Banyule Road
View Bank VIC 3084
Tel: 03 457 5413 Fax: 03 457 6725
Offers accessible farm accommodation list.

ROYAL AUTOMOBILE CLUB OF VICTORIA
550 Princes Highway
Noble Park VIC 3174
Tel: 03 790 2211 Fax: 03 790 2844
Publishes a list of accommodation of
accessible properties.

VICTORIA DEPARTMENT OF CONSERVATION AND ENVIRONMENT
240 Victoria Parade
East Melbourne VIC 3002
Tel: 03 412 4011
Produces a range of brochures on
Victorian national parks, including
information on access.

VICTORIAN RESTAURANT ADVISORY SERVICE
Tel: 03 521 2600
Provides information on access and types
of assistance available in restaurants
around Melbourne.

WHEELCHAIR SPORTS VICTORIA
Unit 4, 75 Mark Street
North Melbourne VIC 3052
Tel: 03 329 5088 Fax: 03 326 8504

AIRPORT
MELBOURNE AIRPORT
Tel: 03 602 6026 (airport)
03 338 2211 (information)
03 805 0111 (reservations)

Car parking
Spaces are reserved for those in
wheelchairs.

Facilities
Terminals: Wheelchair-accessible
facilities include cocktail/refreshment
bars on the first floor, a restaurant on the
second floor, lifts, WCs, telephones,
medical and first aid facilities.

AIRLINE OFFICES
AIR NEW ZEALAND
Tel: 03 654 3311

ANSETT
Tel: 03 653 5709

BRITISH AIRWAYS
Tel: 03 672 1100

CANADIAN AIRLINES
Tel: 03 629 6731

GARUDA INDONESIA
Tel: 03 654 4311

KENDALL AIRLINES
Tel: 03 678 2677

QANTAS
Tel: 03 602 6111 (international)
Tel: 03 665 1333 (domestic)

SINGAPORE AIRLINES
Tel: 03 602 4555

SUNSTATE
Tel: 03 665 3333

ACCESSIBLE TRANSPORT
METROPOLITAN TRANSPORT-DISABILITY SERVICES
Public Transport Corporation
Spencer Street Railway Station
Melbourne VIC 3000

Tel: Monday-Friday 03 619 2355/2354
Weekends 03 617 0900
Toll free within Australia: 008 131 716
The Public Transport Corporation has a section dedicated to assisting customers with special needs. This includes assistance with communication, buying a ticket, moving to the right platform and changing between trains, coaches and trams.
All metropolitan and country trains in the state have a conductor who can assist during a journey. Other facilities include some portable steps, wheelchair ramps and minibus transport.
Telephone and ask for a copy of the Disability Services 24-page information guide to services within Victoria.

TAXIS
MAXI (M50) TAXI
194 Burwod Road
Hawthorn VIC 3122
Tel: 03 819 1911 Fax: 03 818 2000
Provides a taxi service, with vehicles fitted with ramps and hoists.

SPECIALIST TOUR OPERATORS
CENTRAL VICTORIAN OUTDOOR SERVICES
Calder Highway
Bridgewater VIC 3516
Tel: 05 437 3183
Planning service for individuals or groups on camping holidays with a range of activities.

ANGLING EXPEDITIONS VICTORIA
10 Banks Road
Eltham North VIC 3095
Tel: 03 439 4266
Organises outings for large and small groups of people with disabilities to various locations. All fishing equipment including bait and barbecue provided – no boats are used.

ASSIST PERSONNEL SERVICES PTY
Box 83
Lara VIC 3212
Tel: 03 331 3670
Arranges interstate travel or day trips and general holidays – staff will assist with all requirements.

CITY RIVER CRUISES
3 Princes Walk
Melbourne VIC 3004
Tel: 03 650 2214
Toll free within Australia: 008 327 170
Fax: 03 650 1427
One- to two-hour cruises along the Yarra. Suitable for people with disabilities.

GUIDED TOURS OF VICTORIA
31 High Street
Rushworth VIC 3612
Tel: 05 856 1612 Fax: 05 856 1402
Specialises in organising and designing tailor-made tours of one day or more for groups of people with disabilities. Coaches can carry up to 25 wheelchairs.

HUMAN POTENTIAL TRAVEL- ANGEREN TRAVEL PTY LTD
10 Koornalla Crescent
Mt Eliza VIC 3930
Tel: 03 787 1246 Fax: 03 791 3777

TARWIN VALLEY HORSEDRAWN WAGONS
RMB 2491
Foster VIC 3960
Tel: 05 681 2244
Travel on a horsedrawn wagon through the South Gippsland Strezlecki Ranges on a specially designed holiday. No experience needed.

THE CAMPING ASSOCIATION OF VICTORIA
332 Banyule Road
View Bank VIC 3084
Tel: 03 457 5434 Fax: 03 457 5438
Provides a directory of camp sites and a rating for accommodation providing for all the requirements of a wheelchair user.

TT-LINE TASMANIA
PO Box 323
Port Melbourne VIC 3207
Tel: 03 644 5233 Fax: 03 646 7450
Has a specially fitted cabin which is accessible located on B deck. Lifts are available.

COACH OPERATORS
The following have specialised coaches with hydraulic lifts.

CROWN COACHES
228 Mahoneys Road
East Burwood VIC 3131
Tel: 03 803 6000 Fax: 03 803 7900

DAVIS TOURIST COACHES
Norman Street
Ballarat VIC 3350
Tel: 05 331 7777 Fax: 03 706 8971

GRENDA'S BUSLINES
9 Foster Street
Dandenong VIC 3175
Tel: 03 791 2988 Fax: 03 706 8971

MEE'S BUSLINES
139 Northern Road
Heidelberg Heights VIC 3081
Tel: 03 459 3000 Fax: 03 459 8920

RAMBLER TOURS PTY
326 Bell Street
Preston VIC 3072
Tel: 03 480 4444 Fax: 03 480 0715

WHERE TO GO, WHERE TO STAY

APOLLO BAY
A beautifully situated resort west of
Melbourne. Be sure to view the coast
from Mariners Lookout. Fishing is
extremely popular here, together with
music played in pubs, as many musicians
make their home in Apollo Bay.

TOURIST BOARD
APOLLO BAY AND OTWAY INFORMATION
CENTRE
85 Great Ocean Road
Open daily 1000-1800

ARARAT
Close to the champagne region and
briefly famous in 1857 when gold
deposits were discovered.

TOURIST BOARD
TOURIST INFORMATION CENTRE
Barkly Street
Tel: 05 352 2096
Opening hours: Monday-Friday 0900-1700
Saturday and Sunday 1030-1700

BAIRNSDALE
Good base for visiting mountains to the
north and lakes to the south of the town.
Close by is the resort of Paynesville that
has a long nautical history.

TOURIST BOARD
TOURIST INFORMATION OFFICE
Main Street
Tel: 05 152 3444
Opening hours: Monday-Friday 0900-1700
Saturday and Sunday 1000-1600

BALLARAT
Gold-rush town established in 1851.
Much of Victoria's gold came from this
region and there are many reminders of
the gold-rush period still standing. The
town has accessible, designated parking
and designated WC facilities.

TOURIST BOARD
VISITORS' INFORMATION CENTRE
39 Sturt Street
Tel: 05 332 2694
Opening hours: Monday-Friday 0915-1700
Saturday and Sunday 1000-1600

HOTEL
MAIN LEAD MOTOR INN (FL)
312 Main Road
Tel: 05 331 7533 Fax: 05 332 2853
No. of hotel rooms: 25
No. of adapted rooms: 1
Facilities: restaurant; pool; spa
Two persons per night: 95.00
1km from Ballarat CBD and close to
Sovereign Hill Historical Park and Gold
Museum. The surrounding area is flat.

ACCESSIBLE ATTRACTIONS
SOVEREIGN HILL HISTORICAL PARK
In Oven Valley country, the links with
Ned Kelly and the gold rush are evident
in the tree-lined streets.
Visit the 1859 powder magazine, now a
National Trust Museum.

LAKE WENDOUREE AND GARDENS
The shopping complex and beautiful
gardens are very accessible and level.
There is a ramp into the Craft Cottage.

BARWON HEADS
Popular resort area with river and ocean swimming, 95km south west of Melbourne.

HOTEL
VILLAGE BY THE SEA CARAVAN PARK
Corner of Sheepwash Road and River Parade
Barwon Heads VIC 3227
Tel: 03 698 5222 Fax: 03 696 1956
The caravan park has a 10-metre caravan designed and built for use by people with physical disabilities. It accommodates up to six. Accessible for a wheelchair user.

TOURIST BOARD
BEECHWORTH TOURIST ASSOCIATION
Tel: 05 728 1374

ACCESSIBLE ATTRACTIONS
BURKE MEMORIAL MUSEUM
Fully accessible.

CARRIAGE MUSEUM
Accessible but no adapted WC.

CEMETERY
Accessible with central adapted public WC.

BENALLA
On the Broken River. There is a Pioneer museum and an annual Rose Festival.

TOURIST BOARD
TOURIST INFORMATION OFFICE
14 Mair Street
Tel: 05 762 1749
Open daily 0900-1700

BEECHWORTH
278km north of Melbourne, this is a former gold town with its history carefully preserved in many historic buildings.

BENDIGO
An old gold mining town and the third largest city in Victoria. Attractions include a guided tour on a tram. Sadly Bendigo Art Gallery, the Chinese temple built for Chinese miners, and the Sacred Heart Cathedral are not accessible according to Tourism Victoria in Melbourne, but may be worth checking with local tourist board.

TOURIST BOARD
TOURIST INFORMATION OFFICE
Charing Cross
Tel: 05 441 5244
Opening hours: Monday-Friday 0900-1230 1300-1700 Saturday and Sunday: 0900-1230 1300-1600

BRIGHT
Gateway to the snow resorts and also known for its autumn landscape. The town is lined with deciduous trees.

TOURIST BOARD
TOURIST INFORMATION CENTRE
12 Bernard Street
Tel: 05 755 2275
Open daily 1000-1600

HOTEL
HIGH COUNTRY INN MOTEL (FL)
13-17 Gavan Street
Bright VIC 3714
Tel: 05 755 1244 Fax: 05 755 1575
No. of motel units: 32
No. of adapted units: 1
Facilities: restaurant; pool; sauna; spa
Spacious ground floor units beside the Ovens River, with a bright, country feel. The town centre is 500m away. The surrounding area is flat.

CASTLEMAINE
A delightful old gold-rush town with many fine public buildings and private houses. Also famous for Castlemaine Rock.

TOURIST BOARD
TOURIST INFORMATION CENTRE
Duke Street
Pyrenees Highway
Tel: 05 472 3222
Opening hours: weekends 1000-1600

COBRAM
On the Murray River and renowned for its sandy beaches and peaches.

COLAC
There is a very high rainfall here among the volcanic lakes. Alvie and Red Rock lookouts offer fine views over the area.

ECHUCA

Positioned at the confluence of the rivers Goulburn and Murray, Echuca was once a busy inland port. Sights include Paddle-steamers and Port of Echuca Historic area.

TOURIST BOARD
TOURIST INFORMATION CENTRE
Corner of Leslie Street and Murray Esplanade
Tel: 05 482 5252
Open daily 0900-1700

GEELONG

The second largest city in Victoria, Geelong's original exports of wool and wheat were forsaken when a gold rush and the onset of industrialisation began. Over 100 National Trust Buildings, but be sure to visit the National Wool Museum.

TOURIST BOARD
TOURIST INFORMATION CENTRE
Corner of Brougham and Moorabool Streets
Tel: 05 222 2900
Open daily 1000-1700

ACCESSIBLE ATTRACTION
NATIONAL WOOL CENTRE
Geelong Wool Exchange
Corner of Brougham and Moorabool Streets
(Alongside Tourist Board)
Open daily 1000-1700
Still operates as a wool exchange, though only on paper. Exhibits include a mill worker's cottage and a reconstructed shearer's quarters of the early 20th century.

HAMILTON

In the centre of the town is Lake Hamilton. There is also a zoo and botanical gardens.

TOURIST BOARD
DISTRICT TOURIST OFFICE
Lonsdale Street
Open daily 0900-1700

ACCESSIBLE TOURS
AIR ADVENTURE AUSTRALIA
PO Box 339, Hamilton, Victoria
Tel: 05 572 1371 Fax: 05 572 5979
Ten-person aircraft with space for disabled pax. Wheelchair must be of folding variety.

HORSHAM

Main centre for the Wimmera and a good base for the Little Desert National Park. There is also an art gallery and botanical gardens located here.

TOURIST BOARD
WIMMERA TOURISM
O'Callaghan Parade
Tel: 05 382 3778

ACCESSIBLE ATTRACTIONS
ART GALLERY
Ground floor, accessible only by appointment. Accessible WC.

BOTANICAL GARDENS
Accessible with suitable WC.

MELBOURNE

The colony of Victoria became independent of NSW in 1835. Melbourne is Australia's second largest city, with a population almost as large as Sydney's. Situated on the River Yarra, the city is orderly and laid out on a grid system. There is good shopping around Collins and Bourke Streets. Victorian buildings and museums, electric trams and the Melbourne Cup horse race show the city's diversity. Melbourne has a reputation as a city of style where fashion and restaurants, theatres and art galleries, leafy gardens and architectural beauties are hallmarks of an enduring tradition. Winding west of the city, the Great Ocean Road travels along the southern coast of Victoria past rock formations such as the Twelve Apostles. The road is a memorial to the soldiers and sailors of World War I. Melbourne is close to the rolling paddocks of the state's farming districts. 35km east of the town are the Dandenong Ranges, renowned for a host of galleries, restaurants, museums and scenic gardens.

HOTELS
ALL SEASONS SWANSTON HOTEL
195 Swanston Street
Melbourne VIC 3000
Tel: 03 663 4711 Fax: 03 663 8191
No. of hotel rooms: 196

No. of adapted rooms: 3
Facilities: restaurant
Located in the centre of the central business district, the surrounding area is flat.

GRAND HYATT ON COLLINS (HYA)
123 Collins Street
Tel: 03 657 1234 Fax: 03 650 3491
No. of hotel rooms: 580
No. of adapted rooms: 6
Facilities: restaurant; pool; sauna; whirlpool
In the heart of the shopping and business districts. The surrounding area is flat and accessiblity to the town centre is very easy.

LE MERIDIEN (MH)
495 Collins Street
Melbourne VIC 3000
Tel: 03 620 9111 Fax: 03 614 1219
No. of hotel rooms: 241
No. of adapted rooms: 2
Facilities: 2 restaurants; pool; spa; sauna
Two persons per night: 320.00
A National Trust property with a 19th-century Gothic facade. Redesigned in 1993 it now surrounds a 10-storey atrium. Located in the central business district, close to boutique shopping, theatres and parks. The surrounding area is flat.

NOVOTEL ON COLLINS (NOV)
270 Collins Street
Melbourne VIC 3000
Tel: 03 650 5800 Fax: 03 650 7100
No. of hotel rooms: 323
No. of adapted rooms: 4
Facilities: restaurant; pool; sauna; whirlpool
Two persons per night: 240.00
In the town centre, close to the best shops, restaurants and theatres. The beach is 6km away and the surrounding area is flat.

PARKROYAL MELBOURNE (SPHC)
11 Little Collins Street
Tel: 03 659 1000 Fax: 03 659 0999
No. of hotel rooms: 283
No. of adapted rooms: 3
Facilities: restaurant; pool; sauna
Downtown location.

PARKROYAL ON ST. KILDA ROAD (SPHC)
562 St. Kilda Road
Tel: 03 529 8888 Fax: 03 525 1242
No. of hotel rooms: 220
No. of adapted rooms: 1
Facilities: restaurant; pool
Close to the business district.

RADISSON PRESIDENT (RAD)
65 Queens Road
Tel: 03 529 4300 Fax: 03 521 3111
No. of hotel rooms: 385
No. of adapted rooms: 3
Facilities: 2 restaurants; pool; spa; sauna
Opposite Albert Park in the business district. Close to South Yarra and the Botanical Gardens. It has a fully equipped health centre. The surrounding area is flat.

SHERATON TOWERS SOUTHGATE (SH)
One Brown Street
Tel: 03 696 3100 Fax: 03 690 6581
No. of hotel rooms: 388
No. of adapted rooms: 5
Facilities: 2 restaurants; pool; spa
Centrepiece of the Southgate Development, a complex of shops, restaurants and offices on the riverside in the centre of town. The surrounding area is flat and the nearest beach is 5km away from this quality hotel.

SOUTHERN CROSS HOTEL (FL)
131 Exhibition Street
Tel: 03 653 0221 Fax: 03 650 2119
No. of hotel rooms: 426
No. of adapted rooms: 2 twins and 1 suite
Facilities: 2 restaurants; pool; sauna; spa
Two persons per night: 320.00
Opened in 1962 as the first five-star international hotel in Australia and the only resort hotel in the city centre. Close to theatres, shops and extensive gardens. The surrounding area is flat.

THE REGENT HOTEL (LHW)
25 Collins Street
Melbourne VIC 3000
Tel: 03 653 0000 Fax: 03 654 4261
No. of hotel rooms: 363
No. of adapted rooms: 6
Facilities: 4 restaurants; pool; sauna; spa
A hotel in the grand tradition with

Blue skies all the way along the riverside in Southgate, Melbourne.

panoramic views of the city coastline, gardens and the major tourist attractions.

ACCESSIBLE ATTRACTIONS
NATIONAL GALLERY OF VICTORIA
180 St. Kilda Road
Melbourne VIC 3004
Tel: 03 685 0222 Fax: 03 686 4337
Open daily 1000-1630
Houses a fine collection of Aboriginal, Asian, Australian, European and pre-Colombian art. Accessible facilities are available.

MUSEUM OF VICTORIA
328 Swanston Street
Melbourne
Tel: 03 669 9888
Open daily 1000-1700
Ramp for disabled access. Staff take visitors from level to level by an accessible lift.

RAAF MUSEUM
Aviation Point
Point Cook VIC 3029
Tel: 03 368 1443 Fax: 03 368 1629
Opening hours: Sunday-Friday 1000-1600
One of Australia's largest collections of old aircraft with pictorial displays of weapons, uniforms and other articles.

MILDURA
Mildura was the first Murray River irrigation project and a fruit-picking centre. Paddlesteamer expeditions, the Aboriginal Arts Centre and wineries to see.

TOURIST BOARD
MILDURA INFORMATION CENTRE
The Mall
Tel: 05 023 3619
Opening hours: Monday-Friday 0900-1700
Saturday and Sunday 1000-1600

ACCESSIBLE ATTRACTION
ORANGE WORLD
Murquong
Tel: 05 023 5179
Open daily 0900-1600
Avocado and citrus groves.

MORWELL
An industrial town, Morwell was settled in the 1880s as a servicing point for diggers and traders going to the goldfields.

PHILIP ISLAND (COWES)
Home to the famous penguins at Cat Bay and Summerland who may be seen waddling up the beach to their nests at dusk. Kangaroos and seals may be seen. 140km south-east of Melbourne.

HOTEL
SEAHORSE MOTEL
29-31 Chapel Street, Cowes VIC 3922
Tel: 05 952 2003 or 059 52 2269
No. of adapted units: 6
This motel has achieved the ACROD award for units for people with a disability. Set in garden surroundings, close to shops and the beach, the units are on ground floor level with no internal steps and parking in front of each unit.

PORT FAIRY
An old Irish harbour town and crayfishing centre, originally called Belfast. 291km south-west of Melbourne.

TOURIST BOARD
TOURIST INFORMATION CENTRE
Bank Street
Tel: 05 568 1002
Opening hours: Monday-Friday 1000-1600

HOTEL
LADY JULIA PERCY MOTEL
54 Sackville Street
Port Fairy VIC 3284
Tel: 05 568 1800
No. of adapted units: 1
In the middle of a flat shopping area.

PORTLAND
Used by whalers and sealers and settled in 1834, there are several classified buildings.

TOURIST BOARD
TOURIST OFFICE
The Waterfront
Tel: 05 523 2671
Open daily 1000-1600

RUTHERGLEN

Scenic town and centre of wine making area. Renowned for its fortified wines.

TOURIST BOARD
TOURIST INFORMATION CENTRE
The Vintage Cellar
84 Main Street
Tel: 06 032 9784

SHEPPARTON

Fruit and veg. growing area. Visit the Historical Society Museum.

TOURIST BOARD
TOURIST INFORMATION CENTRE
Victoria Park Lake
Goulburn Valley Highway
Tel: 05 832 9870
Open daily 0900-1700

ACCESSIBLE ATTRACTIONS
INTERNATIONAL VILLAGE
Accessible.

SHEPPARTON & GOULBURN VALLEY
HISTORICAL SOCIETY MUSEUM
New wing with ramp access due for completion by the end of 1994.

SWAN HILL

An interesting town on the banks of the Murray River, Swan Hill was once an important shipping and agricultural centre. Now the commercial and agricultural focus for the fertile Malle district and rich irrigation riverlands.

TOURIST BOARD
TOURIST INFORMATION OFFICE
306 Campbell Street
Opening hours: Monday-Friday 0900-1700
Saturday 1000-1300

HOTEL
SWAN HILL RESORT MOTOR INN (FL)
405 Campbell Street
(Murray Valley Highway)
Swan Hill VIC 3585
Tel: 05 032 2726 Fax: 05 032 9109
No. of hotel rooms: 61
No. of adapted rooms: 2

Facilities: restaurant; pools – indoor and out-door; pool-side lounge; sauna; spa; games room
Lush tropical landscaped resort hotel. Close to Pioneer Settlement, Tyntynder Homestead (the first brick veneer structure ever built in Australia in 1850) and other major attractions. Surrounding area is flat.

ACCESSIBLE ATTRACTIONS
SWAN HILL PIONEER SETTLEMENT
Horshoe Bend
Open daily 0830-1700
Reconstruction of pioneering community about 1km from town. The buildings are authentic and many of the shops' assistants are dressed in period costume.

SWAN HILL REGIONAL CONTEMPORARY ART GALLERY
Open daily 0900-1630
Specialises in folk and original art.

DOWLING HOUSE ARTS & CRAFTS
Entrance ramp and accessible WC facilities.

TORQUAY

Famous for surfing, Bells Beach waves can reach six metres. At Easter there is a classic surf competition but if surfing is not for you, there is little else.

TOURIST BOARD
TOURIST INFORMATION BOOTH
Fisherman's Beach
Tel: 05 261 3310

WANGARATTA

Located where the King and Ovens Rivers meet. The bushranger Mad Dog Morgan is buried here.

TOURIST BOARD
TOURIST INFORMATION CENTRE
Corner of Handley Street and Tone Road
Tel: 05 721 5711
Open daily 1000-1600

WARRNAMBOOL

A popular resort with coastal and agricultural landscape and cattle everywhere. Tower Hill, a dormant volcano, is well worth visiting. Warrnambool is a busy city in the downtown area with shopping, museums and old churches.

TOURIST BOARD

TOURIST INFORMATION
600 Raglan Parade
Tel: 05 564 7837
Opening hours: Monday-Friday 0900-1700
Saturday and Sunday 1000-1200, 1300-1600

HOTEL

MID CITY MOTOR INN (FL)
525 Raglan Parade
Tel: 05 562 3866 Fax: 05 562 0923
No. of hotel rooms: 62

No. of adapted rooms: 1
Facilities: restaurant; pool; spa
Two persons per night: 95.00
Three blocks, about 50m, to the beach and Fletcher Jones gardens.
The surrounding area is flat.

ACCESSIBLE ATTRACTION

TOWERHILL GAME RESERVE
Princes Highway
13km west of town
The reserve surrounds the crater lake of an extinct volcano and is known for its bird wildlife.
Drive to the bottom of Towerhill where barbecue facilites are available.

The Diamaru Centre typifies Melbourne style and sophistication.

WESTERN AUSTRALIA

Described by both the first European to land on this coast, Dirk Hartog in 1626, and Englishman William Damper in 1688, as dry and barren, Western Australia was first settled permanently in 1829 at what was to become Perth. In the following years many Aborigines were killed as a result of hunting and disease. The 1890 gold rush accelerated development and the mineral industry is now the basis of much of WA's prosperity.

Among the many different facets of this state, The Kimberley, Australia's Outback frontier, is the area most notable. A land of spectacular gorges and ranges, cascading waterfalls and pools, it is home to the crocodile, Barramundi game fish and many varieties of bird, reptile and wild flower. The region is considered Australia's last frontier.

Bungle Bungle in the north is an isolated area of weird domes and pyramids ringed with striations forming a surrealistic landscape stretching over more than 3000 sq. km of remote wilderness. This awesome natural spectacle is closed between January and March. The great Karris forests are found in the south where the coastline is very rugged. 1600km north of Perth are The Pilbara. The magnificent gorges of the Karijini National Park are one of Western Australia's best-kept secrets.

Time zone
October-March: GMT + 9 hours
April-September: GMT + 9 hours

TOURIST BOARDS
WESTERN AUSTRALIA TOURISM
Western Australia House
115 Strand, London WC2R 0AJ
Tel: 071-240 2881 Fax: 071-379 9826

AUSTRALIAN TOURIST BOARD
WESTERN AUSTRALIA TOURIST CENTRE
Forrest Place
Corner of Wellington Street

Perth WA 6000
Tel: 09 483 1111 Fax: 09 481 0190

WESTERN AUSTRALIA TOURISM COMMISSION
6th Floor
16 St. George's Terrace
Perth WA 6000
Tel: 09 220 1700 Fax: 09 220 1702

BRITISH CONSULATE GENERAL
Prudential Building
95 St. George's Terrace
Perth WA 6000
Tel: 02 322 3200 Fax: 09 481 4755

UNITED STATES TOURIST BOARD
WESTERN AUSTRALIA TOURISM COMMISSION
Suite 1210, 2121 Avenue of the Stars
Los Angeles CA 90067
Tel: 213 557 1987 Fax: 213 557 0322

SUPPORT ORGANISATIONS
INDEPENDENT LIVING CENTRE
OF WESTERN AUSTRALIA
3 Lemnos Street
Shenton Park WA 6008
Tel: 09 382 2011 Fax: 09 382 2896
Information and advisory service on equipment and resources.

PARAPLEGIC & QUADRIPLEGIC
ASSOCIATION OF WA
Selby Street
Shenton Park WA 6008
Tel: 09 381 0111 Fax: 09 382 3687
Charitable organisation providing information and services.

ACROD
Tel: 09 222 2961

DISABILITY RESOURCE CENTRE
Tel: 09 222 2973

WESTERN AUSTRALIAN DISABLED SPORTS
ASSOCIATION INC
PO Box 1108
East Victoria Park WA 6101
Tel: 09 470 5877 Fax: 09 362 4504

ROYAL AUTOMOBILE CLUB OF WESTERN
AUSTRALIA INC
228 Adelaide Terrace
Perth WA 6000
Tel: 09 421 4444 Fax: 09 221 1887
Produces accommodation guide to
properties with accessible facilities.

WA DEPARTMENT OF CONSERVATION AND
LAND MANAGEMENT
50 Hayman Road
Como WA 6152
Tel: 09 334 0333 Fax: 09 334 0466
Produces access to information on
Western Australia's national parks.

DEPARTMENT FOR THE ARTS
Tel: 09 427 1222

DEPARTMENT OF SPORT AND RECREATION
Tel: 09 387 9700

AIRPORT

PERTH INTERNATIONAL AIRPORT
Tel: 047 225 8282 (airport)
047 225 2222 (reservations)

Car parking
Designated spaces are reserved for those
in wheelchairs in the international and
domestic terminals, that are both under
one roof.

Facilities
Terminal: Access is from ground level by
kerb crossovers onto the pavement and
through automatic doors. A cocktail and
refreshment bar is located on the first
floor, and is accessible. Two WCs, male
and female, are located off the lower and
upper lounges and one off the customs
hall. Telephones are NOT at a suitable
height, but can be requested from the
airline staff.
The Airport Traffic Officer holds a first aid
certificate and can attend whilst on duty.
Oxygen and first aid kits are available
from the first aid room. Further oxygen
supplies are available from aircraft if
parked on the tarmac.

ACCESSIBLE TRANSPORT
TAXIS
SWAN TAXIS
Tel: 09 332 0111

BLACK & WHITE TAXIS
Tel: 09 333 3333

TRANSPERTH (Public Transport in WA)
Tel: 09 425 2525

WESTRAIL (Railways of WA)
Tel: 09 326 1200
BUDGET RENT A CAR PERTH
Tel: 09 481 1044

SPECIALIST TOUR OPERATORS
TARDIS TRAVEL
The Royal Institute for the Blind
6th Avenue
Maylands WA 6051
Tel: 07 272 6700

WHERE TO GO, WHERE TO STAY
ALBANY
This, the first settlement in Western
Australia, dates from 1826. There are
some fine restored buildings, including
the 1851 Old Gaol Museum. Located on
the picturesque Princess Royal Harbour,
Albany was originally a whaling port.
Good views from the Twin Peaks.

TOURIST BOARD
ALBANY TOURIST OFFICE
Peel Place
off York Street
Tel: 09 841 1088
Opening hours: Monday-Friday 0830-1730
Saturday and Sunday 0900-1700

BADGINGARRA

HOTEL
WADDI FARMS RESORT
Koonah Road
Tel: 09 652 9071 Fax: 09 652 9082
No. of chalets/cabins: 10
No. of adapted chalets: most
Facilities: restaurant; pool

Premier wildflower and emu farming stud in a genuine country setting. Emus can be approached and patted on this interesting and fascinating farm.
Waddi is a short drive from the Cervantes Pinnacles and the Indian Ocean (40km). Accommodation is in cabins, chalets and the main house.

BROOME

The pearl capital of the world. Founded more than 100 years ago when fleets of pearl luggers from Japan, Timor, the Philippines and Malaya discovered gem pearls here. The town still reflects that early polyglot community with a thriving Chinatown.
Each year many wading birds land at Broome from the Arctic. Between September and April Broome becomes a naturalists' home. It has the best beach in NW Australia and is a very popular resort particularly during the Festival of the Pearl in late August and early September.
Shopping in town generally is difficult except in the Roebuck Bay complex, but the town is level for the most part and it is possible to drive to beaches at low tide.

TOURIST BOARD
BROOME TOURIST OFFICE
Corner of Bagot Street and Broome Road
Tel: 09 192 2222
Opening hours: Monday-Friday 0800-1700,
Saturday 0900-1300, Sunday 0900-1700

HOTEL
CABLE BEACH CLUB (FL)
Cable Beach Road
Broome WA 6725
Tel: 09 192 0400 Fax: 09 192 2249
No. of hotel rooms: 263
No. of adapted rooms: 2, plus a further 20
with easy access.
Facilities: 4 restaurants; pool (hotel advise assistance is required)
A deluxe resort on the beach in ten hectares of lush surroundings.

BUNBURY

Bunbury has wide, golden beaches, caves and inlets, good restaurants, beach and sea fishing. Drive along the harbour up to Koombana Bay. Bunbury is also a natural centre for touring the south with its amazing karri forests, coastline and rolling grassland.

TOURIST BOARD
BUNBURY TOURIST OFFICE
Old Railway Station
Carmody Place
Tel: 09 721 7922
Opening hours: Monday-Friday 0830-1730,
Saturday 0900-1700, Sunday 0930-1730

HOTEL
CHATEAU LA MER MOTOR LODGE
99 Ocean Drive
Bunbury WA 6230
Tel: 09 721 3166 Fax: 09 721 3963
No. of hotel rooms: 26
No. of adapted rooms: 1
Facilities: units have fridges and tea, coffee and toast-making facilities; pool
Central location right by sea.

THE LORD FOREST HOTEL
Symmons Street
Bunbury WA 6230
Tel: 09 721 9966 Fax: 09 721 1845
No. of hotel rooms: 115
No. of adapted rooms: 3
Facilities: 2 restaurants; karaoke lounge; Scandals night club and cocktail lounge; pool; sauna; spa
Two persons per night: from 155.00
Luxury four-star hotel with commanding views 500m from the town centre and 700m from the nearest beach.
The location is ideal for exploring the towering karri forests, vineyards and the spectacular coastline. The surrounding area is flat.

BUSSELTON

Charming coastal resort, with some minor attractions and an Oceanarium. Ideal family location with a safe beach.

CARNARVON

Delightful fishing town providing much of WA's delicious prawns. Also famed for tropical fruit and as a NASA station tracking space shots. 450km inland is Mount Augustus, the world's largest monocline–twice the size of Uluru (Ayers Rock).

TOURIST BOARD
TOURIST INFORMATION CENTRE
Robinson Street
Tel: 09 941 1145
Open daily 0900-1700

CERVANTES
Cervantes is situated at the only entrance to the Nambung National Park that contains the Pinnacles, calcified spires that rise vertically like monuments–the remains of an ancient forest that stretch eerily across the desert landscape.

HOTEL
CERVANTES PINNACLES MOTEL
7 Aragon Street
PO Box 20
Cervantes WA 6511
Tel: 09 652 7145 Fax: 09 652 7214
No. of hotel rooms: 40
No. of adapted rooms: 1, (hotel advises all others are accessible)
Facilities: restaurant; pool; all units have refrigerators
Close to the beach and 200m from town. The surrounding area is flat.

DAMPIER
The town looks towards the island of the Dampier Archipelago, and is now an iron town with a liquefied natural gas terminal.

TOURIST BOARD
DAMPIER TOURIST OFFICE
Bay Holiday Village Reception
138 The Esplanade
Tel: 09 183 1400
Open daily 0700-2100

DENHAM
The most westerly town in Australia, once a pearling port, but now famous for prawns. Near the town is the tiny community of Monkey Mia, with an almost tame school of dolphins.
Although there are no specific facilities for

those in wheelchairs in Shark Bay, some shops are level and most footpaths along the waterfront are paved.

TOURIST BOARD
DENHAM TOURIST OFFICE
83 Knights Terrace
Tel: 09 948 1253

HOTEL
NANGA BAY HOLIDAY VILLAGE
c/o PO Box Denham
Shark Bay WA 6537
Tel: 09 948 3992 Fax: 09 948 3996
No. of hotel rooms: 24
No. of adapted rooms: None
Facilities: restaurant; pool
NB: NONE OF THE ROOMS IS SPECIFICALLY ADAPTED BUT ALL FACILITIES AND BEDROOMS APPEAR ACCESSIBLE.
The village is situated on a 500,000-acre sheep station, 200m from the beach and almost completely surrounded by land. The bay is shallow and calm. In front of the homestead is a large patio. You must visit Nanga Station, Shark Bay and a 40-minute drive via Denham brings you to the dolphins at Monkey Mia.

DUNSBOROUGH
Attractive coastal resort 21km from Busselton. 14km to the northwest is Cape Naturaliste.

ESPERANCE
Named after a French naval vessel that in 1863 took shelter a few kilometres from the present town. The beautiful bays and beaches look out onto a group of offshore islands famous for fishing and seals. Since the 1950s when trace elements were found in the soil, Esperance has become an increasingly popular agricultural base.

TOURIST BOARD
ESPERANCE TOURIST OFFICE
Museum Village, Dempster Street
Tel: 09 071 2330
Opening hours: Monday-Friday 0845-1700
Saturday and Sunday 0900-1700

HOTEL
CAPTAIN HUON MOTEL
5 The Esplanade
Tel: 09 071 2383 Fax: 09 071 2358
No. of motel units: 21
No. of adapted units: 1
Facilities: restaurant; pool
Note: THERE IS A SMALL STEP INTO
THE RESTAURANT, AND ALSO INTO
SHOWER AREA OF THE BATHROOM.
Self-contained motel units on the
beachfront with the adapted unit on the
ground floor.

EUCLA
An area known for its caves, notably the
Koonalda Cave. The town contains the
ruins of an old weather station.

EXMOUTH
Big game fishing and prawning centre
with good beaches and the Yardi Creek
Gorge. It is also the site of a US Navy base
with 13 transmitter stations, 12 of them
taller than the Eiffel Tower. These
support the 13th that, at 396m, is the
tallest structure in the southern
hemisphere.

FREMANTLE
20 minutes southwest of Perth and now
part of the suburbs of the port, Fremantle
has a great sense of history and a
cosmopolitan and exotic flavour, with
night spots, old world haunts, ethnic
restaurants, pubs and quaint old cottages.
Most of the historic buildings were built
with convict labour.

TOURIST BOARD
FREMANTLE TOURIST OFFICE
88 St John's Square
Tel: 09 430 2346
Opening hours: Monday-Friday 0900-1700,
Saturday and Sunday 0900-1200, 1300-1700

HOTEL
FREMANTLE ESPLANADE HOTEL
Corner of Marine Terrace and Essex Street
Fremantle WA 6160
Tel: 09 430 4000 Fax: 09 430 4539
No. of hotel rooms: 141

No. of adapted rooms: 1
Facilities: 3 restaurants; bar; pool; sauna; spa
4-star, historic hotel in the city centre.
The beach is two minutes away and the
surrounding area is flat.

PIER 21 RESORT
7-9 John Street
North Fremantle WA 6159
Tel: 09 336 2555 Fax: 09 336 2140
No. of hotel rooms: 47
No. of adapted rooms: 2
Facilities: restaurant; pool; sauna; spa
Deluxe self-catering on the river front,
with all rooms overlooking the Swan
River and entrance to the Indian Ocean.
Fremantle is 4km away, the nearest beach
3km and the surrounding area is flat.

ACCESSIBLE ATTRACTION
MARITIME MUSEUM
Level entry from designated car parking,
and accessible WC facilities. Service lift is
used for access to the second floor.

GERALDTON
The major town of the midwest region on
a superb coastline. A lively, attractive
town with ample sunshine all year round
and a wide choice of activities.

TOURIST BOARD
GERALDTON TOURIST OFFICE
Bill Sewell Complex
Champan Road
Tel: 09 921 3999
Opening hours: Monday-Friday 0800-1730,
Saturday 0800-1700, Sunday 0900-1700

ACCESSIBLE ATTRACTION
MARITIME MUSEUM
All on ground level.

HYDEN
The aborigines were the first inhabitants
of the Hyden area and many stones have
been found from their campsites and
painted handmarks can still be seen on
rocks at the Humps and Wave Rock, just
4km away. The Sandalwooders are
believed to have been the first white men
in the area and the earliest recorded

farming was in 1922. The descendants of these settlers still live in Hyden.
Wave Rock is a granite formation 2,700 million years old with vertical bands of colour formed by rain washing chemicals down the rock face. There are other formations in the area also worth seeing, including Hippos Yawn, The Falls and The Breakers.

TOURIST BOARD
TOURIST INFORMATION SERVICE
Tel: 09 880 5182

HOTEL
HYDEN MOTEL
2 Lynch Street, Hyden WA 63
Tel: 09 880 5052 Fax: 09 880 5165
No. of hotel rooms: 47
No. of adapted rooms: none
Facilities: restaurant
Located in the town centre, the surrounding area is flat.
THIS MOTEL DOES NOT HAVE ANY SPECIALLY ADAPTED ROOMS, BUT THE STAFF HAVE INDICATED A GREAT WILLINGNESS IN ACCOMMODATING GUESTS IN WHEELCHAIRS. ALTHOUGH THE PRIVATE ROOMS' FACILITIES DO NOT MEET THE CRITERIA REQUIRED, THE STAFF WILL ASSIST. OBVIOUSLY THE MOTEL IS SUITABLE FOR GUESTS WHO ARE ACCOMPANIED.

KALBARRI
A pleasant holiday resort famed for the grandeur of its coastal gorges: Red Bluff, Alley Gorge and Hawke's Head. Also notable for its position where the meandering Murchison River empties into the Indian Ocean.
Shopping in Kalbarri town is easy and in the park some views are accessible from the car. There are some flat paths near the beach and sea birds can be accessibly viewed at Red Bluff. The Bird Sanctuary here is paved and has good access.

TOURIST BOARD
KALBARRI TOURIST OFFICE
Allen Centre

Grey Street
Tel: 09 937 1104
Open daily 0830-1730

KALGOORLIE
A thriving gold mining town where visitors may explore an old mine and pan for themselves. Visit the Hainault Tourist Mine and the Golden Mile Museum. There are also many fine public buildings. Kalgoorlie is the fastest-growing gold-producing town in the world.

TOURIST BOARD
KALGOORLIE TOURIST OFFICE
250 Hannan Street
Tel: 09 021 1966
Opening hours: Monday-Friday 0830-1700
Saturday and Sunday 0900-1230 1330-1700

KUNUNURRA
The centre of the Ord River irrigation scheme and a fisherman's and birdwatcher's paradise. Ancient rocks covered with Aboriginal paintings can be seen in the Hidden Valley. The town is modern and includes the Waringarri Aboriginal Arts Centre. Be sure to see the Zebra Rocks that have red stripes on a white base.

TOURIST BOARD
VISITORS' CENTRE
Koolibah Drive
Tel: 09 168 1177
Open daily 0800-1700

HOTEL
KIMBERLEY COURT HOTEL
PO Box 384
Kununurra WA 6743
Tel: 09 168 1411 Fax: 09 168 1055
No. of motel units: 21
No. of adapted units: 1
Facilities: pool; fully equipped kitchen for guests' use. Breakfast is served on the kitchen terrace and there are 13 eating places within five minutes of the motel.
Two persons per night: 94.00
Small and privately owned, the motel is in the centre of Kununurra with a large shopping complex immediately opposite.

MANDURAH
Seaside resort town an hour's drive south of Perth, situated at the mouth of the enormous Serpentine River estuary. Coastal salt lakes nearby offer opportunities to see bird life and dolphin activity.

MARGARET RIVER
This is a charming town in the centre of the south west's successful wine-growing region. Vineyards welcome visitors for tastings. The location also offers wonderful surf.

TOURIST BOARD
TOURIST OFFICE
Bussell Highway
Tel: 09 757 2911
Open daily 0900-1700

MERREDIN
An interesting National Trust Homestead and old preserved railway station worth a visit. There are some fascinating rocks north of the town around Koorda.

MOUNT BARKER
First settled in the 1830s, nearby Kenderup was the site of WA's first gold discovery. There is a huge TV tower on the top of Mount Barker.

TOURIST BOARD
TOURIST OFFICE
Lowood Road
Tel: 09 851 1163

MUNDARRING (Perth suburb)
See the damming of the Helena River, built to supply water to the gold fields 500km to the east.

NORSEMAN
Gold put Norseman on the map in 1894, and it still remains important, mining the richest quartz reef in Australia.

TOURIST BOARD
NORSEMAN TOURIST OFFICE
Robert Street
Tel: 09 039 1071
Open daily 0900-1700

PEMBERTON
Old timber town surrounded by wooded hills and valleys in the karri forest.

TOURIST BOARD
PEMBERTON TOURIST INFORMATION
Brockman Street
Tel: 09 776 1133
Open daily 0900-1700

PERTH
PERTH METROPOLITAN
The city was originally founded in 1829 and became known as the Swan River Settlement. Development was very slow until 1850 when convict labour became readily available and then increased dramatically following the discovery of gold in the 1890s.

Modern skyscrapers now tend to overshadow colonial buildings, but situated as it is on the banks of the scenic Swan River, Perth enjoys a glorious climate and superb location.

The river foreshore and the lovely beaches are very popular. There are several delightful attractions including Pioneer World and Kings Park that is a must. Manly and Hay streets are good for shopping. South of the city and easily reached by car, are picturesque farmlands, magnificent forest and scenic wine-growing areas producing some excellent world-class wines. East of Perth is the gold-mining town of Kalgoorlie.

TOURIST BOARD
TOURIST OFFICE
Forrest Chase Precinct (nr. Wellington St.)
Perth
Tel: 09 483 1111

AIRLINE OFFICES
BRITISH AIRWAYS
Tel: 09 483 7711

GARUDA INDONESIA
Tel: 09 481 0963

QANTAS
Tel: 09 225 2222

SINGAPORE AIRLINES
Tel: 09 483 5777

ANSETT AIRLINES
Tel: 09 325 0401

HOTELS
HILTON PERTH PARMELIA (HH)
Mill Street
Perth WA 6000
Tel: 09 322 3622 Fax: 09 481 0857
No. of hotel rooms: 274
No. of adapted rooms: 1
Facilities: 3 restaurants; pool; sauna; spa
Two persons per night: 215.00
De luxe hotel in CBD, with award-winning restaurant. The surrounding area is flat.

HYATT REGENCY HOTEL (HYA)
99 Adelaide Terrace
Perth WA 6000
Tel: 09 225 1234 Fax: 09 325 8899
No. of hotel rooms: 364
No. of adapted rooms: 8
Facilities: 3 restaurants; pool; sauna; spa
Five-star hotel in CBD on the Swan River. The nearest beach is 17km away and the surrounding area is flat.

QUALITY LANGLEY HOTEL (CHI)
221 Adelaide Terrace
Tel: 09 221 1200 Fax: 09 221 1669
No. of hotel rooms: 252
No. of adapted rooms: 1
Facilities: 2 restaurants; lobby bar; Irish theme public bar; pool; sauna; whirlpool
Two persons per night: 150-290.00
Four-star, city-centre hotel with excellent views of the Swan River. The beach is 20 minutes away.

PERTH INTERNATIONAL HOTEL
10 Irwin Street
Tel: 09 325 0481 Fax: 09 221 3344
No. of hotel rooms: 229
No. of adapted rooms: 2
Facilities: 2 restaurants; pool (none of the facilities is accessible)
500m from town centre, and 12km from the nearest beach. The surrounding area is flat.

SHERATON PERTH HOTEL (SH)
207 Adelaide Terrace
Tel: 09 325 0501 Fax: 09 325 4032
No. of hotel rooms: 391
No. of adapted rooms: 1
Facilities: 2 restaurants; pool; sauna
This is a prominent five-star hotel 1km from the town centre and 10km from the nearest beach. All the rooms have a view of the Swan River. There is a hill sloping away from the hotel otherwise the surrounding areas are flat.
Note: THE ROUTE FROM THE CAR PARK TO THE HOTEL IS STEEP SO PARK AT THE HOTEL'S MAIN ENTRANCE AND THE DOORMAN WILL TAKE CARE OF YOUR CAR.

THE MOUNT STREET INN (FL)
24 Mount Street
Tel: 09 481 0866 Fax: 09 321 4789
No. of suites: 100
No. of adapted suites: 5
Facilities: restaurant; pool; spa; sauna
Two persons per night: 105.00
Self catering – all suites are equipped with a microwave oven. The inn has a central location in a quiet cul-de-sac between the CBD and tranquil Kings Park. The beach is 6km away and the surrounding area is flat.

PINGARRING
TURRAMA FARM
Hyden and Newgidate Roads
Pingarring WA 6357
Tel: 09 866 8066
Shearers' quarters and farm-style bed and breakfast. About 40km south of Wave Rock (Hyden). The rock is 2,700 million years old and was formed by weathering processes and by erosion creating the distinctive undercut surface.
The owners of Turrama advise us they have a small cottage close to the farmhouse, both are accessible, as is the bathroom in the cottage, but a commode may be required for the WC.
They have hosted a quadriplegic guest for a ten-day period, and are confident of assisting more such guests. Meals are taken in the farmhouse that is accessible.

PORT HEDLAND
Situated on an inlet surrounded by mangrove, ore is shipped from here to Japan. Plenty of fish, oysters and birds surround the inlet.

TOURIST BOARD
TOURIST OFFICE
Wedge Street
Tel: 09 173 1711
Opening hours: Monday-Friday 0830-1700
Saturday and Sunday 0900-1700

RAVENSTHORPE
Explore the copper mine near this tiny town that was once at the centre of the Philips River gold field.

ROTTNEST ISLAND
Discovered in 1696 by Vlaming, a Dutch explorer, who called it Rat's Nest because of what he thought were a plague of enormous rats inhabiting the island. They were in fact quokkas.
30 minutes by ferry from Perth, only limited development is allowed in order to protect wildlife and ecology. There is little activity except fishing and boating.

TOURIST BOARD
ROTTNEST INFORMATION OFFICE
Thompson Bay Jetty
Tel: 09 372 9752
Opening hours: Monday-Friday 0830-1700
Saturday 0900-1600 Sunday 1000-1200
and 1430-1600

SCARBOROUGH (Perth suburb)
HOTEL
INDIAN OCEAN HOTEL
27 Hastings Street
Scarborough
Tel: 09 341 1122 Fax: 09 341 1899
No. of hotel rooms: 59
No. of adapted rooms: none
Facilities: restaurant; pool; spa
Note: Although there are no specifically adapted rooms, general facilities are easy to negotiate.
There is a ramp approach with a five-degree gradient at the main entrance, restaurant and bedrooms. There are no grab rails or shower seat in the shower. The town centre is 200m away and the beach 300m. The surrounding area is flat.

TOM PRICE
Highest town in Western Australia and centre of the mining region of the Pilara. You can explore the Hamersley Range from here. Take the extremely steep drive up to the peak of Mt Nameless.

TOURIST BOARD
TOM PRICE TOURIST OFFICE
Central Road
Tel: 09 189 2375
Opening hours: Monday-Friday 0800-1700

TOODYAY
Many old buildings, built by convicts who were frequently incarcerated in the still-standing Old Newcastle Gaol, may be seen.

TOURIST BOARD
TOODYAY INFORMATION CENTRE
Connors Mill, Stirling Terrace
Opening hours: Monday-Saturday 0900-1700
Sunday 1000-1700

WALPOLE
Coastal town with giant karri trees in the Valley of the Giants.

YANCHEP (Perth suburb)
An hour's drive from Perth itself, Yanchep National Park is the home of the koala bear as well as Loch McNess, a freshwater lake teeming with wild fowl. Yanchep Sun City is an important marina and base for The America's Cup Challenge. Visit the Atlantis Marine Park to see sharks, seals and dolphins.

HOTEL
CLUB CAPRICORN
2 Rocks Road
Tel: 09 561 1106 Fax: 09 561 1163
No. of hotel rooms: unknown
No. of adapted rooms: 1
Facilities: restaurant; pool
Coastal resort with lodge and chalets and superb ocean views.

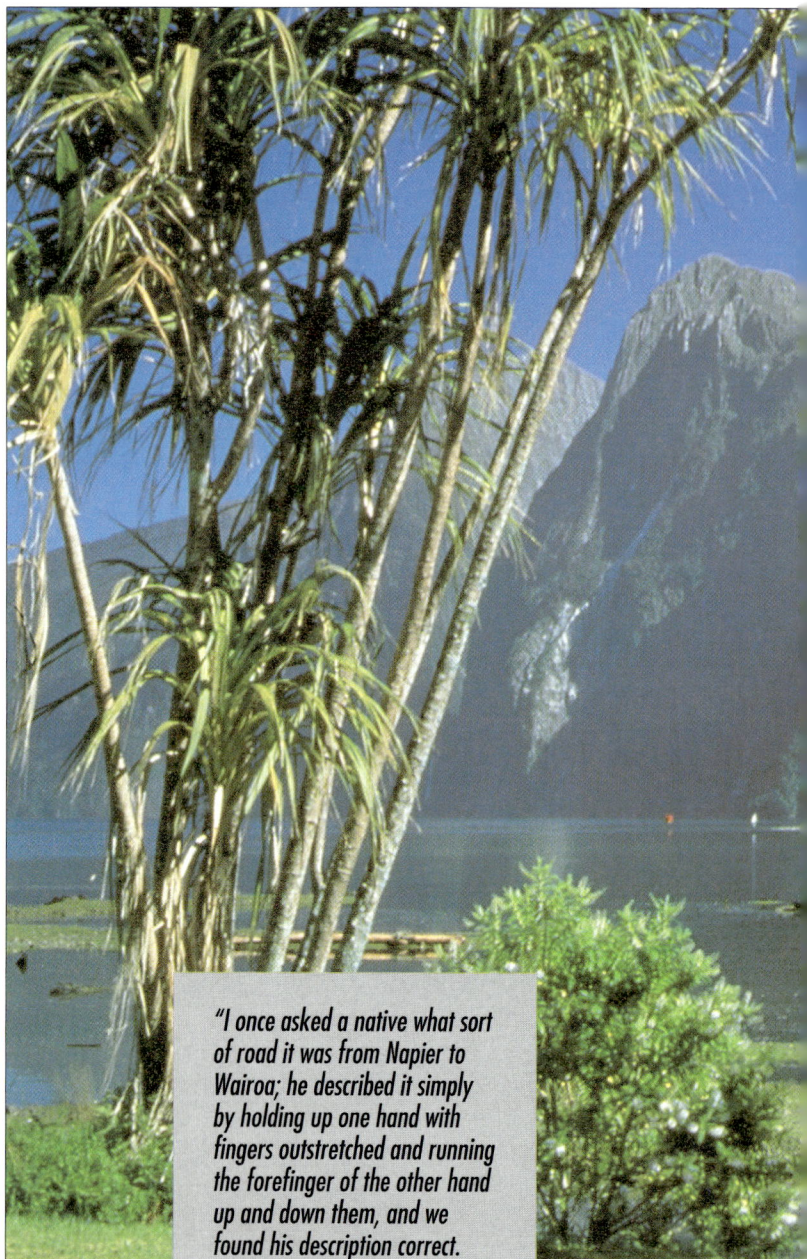

"I once asked a native what sort of road it was from Napier to Wairoa; he described it simply by holding up one hand with fingers outstretched and running the forefinger of the other hand up and down them, and we found his description correct. Lofty ranges, on the summit of which crops out a hard shelly conglomerate, and deep glens constitute the character of the country."

Lt. Col. J. St. John
"Pakeha Rambles through Maori Lands" 1879

NEW ZEALAND

A REAL SLICE OF HEAVEN *BY ANNE HUNTER "TABS ON TRAVEL" – AUCKLAND*

Time was when pilots touching down in New Zealand would advise their passengers to put their watches back 20 years. Witty colleagues were prone to add, "Sorry folks, New Zealand's closed".

That was all a while back when, to most northern hemisphere folk, New Zealand was two tiny dots on the edge of the map somewhere near the end of the world – next stop Antarctica. If it had other claims to fame they were for sheep and macho rugby players. Since then this 'real slice of heaven' has woken up, appreciated its assets and opened its doors and hearts to tourists with a warm and unique welcome.

Today New Zealand's whereabouts is well charted and recognised the world over. The country's population exceeds three million by a whisker and last year more than one million visitors made the trip. This achievement so elated the NZ Tourism Board that it's now targeting three million tourists by the end of the year 2000.

But never fear, New Zealand is far from overrun by tourists, or people for that matter. As you've no doubt heard, sheep greatly outnumber people. And New Zealanders are a friendly lot – Maori and Pakeha both. They are frequently compared with the Irish and my husband loves to recall a sojourn in an Irish pub in County Cork when his praise for the country and its people was greeted with this memorable response from a local: "Ah well to be sure, this is the country where the grass is friendly and the people are green!" Albeit some 12000 miles away from Ireland, the same can be said of New Zealand.

The locals apart, this is the place to commune with nature and share your life with a penguin, albatross, kiwi, tui or whale – you name it and NZ has the bird, beast or mammal to find favour with you!

If it's a case of which first – good news or bad – let's take the only negative about travelling to New Zealand. It's a long way from anywhere except Australia and the islands of the South Pacific. The big tip is to choose your airline carefully. Being delayed 12 hours in Honolulu is no fun if you want to arrive happy and fit.

With its gentle welcome, Aotearoa, the Maori name for New Zealand, comprises two islands, north and south. They form a country of enormous contrasts inspiring such descriptions as Switzerland by the sea, Ireland in the sun, scrubbed Vermont and many more, but New Zealand is very much its own country and for those who wish to live, understand and appreciate what it is today then the Maori history and legends are compulsive reading.

Nestled in the sparkling clear waters of the South Pacific and boasting 16000km of spectacular coastline, New Zealand is justifiably proud of its environmentally conscious image now successfully encapsulated as the 'clean green Down Under'.

Its magical coastline, lakes, rivers and mountains paint a perfect scenic backdrop; its temperate climate provides a tourists' paradise and from the sub-tropical north to the snow-capped peaks, glaciers and fjords of the south, New Zealand is a splendidly scenic and geological wonderland.

While hissing geysers puff their boiling steam from volcanic rock and boiling mud spurts its welcome midst vast tracts of native bush and forestation, New Zealand's prime exports– cows and sheep – munch happily away on lush green paddock and hillside grass. Never far from their agricultural heritage, city dwellers successfully combine commercialism with an enviable standard of quality laid-back living, including some of the best food and wine to be had anywhere in the world.

On a whistle-stop tour down the country we start at Northland and Cape Reinga at the northernmost tip of the North Island where the Tasman and Pacific meet in a grandly visible clash. On then down the east coast to the picturesque and historic Bay of Islands. Renowned for its sailing and big game fishing, it is here at Waitangi that the famous treaty between the British and the Maori was formalised. Heading west, make a short diversion through the Waipoua Forest to pay homage to its kings – the giant Kauri trees.

Of the three million plus population in New Zealand, 850,000 live in Auckland, the country's commercial centre, known as the city of sails. Aucklanders enjoy a lifestyle that boasts more pleasure boats per capita than anywhere else in the world.

Moving on south to one of the country's foremost Maori cultural centres, Rotorua offers its unique geysers, boiling, bubbling mud pools and thermal valleys. Many of the thermal attractions are easily accessed and don't miss the opportunity to bathe in the natural mineral water and enjoy its magical qualities. The Agrodome with its super slick presentation by a multi-talented cast of woolly stars and their guardian sheepdogs is also a must.

There's a lot more to see en route to Wellington and the southern tip of the North Island. The capital with its beehive-shaped seat of government sits high on hills overlooking a picturesque harbour. Take an accessible cablecar ride up past the university and enjoy the views.

Southward by ferry or air across Cook Strait to Picton and Marlborough, pause to enjoy another of New Zealand's very fine wine-making regions. Through magnificent scenery press on to the very English city of Christchurch with its cathedral and River Avon complete with punts as testament to the city's colonial past. Just north of Christchurch you can watch the whales blow their spouts in friendly greeting off the coast at Kaikoura.

Moving west to Queenstown, you may enjoy one of the world's most scenic flights over the Southern Alps and Mt. Cook, New Zealand's highest mountain at 3764 metres. Queenstown and neighbouring Arrowtown are steeped in 1930s gold prospecting history and are among New Zealand's most scenic gems. Nestled beneath The Remarkables mountain range, Queenstown is the adventure capital of the southern hemisphere offering every imaginable adrenalin-pumping activity from bungy jumping to white water rafting. But there are gentler pursuits to be enjoyed such as a cruise on Lake Wakatipu aboard a Scottish-built steam ship to visit a working sheep station for lunch and experience friendly Kiwi hospitality.

South lies the wonderful wilderness of New Zealand with Milford Sound and Fiordland offering breathtaking and incomparable scenery. Even farther south, the Scottish settlement, Dunedin, is the seat of New Zealand's first university. Here you can visit the penguins and the albatross colony or relax with the locals and enjoy a wee dram of New Zealand's own Scotch whisky.

Haere Mai!

Customary greetings are the order of the day at Whakarewarewa, Rotorua.

FINDING YOUR WAY

TRAVEL DETAILS AND GENERAL INFORMATION

INTERESTING SNIPPETS
Sheep outnumber people by 30 to 1.
Two thirds of the country is farmland.
The Gold Rush in New Zealand started in Arrowtown, and miners still go there to sell their gold.
The gold industry is still producing a national income of over NZ$90 million per annum.
New Zealand is the same size as Britain, with a population half that of London (3.5 million).
New Zealanders are the world's greatest travellers with 25 percent of the nation's under 30s abroad at any one time.

Passport and visa requirements
A British 10-year passport is required.
No visa is necessary for a visit up to six months, but evidence of sufficient funds and an onward return ticket is required. No visa is necessary for citizens of the United States or Canada, but evidence of an onward return ticket is required.

Currency
The New Zealand Dollar (NZ$) = 100 cents. There are no restrictions on the amount of currency imported. Most major credit cards are accepted as are most major currencies in traveller-cheque form.

Climate
Sub-tropical in the North Island, temperate in the South Island.
The north has few extremes of heat or cold, but the southern winter can be cool with snow on the mountains.
Most rain falls in winter (April-September) and is extremely plentiful on the west coast of the South Island.
The east coast of both islands is far drier. The wind can be fierce throughout. Wellington records the windiest conditions, but the Auckland and Christchurch areas also suffer.
All New Zealand is subject to earth tremors, being very seismic, although the risk varies regionally. A fault line running the entire length of both islands bisects Wellington. The volcanoes of the North Island are dormant and unlikely to erupt, but care should be taken when visiting the thermal activity areas surrounding them.

Time
Throughout the country GMT + 12 hours. (GMT + 13 hours from the last week of March to the first week of October.)

Electricity
230 volts AC, 50Hz. Plugs of a flat 3-pin type, but dissimilar to those in use in the UK, and an adaptor will be required.

129

CONSULATES

HIGH COMMISSION OF NEW ZEALAND
New Zealand House
80 Haymarket
London SWIY 4TQ
Tel: 071-930 8422

BRITISH HIGH COMMISSION
9th Floor, Reserve Bank of NZ
9 The Terrace
Wellington New Zealand
Tel: 04 72 6049

BRITISH CONSULATE-GENERAL
151 Queen Street
Auckland New Zealand

BRITISH CONSULATE-GENERAL
The Dome
Regent Theatre Building
Cathedral Square
Christchurch New Zealand

MEDICAL NOTES

Reciprocal benefits apply for British or European Union subjects with free prescriptions and consultations in public hospitals. A consultation with a GP is chargeable. Pharmaceutical products obtained without a prescription are expensive.

To summon help dial 111 in all cities. There are almost no snakes or insects but Mako sharks, that are not really dangerous, occasionally come close inshore. Jellyfish and sandflies can be a nuisance and very obtrusive.

Wasps can also be a problem on the west coast of South Island and carrying medication is recommended.

TOURIST BOARDS

UK TOURIST OFFICE
NEW ZEALAND TOURIST OFFICE
New Zealand House, Haymarket
London SW1Y 4TQ
Tel: 071-973 0360 Fax: 071-839 8929

NEW ZEALAND TRAVEL INFORMATION SERVICE
94 Fulham Palace Road
London W6 8JA
Tel: 081-748 4455 Fax: 081-748 2274

SPECIALIST TOUR OPERATORS

DISABLED KIWI TOURS
East Coast Highway
PO Box 550, Opotiki
Tel: 07 315 7867 Fax: 07 315 5056

AIRLINES

ANSETT AIRLINES NEW ZEALAND
New Zealand Head Office, PO Box 4168
Auckland
Tel: 09 309 6235 Fax: 09 309 6434

London Office
4th Floor, Heathcote House
20 Savile Row
London W1X 2AN
Tel: 071-434 4071 Fax: 071-734 4333

Ansett operates an Ansacare programme for travellers using wheelchairs. Details are available from the airline. Passengers using their own wheelchairs are asked to transfer to an Ansett customised chair for boarding Ansett jet services. These are designed for movement down the aircraft aisles. Passengers' wheelchairs are then boarded.

MOUNT COOK AIRLINES
Airline/Landline Head Office
PO Box 4644
Christchurch
Tel: 03 348 2099 Fax: 03 377 5786
RESERVATIONS ARE MADE THROUGH AIR NEW ZEALAND.

Hawker Siddeley HS748 aircraft are used. Passengers use the airline's wheelchairs for boarding. Special requirements should be notified at the time of reservation. Passengers with disabilities cannot be carried when Chieftain aircraft are used on the Auckland-Kerikeri route.

Air travel between the major centres of Auckland, Wellington, Christchurch and Dunedin by jet aircraft is aided by the use of covered airbridges. At other airports alternative arrangements have to be made. Terminals with airbridges also have lifts to upper levels.

Terminals throughout New Zealand have lifts and accessible WCs throughout. Further information is listed under individual airports.

Both airlines offer special passes. Sample journey times are:
Auckland/Wellington 1 hour.
Auckland/Rotorua 40 minutes.
Auckland/Christchurch 1 hour 20 minutes.
Christchurch/Queenstown 1 hour 15 minutes.

G'DAY PASS – see page 32 for full details of this excellent Australian air travel pass.

FERRIES

INTER-ISLANDER
INTER ISLAND FERRY SERVICE
New Zealand Rail Ltd
Bunny Street
Wellington
Tel: 0800 658 999 call free
03 498 3949 local

The ferry service operating between the North and South Islands, Wellington to Picton, is designed to meet the needs of the less able. There are two wheelchair-accessible ferries, *Arahura* and *Aratika*. Lifts connect all passenger decks, although some assistance may be required from staff whilst boarding. The journey between the islands takes three hours and operates daily, morning, afternoon and evening.

RAIL
INTERCITY-NEW ZEALAND RAIL
UK Agent
COMPASS
Tel: 07 335 1780

New Zealand Rail
Tel: 0800 802 802 call free
03 498 3949 local

Passengers on board main line trains can request a special chair to negotiate narrow aisles. WC facilities are accessible only to those with a reasonable degree of mobility, as limited space excludes chairs from entering the toilet area.
ACCESS FROM PLATFORMS TO LONG-DISTANCE TRAINS REMAINS DIFFICULT AT EVERY STATION. IT IS THEREFORE RECOMMENDED THAT RAIL JOURNEYS BE UNDERTAKEN ONLY WITH A COMPANION.

RAIL ITINERARIES
OVERLANDER EXPRESS
The day-time services between Auckland and Wellington afford great views of the constantly changing North Island landscape including Raurimu Spiral, a famous piece of railway engineering. Journey time is 10 hours.

TRANS ALPINE EXPRESS
This service crosses the South Island's Southern Alps, and provides a spectacular scenic journey from Christchurch to Greymouth. Journey time is five hours.

COASTAL PACIFIC
This meets the inter-island ferries at Picton and travels on to Christchurch via the eastern coast. Journey time is five hours 20 minutes.

KAIMAI EXPRESS
Auckland to Tauranga, an evening journey, returning in the morning. Journey time is three hours 15 minutes.

GEYSERLAND EXPRESS
Auckland/Rotorua/Auckland.
Journey time is four hours each way.

BAY EXPRESS
A daytime service between Wellington and Napier. Journey time is five hours 30 minutes.

SOUTHERNER EXPRESS
Overnight journey between Christchurch and Invercargill. Journey time is nine hours 30 minutes.

COACH
There are no coaches fitted with hoists, nor are there any special areas on board that can accommodate a person in a wheelchair, the aisles being too narrow.

CAR HIRE
AVIS RENT-A-CAR
Private Bag
Wellesley Street
Auckland
Tel: 09 525 1982
Hand controls can be fitted to some models.

BUDGET RENT A CAR
Tel: 03 366 0072
In Christchurch Budget have two hand-controlled cars for the whole country, so they must be reserved well in advance.

HORIZON HOLIDAYS
530-544 Memorial Avenue
PO Box 14068
Christchurch Airport
Tel: 03 535 5600 Fax: 03 353 5646
A Paravan is available for hire fitted with an electric hoist. The rear seat of a twin cab is removed so that a wheelchair driver can sit behind the seat, secured by wheelchair clamps.

TAXIS

Throughout the country there are 80 Maxi Taxis (Toyota Hiace vans) operating under the Total Mobility Taxi Service.

DUNEDIN TAXIS
Tel: 03 477 7777

Offer a van with a wheelchair hoist.

NORTHLAND DISABILITIES RESOURCE CENTRE
18 Vine Street
Whangarei
Tel: 09 430 0988
Fax: 09 438 9468

Runs two vans converted to wheelchair vehicles. To book one call the above number, or leave a message on the answerphone (09 430 0988).

KIWI CABS
Tel: 09 438 2299

Taxi service with van equipped with hoist.

Auckland's Westhaven Marina with Harbour Bridge in the background.

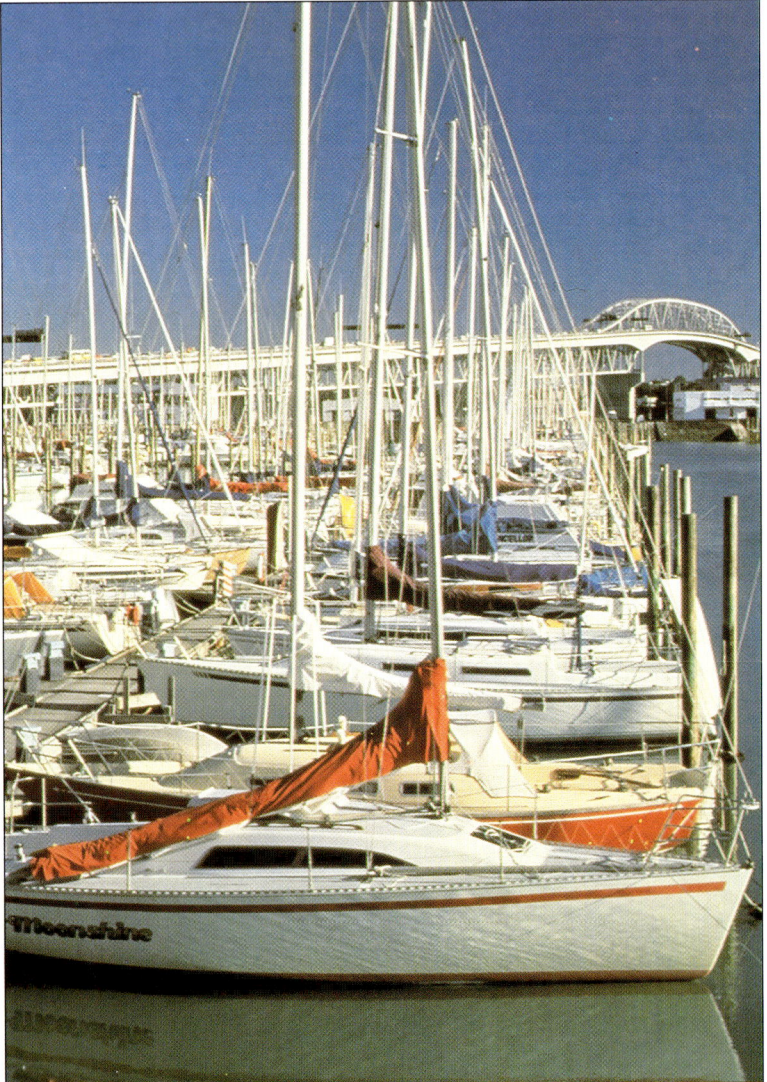

NORTH ISLAND

SUPPORT ORGANISATIONS
DISABILITY RESOURCE CENTRE
PO Box 24-042
14 Erson Avenue
Royal Oak
Auckland 3
Tel: 09 625 8069 Fax: 09 624 1633

AIRPORT
AUCKLAND INTERNATIONAL AIRPORT
Tel: 09 275 0789 Fax: 09 275 0789

Car Parking
Designated parking areas in metered car
park.

Facilities
International Terminal: There is a
restaurant on the ground floor with good
access. Phones are mounted low throughout the terminal and also at coffee-table
level in Ansett's Golden Wing Lounge.
Ansett provides an easy access lift to the
first floor for airbridge boarding. There is
one male and one female accessible WC.
Air New Zealand have airbridges installed
in both terminals.

AIRLINE OFFICES
AIR NEW ZEALAND
Quay Street
Auckland
Tel: 09 366 2400

ANSETT NEW ZEALAND
75 Queen Street or
50 Grafton Road
Auckland
Tel: toll-free 09 307 6950

GREAT BARRIER AIRLINES
Tel: 09 275 9120

WHERE TO GO, WHERE TO STAY

AUCKLAND
Founded in 1840 and by far the largest
city in NZ, Auckland's low-rise buildings
spread haphazardly over once-active
volcanoes. Boasting two attractive
harbours and over 300 parks, it is
considered the queen city of NZ. The
main shopping areas are Queen Street
and Karangahape Road and, for the more
adventurous, the Chinese and bustling
Victoria markets.
Auckland is the liveliest city in the
country with good restaurants on Parnell
and Ponsonby Roads. Parnell village has
painted colonial villas, designer stores
and stylish craft shops.
The Museum of Transport and

133

*Prepare to be constantly invigorated by
New Zealand's majestic scenery.*

Technology has an impressive collection of planes and trains. The zoo, unquestionably the best in NZ, contains many rare examples of local fauna, including the kiwi. Albert Park and the university stand in the very heart of the city and fine views can be had from One Tree Hill and Mount Eden, both accessible on good roads.

There are many fine bathing beaches and the Aucklander's sea-based culture is served by a myriad of small boats and craft. Auckland has more boats per capita than anywhere else in the world, and is often called The City of Sails.

Outlying islands can be reached by ferry and the 3500ft-long Harbour Bridge transports you to the North Shore.

Sir John Logan Cambell is the father of Auckland's cottage that was built in 1843 and still stands in Cornwall Park. Explore the towns of Takapuna and Northland and visit the Waitakere Hills and the Savage Memorial.

Auckland has the third lowest rate of obesity of all world cities.

ACCESSIBLE TRANSPORT
NEWMANS RENTALS
Richard Pearse Drive
Po Box 73 125
There is a Paravan available for rental. It is fitted with electric hoists, side-mounted and powered by the van's own master battery. The rear seat of a usual twin cab is removed and anchor bolts and sufficient padded head room are provided.

AVIS RENT-A-CAR
Private Bag
Wellesley Street
Hand controls can be fitted to some rental models.

BUDGET RENT A CAR
8 Beach Road
Tel: 09 379 6768 Fax: 09 394 180
A VN Commodore Ford Falcon equipped with hand controls is available for rental.

SPECIALIST TOUR OPERATORS
ATLANTIC & PACIFIC TOURS
2nd Floor
164 Parnell Road
Parnell
Auckland
Tel: 09 377 0660 Fax: 09 307 9328

WHITTA TOURS
57 Ridge Road
Howick
Auckland
Tel: 09 537 3300

HOTELS
AIRPORT HARBOUR VIEWS MOTOR LODGE
6 Onehunga Harbour Road
Onehunga
Auckland
Tel: 09 634 5300 Fax: 09 634 5304
No. of hotel rooms: 17
No. of adapted rooms: 2
Facilities: room service is available; pool; spa bath in some rooms
Two persons per night: 90.00
Park setting with views of the harbour.

AUCKLAND PARK ROYAL HOTEL (SPHC)
8 Customs Street
PO Box 1707
Tel: 09 377 8920 Fax: 09 307 3739
No. of hotel rooms: 187
No. of adapted rooms: 4
Facilities: restaurant; 2 bars
Located in the city centre, 10 minutes from the beach and 30 minutes from the international airport. The surrounding area is flat.

KINGSGATE LOGAN PARK HOTEL GREENLANE
187 Campbell Road
Greenlane
Auckland
Tel: 09 634 1269 Fax: 09 636 8115
No. of hotel rooms: 220
No. of adapted rooms: 1
Facilities: restaurant; pool; 2 private spas
Adjacent to peaceful Cornwall Park, midway between the international airport and downtown Auckland, the hotel is set in landscaped gardens. 7km from the city centre and 5km from the beach, the

Selecting duty frees in Coromandel could turn into a barrel of laughs.

surrounding area is flat.
There is a flat internal courtyard garden by the pool area.

PENINSULA MOTOR HOTEL
18 Elm Street
Avondale
Auckland
Tel: 09 828 2761 Fax: 09 828 3496
No. of hotel rooms: 48, plus 2 suites
No. of adapted rooms: 2
Facilities: restaurant; pool; spa
Two persons per night: 120.00
On the west side of the city with attractive views and an accent on "green". The town centre is 15km by motorway and the beach eight minutes' drive away. The surrounding area is flat.

QUALITY HOTEL AIRPORT AUCKLAND
Corner of Kirkbride and Ascot Roads
Mangere Auckland
Tel: 09 275 7029 Fax: 09 275 3322
No. of hotel rooms: 160
No. of adapted rooms: 6
Facilities: restaurant; bar; pool; sauna; gym; garden
15km from the town centre and from the beach. The surrounding area is flat.

REGENT HOTEL (LHW)
Albert Street
Tel: 09 309 8888 Fax: 09 379 6445

No. of hotel rooms: 332
No. of adapted rooms: 3
Facilities: restaurant; heated rooftop pool
Two persons per night: 350.00
Situated in the shopping and entertainment area and close to Waitemata Harbour. It is 2km to the beach and the surrounding area is flat.

SHERATON AUCKLAND HOTEL (SH)
83 Symonds Street
Tel: 09 379 5132 Fax: 09 377 9367
No. of hotel rooms: 407
No. of adapted rooms: 6
Facilities: 3 restaurants; pool; sauna; spa.
(Access to sauna and spa is by three steps)
Two persons per night: 290.00
Central location within easy reach of harbour, parks and restaurants.
The surrounding area is reasonably flat.

WAIPUNA HOTEL AND CONFERENCE CENTRE
58 Waipuna Road
Mt. Wellington
Auckland 6
Tel: 09 527 3114 Fax: 09 527 1937
No. of hotel rooms: 155
No. of adapted rooms: 8
Facilities: 2 restaurants; hotel bar; pool; whirlpool
Two persons per night: 170.00

Delightful hotel set in 6.25 acres of

parkland overlooking the lagoon. 10km from the international airport and 8km from the town centre, the beach is 15 minutes away and the surrounding area is flat.

ACCESSIBLE ATTRACTIONS
AUCKLAND VISITOR CENTRE
Tel: 09 366 6888

KELLY TARLTONS UNDERWATER WORLD
23 Tamaki Drive
Open 0900-2100
Wheelchair access from the car park, where there is designated car space. A 1200m underwater acrylic tunnel has a moving walkway that exposes to view more than 1500 marine animals. It is currently accessible. WCs are not available at present but major building work now in progress includes new WC facilities.

KELLYS CAFE
On the waterfront above the aquarium. Delightful eating with superb views – ideal for lunch.

MUSEUM OF TRANSPORT AND TECHNOLOGY
Great North Road, Western Springs
Open 0900-1700
Wheelchair access is via Stadium Road, although there is no specific parking area. With prior notification, vehicles are allowed to park inside the museum complex. There are accessible WCs.

PAVILION OF NEW ZEALAND
Montgomerie Road (near airport)
Open 0900-1700
The New Zealand exhibit for the 1988 Brisbane EXPO. Accessible WCs and designated parking space.

REGIONAL BOTANIC GARDENS
102 Hill Road, Manurewa

AUCKLAND ZOO
Motions Road, Western Springs
Designated parking and accessible WCs.

TOP OF ONE TREE HILL
Mt. Victoria and Mt. Eden.

Wonderful scenic views although there is no designated parking and there is no WC at the top of the hill. However there is a restaurant within the One Tree Hill Park that does have accessible WCs.

PARNELL ROSE GARDEN
Gladstone Road, Parnell
Tel: 09 302 1252
No specified designated parking. WCs not accessible, but some are planned.

ACCESSIBLE WALKING TRACKS AND PICNIC AREAS
KING EDWARD PARADE, DEVONPORT
1km, one-way seafront walk from the ferry terminal. For information phone 09 452 205.

CHELTENHAM BEACHFRONT
Access to grassy area and concrete esplanade. Watch the camber. For information phone 09 452 205.

CORNWALL PARK
Greenlane Road, Epsom
Urban farm park and gardens with some areas accessible. For information phone 09 546 442.

AUCKLAND DOMAIN
Central city picnic area with several accessible paths. For information phone 09 792 020.

MILFORD BEACH PARKWAY
Ocean Front Road, Milford
A concrete walkway overlooking the beach.

NORTHERN WALKWAY, PAPAKURA
Over 6km of bush walks with views of early settlement buildings. Bush walks may be undertaken individually using a car to link them. Fairly accessible.
For information phone 09 299 8870

GISBORNE
Settled in 1852, Gisborne is the main city of Poverty Bay on the East Coast. The Maori name for the Eastland district is Tairawhiti, meaning the coast upon which the sun shines across the water. This is the

most easterly city in the world and the first to see the sun rise every day. Gisborne and its surrounding hills were Captain Cook's first sighting of New Zealand and a memorial to Captain Cook, celebrating his first friendly contacts with the Maoris in 1769 and 1777, has been erected. There is a fine view from Kaiti Hill over the city and, out to sea, Young Nick's Head may be seen. The area has one of the country's highest number of sunshine hours that facilitates fruit growing, especially grapes, and enhances some wonderful beaches. Some of the best carved Maori meeting houses (Whare-runangas) and churches are found in this area. South of Gisborne, Wairoa is the gateway to Lake Waikaremoana and some of the most unspoilt scenery in the Urewera National Park.

The city exports frozen meat, lime, fertiliser and tallow. There are pleasant seaside resorts nearby including Wainui Beach, Tatapouri and Tolaga Bay.

TOURIST BOARD
EASTLAND PROMOTION COUNCIL
209 Grey Street, PO Box 170
Tel: 06 868 6139 Fax: 06 868 6139

ACCESSIBLE TRANSPORT
GISBORNE TAXIS
Tel: 06 867 2222

ACCESSIBLE ATTRACTION
TE POHO O RAWIRI
Queens Drive
Tel: 06 867 2835
This, one of the largest Maori meeting houses in the country, is advised by the Promotion Council as accessible. There are two steps at the entrance, but staff will assist.

HAHEI BEACH
Seaside locality on the east coast of Coromandel Peninsula. Mercury Bay is renowned for its deep-sea fishing. In earlier years the area was made famous by a gold rush and for supplying timber for ships' masts. Legend has it that this timber gave Nelson the advantage over

the French and Spanish at Trafalgar. In 1971 the Coromandel State Forest Park was established. The Maoris were well settled here when the first Europeans arrived and the area is often described as part of Polynesia.

HAMILTON
This is the centre of the rich Waikato dairy area. The city straddles the Waikato River, once an important waterway for Maori canoes and colonial steamboats. History is recaptured each March at the annual Maori war canoe regatta. Hamilton is a good base for exploring the small prosperous towns of Cambridge, famous for its English trees; Te Awamutu, renowned for rose gardens and the historic St. Johns Anglican Church of 1854, and Otorohanga whose zoo boasts the largest walk-through aviary in the southern hemisphere. The headquarters of the Waikato tribes, Turangiwaiwai, has a fine collection of Maori carved buildings including a beautiful palace.

In the centre of town Lake Hamilton provides an ideal place for youngsters learning to sail.

137

SUPPORT ORGANISATIONS
DISABILITY RESOURCE CENTRE (Waikato) TRUST
20 Palmerston Street
PO Box 146
Hamilton
Tel: 07 839 5506 Fax: 07 834 9982

NZ PARAPLEGIC AND PHYSICALLY HANDICAPPED ASSOCIATION
Po Box 610
Hamilton
Tel: 07 838 2207

EASTWOOD MANOR (HAMILTON EAST)
209 Gray Street
Hamilton East
Tel: 07 856 9029 Fax: 07 856 9028
No. of hotel rooms: 31
No. of adapted rooms: 3
Located near restaurants, Hamilton East Shopping Centre and close to all the major attractions.

ACCESSIBLE ATTRACTIONS
WAIKATO MUSEUM OF ART AND HISTORY
1 Grantham Street
Open 1000-1600

Tainui Maori cultural and Waikato social history plus travelling exhibitions. There are two designated car parks situated in a driveway left off Grantham Street. Male and female WCs are fully accessible.

M.V. WAIPA DELTA
Memorial Park

A paddlesteamer cruises on the Waikato River daily. Cruises last from one and a half to four hours. Ramp access from shore to vessel involves one step over the safety rail and assistance here is essential, but staff are always available. There is a paraplegic WC on the dining deck.

HAMILTON GARDENS
Cobham Drive

One of NZ's premier gardens with new Japanese and Georgian Flower Gardens. About ten percent is not accessible.

ACCESSIBLE WALKING TRACKS AND PICNIC AREAS
LAKESIDE WALK, LAKE DOMAIN

2km cobblestone path around Lake Rotorua. For information phone 06 386 699

HASTINGS (Hawkes Bay)

Market gardening and fruit growing area. Hastings is the centre of the region's orchards and vineyards. The surrounding rolling countryside is given over to sheep stations and burnt almost white by the bay's hot dry summers.
At Fantasyland, there is a special garden in which beds are raised to be accessibly scented.
The town was named after Warren Hastings, Governor of India, and many of the surrounding areas here are associated with that country. Like Napier, Hastings was devastated by an earthquake in 1931. A building of special interest is the Municipal Theatre, built in the style of a Spanish mission.

TOURIST BOARD
HASTINGS DISTRICT INFORMATION CENTRE
Tel: 06 878 0510

ACCESSIBLE TRANSPORT
HASTINGS TAXIS
Tel: 06 878 5055

HOTEL
HOLIDAY PARK
Windsor Avenue
Tel: 06 878 6692
No. of flats and family cabins: 29
No. of adapted cabins: 1, totally self-contained
Facilities: restaurant: pool - adjacent

Adjacent to Fantasyland, set in 27 hectares of Windsor Park. The park offers a selection of tourist and family cabins, caravan and camping facilities.

ACCESSIBLE ATTRACTION
FANTASYLAND
Grove Road
Tel: 06 876 9856

A leisure park that is accessible to wheelchairs and most of the features and rides can be enjoyed. Two wheelchairs are available for visitors at no charge. There is one accessible WC.

MASTERTON

This is the main centre of a rich sheep-farming district. Near Martinborough to the south-east, vineyards flourish. 16km north at Mount Bruce is the National Wildlife Centre where rare and endangered birds are studied and bred. Here visitors may see kiwis, giant wetas (the world's heaviest insect), native bats and the takahe, thought to be extinct until the 1950s.
Queen Elizabeth Park gardens offer tranquillity in the shade of their old trees. There is no designated parking or accessible WC in the gardens.
For the more active, Masterton is a starting off point for the Mount Holdsworth Recreation Area noted for its rugged hills and rushing waters.

Sun-blessed Napier casts the right light on its superb art-deco townscape.

ACCESSIBLE WALKING TRACKS AND PICNIC AREAS
RIVERBANK RESERVE

Lawn and barbecue area with about 500m of tracks by Waipoua River. It adjoins Queen Elizabeth Park at the northern end of town. For information phone 84 199.

QUEEN ELIZABETH PARK
Lakeside Park

For information phone 84 199.

RITIMONA RESERVE

Grassy area beside a stream with 500m of tracks. There is a good picnic spot between Forth Street and Stamford Place. For information phone 84 199.

ROBINSON PARK

Quiet garden and lawn reserve beside a stream at the north end of town. For information phone 84 199.

MATAMATA

Small rural township in the Waikato area, close to Hamilton. Once the home of the chief Te Waharoa, the town is now a holiday resort, well known for it natural hot springs at Okauia 6km away.

NAPIER (Hawkes Bay)

Main centre of Hawkes Bay area. Art Deco buildings, farming, market gardening and fruit growing region. Kennedy Park has a garden designed for visitors in wheelchairs, similar to Fantasyland in Hastings. There are a number of accessible vineyards including McDonald Winery, Mission Winery, Sacred Hill Winery and Te Mata Estate. Greenmeadows Game Farm and Trout Hatchery is accessible, as is the first floor of the Aquarium.

Napier is a city blessed with generous hours of sunshine and one of NZ's leading holiday resorts with a two-mile esplanade lined with Norfolk Pines. Once restricted by lack of land, Napier gained 8000 acres during the 1931 earthquake. The city boasts a busy port and a long breakwater.

SUPPORT ORGANISATION
DISABILITY INFORMATION CENTRE
HAWKES BAY
22 Munroe Street
PO Box 506
Napier
Tel: 06 835 0781 Fax: 06 835 0421

HOTEL
PARKWOOD MANOR INN
Karanema Drive
Havelock North
Hawkes Bay
Tel: 06 877 8005 Fax: 06 877 4758
No. of hotel rooms: 60
No. of adapted rooms: 3
Facilities: restaurant; pool
Set is five acres of park-like grounds, this hotel is 20 minutes' drive south of Napier's Marine Parade and located alongside the Karamu Stream.
All accommodation is on the gound floor.

ACCESSIBLE TRANSPORT
TAXIS
NAPIER TAXIS
Tel: 06 835 7777

ACCESSIBLE ATTRACTIONS
HAWKE'S BAY MUSEUM
Marine Parade
Open 1000-1630
The museum houses art exhibitions, craft and art of the Ngati Kahungungu people and a 1931 earthquake audio visual show. The museum is currently accessible only in certain areas, but alterations are in hand. There is an accessible lift to the first floor but no accessible WC.

THE McDONALD WINERY
200 Church Road
Taradale
Open Monday-Saturday 0900-1700
Shop and wine tasting. The wine shop is accessible.

MISSION VINEYARDS
Church Road
Greenmeadows
Tel: 06 844 2259 Fax: 06 844 8138
There is designated parking and accessible WC facilities.

ACCESSIBLE WALKING TRACKS AND PICNIC AREAS
MARINE PARADE
Seafront walk of about 3.5km with some accessible attractions. For information phone 57 579.

ANDERSON PARK, TARADALE
2km circular walk with grassed access to barbecue and picnic areas. For information phone 57 579.

NEW PLYMOUTH
On the west coast with a rugged coastline pounding surf on to iron sand beaches, and dominated by the near-perfect cone-shaped Mt. Egmont, (8.260 ft). Mt. Egmont is frequently compared to Japan's Mount Fuji and is at the centre of an 88,000-acre national forest park.
This is also the centre of the Taranaki dairy area. The rich volcanic soil has made the area renowned for beautiful parks and gardens with dazzling arrays of rhododendron and azalea.
Pukekura Park, in the centre of town, contains two natural amphitheatres in which sports and entertainment events are held.
In St. Mary's Anglican Church, the first stone church in the country dating from 1845, lie the graves of the pioneers, soldiers and sailors who fell in the Maori wars, defending the early settlement. Govett-Brewster gallery contains one of NZ's finest collections of contemporary NZ art. The main street in New Plymouth, Devon Street, is reputed to be NZ's longest.

SUPPORT ORGANISATION
TARANAKI DISABILITIES RESOURCE CENTRE
28 Young Street
PO Box 5015
New Plymouth
Tel: 06 768 0982 Fax: 06 757 8789

TOURIST BOARD
NEW PLYMOUTH INFORMATION CENTRE
Corner of Leach and Liardet Streets
PB 2025
Tel: 06 758 6086 Fax: 06 758 1395

ACCESSIBLE TRANSPORT
NEW PLYMOUTH TAXIS
Tel: 06 757 5665

ACCESSIBLE ATTRACTIONS
PUKEITI RHODODENDRON TRUST
Carrington Road

Tel: 06 752 4141
Open 0900-1700
20km from the city centre, these world-famous gardens are set in 350 hectares of native bush. Special male and female WC facilities. There is no designated car parking, but usually there is plenty of space and with prior notification drivers may use the private driveway. Note: If the ground is wet underfoot, people in wheelchairs may require someone to push their chair in order to negotiate the walkways. Pukeiti does have a wheelchair available, and a tour can booked on their Howdah that is secured to a trailer and towed around the gardens.

CEDAR NURSERIES
63 Egmont Road
Tel: 06 755 0369
Open daily
Specialists with one of NZ's largest collections of conifers. The WCs are not accessible. There is no designated parking, but usually there is plenty of parking space.

ST MARY'S CHURCH
Vivian Street
Tel: 06 758 3111
Open daily
The oldest stone church in NZ with an historic graveyard. WCs are accessible as is the top floor – from outside – where there is a suitable unisex WC. The ground floor is accessible with male and female WCs. There is no designated parking, but there is a covered set-down area at the front entrance.

GOVETT-BREWSTER GALLERY
Queen Street
Tel: 06 758 5149
Open Monday-Friday 1000-1700
Saturday and Sunday 1300-1700
One of the country's best collections of contemporary arts. Home of the Len Lye Sculpture Exhibition.
There are separate accessible WCs. There is parallel parking in the street in front of the building, but the gutter will have to be negotiated. If notified prior to a visit staff will come out to assist. They will also allow use of their private car park. Cafeteria facilities are accessible.

TARANAKI MUSEUM AND NEW PLYMOUTH LIBRARY
Ariki Street
Tel: 06 758 9853
Accessible WC is in the library area and therefore not available when the library is closed after 1200 on Saturday and all day Sunday.

LAKE MANGAMAHOE
State Highway 3, south of the city
Tel: 06 758 8099
A reserve famous for its view and reflections of Mt. Egmont/Taranaki. There are neither accessible WCs nor designated car parking spaces.

PUKEKURA PARK
Fillis Street
Tel: 06 758 8099
Accessible WCs and designated car parking space are available at the park.

ACCESSIBLE WALKING TRACKS
BROOKLANDS PARK AND ZOO
Brooklands has a section of native bush and the zoo contains otters, monkeys, wallabies and exotic birds. Adjacent to Pukeiti Park. For information phone 84 242.

LEE BREAKWATER, PORT TARANAKI
Accessible for about 500m up to the barrier. Good fishing. Ngamotu Beach is close by and is a good spot for a picnic. For information phone 84 242.

OHOPE (BAY OF PLENTY)
Close to Whakatane and attracts many holidaymakers to enjoy the weather, miles of safe beaches and picturesque countryside.

HOTEL
SURFS REACH HOTEL
52 West End, Ohope
Tel: 07 312 4159 Fax: 07 312 4995
No. of hotel units: 10
No. of adapted units: 1 THIS UNIT HAS ONE

141

ROOM WITH A DOUBLE BED, TV, CHAIRS, TABLE AND A KITCHEN ALCOVE WITH MICROWAVE, SINK, CROCKERY AND CUTLERY.
Facilities: self-catering
Two persons per night: 80.00
10 modern units with kitchens and new furniture. A few minutes' scenic drive from Whakatane. Quiet, sheltered panoramic surroundings that are flat. The hotel is adjacent to safe and sandy Ohope beach that has wheelchair access.

OMAPERE
Gateway to the 42,000 acres of Waipoua State Forest that contains the last great stands of kauri trees, famous for their gum. One of the trees, Tane Mahuta, or Father of the Forest, towers to the sky only a short distance from the main road.

HOTEL
OMAPERE TOURIST
Main Road, PO Box 19
Omapere
Tel: 09 405 8737 Fax: 09 405 8801
No. of hotel units: 17
No. of adapted units: 1 and 5 new rooms that are adaptable
Facilities: restaurant; pool
Two persons per night: 75.00
Sub-tropical setting, with all self-contained units having a seaview, and located right on the safe and sandy beach. Good views of Hokianga Harbour and good native bush walks in an area steeped in history.

OPONONI
Explore the Waipoua State Forest and the hot medicinal springs of Ngawha.
The story of Opononi's tame dolphin that carried children on its back in 1956 has passed into legend; a monument by a distinguished sculptor is above the dolphin's grave on the seafront.

HOTEL
OPONONI RESORT HOTEL (BW)
State highway 12
Tel: 09 405 8858 Fax: 09 405 8827
No. of hotel rooms: 10
No. of adapted rooms: None specific,

but full assistance is given and the hotel has been passed by an independent assessor
Facilities: restaurant
Two persons per night: 80.00
Panoramic sea views.

PAIHIA (BAY OF ISLANDS)
This pretty seaside town looks across to the historic settlement of Russell and caters for all tastes with safe swimming, sandy beaches, fishing, boating and historical attractions. In the chart of the Bay of Islands, it is only a few minutes from Waitangi with its Treaty House and museum, formally the home of James Busby. Here in 1840 the Treaty of Waitangi was signed representing the birth of New Zealand as a member of the Commonwealth. The town is therefore regarded as the cradle of New Zealand. The first Christian marriage was recorded at the Meeting House in 1823, the first printing press operation in New Zealand also took place here, printing copies of the treaty and of a Maori dictionary.
A popular holiday resort, Paihia is well served by ferries, cruise launches and tour companies and is an ideal bay from which to explore the Bay of Islands and Northland.
Approximately 33km southeast of Paihia is the historic township of Keri Keri, clustered around a picturesque inlet. Often called the fruit bowl of the north, the area has a sub-tropical climate and the surrounding orchards produce citrus and the famous KK oranges, kiwi fruit and many vegetables as well as macadamias.

TOURIST BOARD
INFORMATION BAY OF ISLANDS
PO Box 70
Paihia
Bay of Islands
Tel: 09 402 7426 Fax: 09 402 7301

HOTELS
BEACHCOMBER RESORT (FL)
1 Seaview Road, Paihia
Bay of Islands
Tel: 09 402 7434 Fax: 09 402 8202

No. of hotel rooms: 47
No. of adapted rooms: 3
Facilities: restaurant; pool; sauna; whirlpool
Two persons per night: 130.00
All rooms overlook the sea and there is a safe, private, sandy beach and two acres of garden. Secluded and quite glorious.

PAIHIA PACIFIC RESORT
27 Kings Road
Tel: 09 402 8221 Fax: 09 402 8490
No. of hotel rooms: 35
No. of adapted rooms: 2
Facilities: pool; sauna
Two persons per night: 90.00
NB. THERE ARE TWO SMALL STEPS TO AN OTHERWISE MOST ACCESSIBLE APPROACH AND THREE STEPS TO RECEPTION. ACCESS TO THE RESTAURANT IS BY FIVE STEPS AND SOME DEEP GRAVEL. OTHERWISE THIS PROPERTY IS ACCESSIBLE.
The town centre is ten minutes' walk on the flat, and the beach is two minutes away over similar terrain. The surrounding area is also flat.

ACCESSIBLE ATTRACTION
BOAT TRIPS ON BAY OF ISLANDS
FULLERS NORTHLAND
PO Box 145, Paihia
Tel: 09 402 7421 Fax: 09 402 7831
All vessels are accessible except *R. Tucker Thompson Tall Ship Sailing*
On the *Cape Brett Hole* on the Rock cruise, and the *Cream Trip*, the crews are reportedly well practised in embarking and disembarking passengers confined to wheelchairs and passengers can either remain in their own chairs or take an ordinary seat on board.
This also applied to Fullers *Cape Reinga* coach trip where special seats are allocated and wheelchairs are stored in lockers. We have heard good reports about this company from two independent sources.

PALMERSTON NORTH
The hub of the Manawatu district and the largest city in the region with pleasant city-centre gardens. At the esplanade,

native trees by the river and a cherry tree drive attract many visitors at blossom time. Across the river, on higher land, are the fine grounds of Massey Agricultural College, established in 1926 it became the Massey University of Manawatu in 1963. The city is surrounded by rich farming land where some of the country's finest sheep are reared and the Manawatu River emerges from the Manawatu Gorge not far away. Do not miss the Maori Battalion Memorial Building in Cuba St. Fortress-like with a suggestion of an eastern temple, this modern work also makes effective use of Maori carving.

SUPPORT ORGANISATION
NZ DISABILITIES INFORMATION BUREAU
840 Tremaine Avenue
Tel: 06 356 2311 Fax: 06 355 5459

TOURIST BOARD
VISITOR INFORMATION CENTRE
Civic Centre, The Square
PO Box 474
Tel: 06 358 5003 Fax: 06 356 9841

ACCESSIBLE TRANSPORT
PALMERSTON NORTH TAXIS
Tel: 06 357 6076

SPECIALIST TOUR OPERATORS
DISABLED TOURS
No. 6 Road
Tel: 06 323 7167

HOTEL
HACIENDA MOTOR LODGE
27 Victoria Avenue
Tel: 06 357 3109 Fax: 06 355 1455
No. of hotel rooms: 16
No. of adapted rooms: 2
Facilities: restaurant; pool; spa
Two persons per night: 100.00
Central, but quiet, location close to hospitals, doctors and shops and 20 minutes' drive from the nearest beach. The surrounding area is flat.

ACCESSIBLE ATTRACTIONS
MAORI BATTALION MEMORIAL BUILDING
138 Cuba Street

Tel: 06 354 0883
Run mainly as a functions and catering centre called Portofino. Access to the ground floor only.

ACCESSIBLE WALKING TRACKS
THE ESPLANADE
Urban park and a riverbank of about 1.5km For information phone 68 199

PARAPARAUMU
A pleasant seaside town 51km north-east of Wellington. Off the coast is the bird sanctuary of Kapiti Island, once the base of the Maori warrior chief Te Rauparaha who raided the mainland in the 1820s. Farming, market gardening and fruit growing area.

SUPPORT ORGANISATION
KAPITI ABILITIES RESOURCE CENTRE
7a Epiha Street
Paraparaumu
Tel: 04 298 2914

HOTEL
OCEAN MOTEL
42-44 Ocean Road
Tel: 04 298 6458 Fax: 04 298 6458
No. of self-contained villas: 5
No. of adapted villas: 5
Facilities: pool; spa
Delightful park setting, two minutes from the beach, village and boutiques. The surrounding area is flat.
Note: This property is wholly owned by the New Zealand CCS Wellington and all profits go to support the provision of services for people with disabilities.

ACCESSIBLE ATTRACTION
SOUTHWOODS MUSEUM TRUST
Designated parking and accessible WCs available.

ROTORUA
Famous for its volcano and a good base for exploring geysers and thermal zones. Visit the Agrodome, an amazing display of trained sheep, working dogs and agricultural exhibitions.
A busy tourist spot, the city is on the lake from which it takes its name. Cultures intermingle here with the Maori village of Ohinemutu with its magnificently carved meeting place standing not far from the small Anglican church of St. Faiths. Tudor Towers in Government Gardens offer many leisure activities.
A short way to the south of the town are the best known thermal attractions Whakarewarewa, known locally as Whaka, where guides are always on hand to lead people through the reserve.
Among other attractions are Fairy and Rainbow Springs, where Rainbow and Brown Trout can be viewed in their hundreds.
The buried village covered by the eruption of Mount Tarawera that caused the loss of many lives, is also worth a visit.
Further attractions include the Waiotapu Thermal Reserve in which the main geyser, Lady Knox, plays to a height of 60 feet and Orakei-Korako, perhaps the most colourful and interesting of thermal areas.

ACCESSIBLE TRANSPORT
ROTORUA TAXIS
Tel: 07 348 5079

HOTELS
KINGSTATE ROTORUA
Corner of Hinemaru and Eruera Streets
Tel: 07 347 1234 Fax: 07 348 1234
No. of hotel rooms: 227
No. of adapted rooms: 1
Facilities: 3 restaurants; pool; sauna; spa
Located in the business district close to the Polynesian Pools. The surrounding area is flat.

SHERATON HOTEL (SH)
Fenton Street
Tel: 07 348 7139 Fax: 07 348 8378
No. of hotel rooms: 130
No. of adapted rooms: 1
Facilities: 2 restaurants; heated outdoor pool; sauna; individual grotto spas
Two persons per night: 215.00
NB: THE CONVENTIONS MANAGER'S SON IS IN A WHEELCHAIR AND REGULARLY USES THE HOTEL'S FACILITIES.

Close to the Lake, Rainbow Trout Springs and Maori Craft Centre.

THE ROTORUA (SPHC)
Corner of Tyron and Froude Streets
Tel: 07 348 1189 Fax: 07 347 1620
No. of hotel rooms: unknown
No. of adapted rooms: 1
Facilities: restaurant; pool; spa
Overlooking Whakarewarewa thermal activity, (5km).

ACCESSIBLE ATTRACTION
RAINBOW SPRINGS
Fairy Springs Road
Open 0800 till late
5km from town; a natural trout sanctuary and wildlife park with a nocturnal kiwi house.

AGRODOME LEISURE PARK
Western Park
Ngongotaha
Open daily from 0900
10km north; features various sheep breeds and other farm animals.

MAORI ARTS AND CRAFTS INSTITUTE
Hemo Road
Open daily 0830-1700
The institute is accessible but Whakarewarewa Thermal Reserve does have steep paths and some steps. To view Pohutu Geyser go to lookout by the entrance to Geyserland Hotel in Fenton Street. Assistance here is recommended.

ACCESSIBLE WALKING TRACKS, PICNIC AREAS AND PARKS
WAIOTAPU THERMAL PARK
State Highway 5
Open daily 0830-1700
5.3km south of town, The Lady Knox Geyser erupts at 1030 daily and is accessible. For the remainder–silica terraces, champagne pools and craters – assistance is recommended. NZ's largest mud pool is on the access road.

No sheepish behaviour from this human visitor to The Agrodome – 10km north of Rotorua.

Pohutu Geyser, Whakarewarewa Thermal Reserve.

WAIMANGU THERMAL VALLEY
Open 0900-1700
20 minutes south off State Highway 5.
This is the southern end of the 1886 Mt.
Tarawera eruption. Paths run downhill
but park transport will return wheelchair-
bound visitors to the entrance.

KUIRAU PARK
Ranolf Street
Accessible paths and scented garden.
Unique public foot-pools. For information
phone 84 199.

HELLS GATE
Tikitere
Open 0900-1700
16km on State Highway 30. Thermal
reserve of mud pools, sulphurous steam
vents and other formations. One steep
slope, but otherwise access is good.

HAMURANA PARK
2km walk to springs on northern side of
lake. For information phone 479 179.

GOVERNMENT GARDENS
There are accessible paths near thermal
pools on Hinemaru Street. For
information phone 84 199.

WHAKAREWAREWA STATE FOREST
1km forest walk from Park HQ to
Redwood Grove. For information phone
83 839.

RUSSELL (BAY OF ISLANDS)
Popular resort town in Bay of Islands.
Boating, big-game fishing and several
historic buildings.
Formally known as Kororareka, Russell
was the site of NZ's first capital and a
trading post for sailing ships. No other
place in the country is richer in
atmosphere and history. The Duke of
Marlborough Hotel stands on the site of
the first recorded land purchase and the
cutting down of the famous flagstaff by
Hone Heke sparked off the first Maori war.
Be sure to visit Pompallier House built in

1839, formally a Roman Catholic monastery and one of the few buildings to survive the Maori war.

TOURIST BOARD
INFORMATION BAY OF ISLANDS
PO Box 70, Paihia
Bay of Islands
Tel: 09 402 7426 Fax: 09 402 7301

HOTEL
HANANUI LODGE MOTEL
The Strand
Russell
Tel: 09 403 7875 Fax: 09 403 7697
No. of hotel units: 10
No. of adapted units: 2
Facilities: self-catering
Located on the waterfront with delightful coastal views. Ten fully self-contained units and the surrounding area is flat. Close to licensed restaurants, shops, historic Pompallier House, Captain Cook Memorial Museum.

ACCESSIBLE ATTRACTION
POMPALLIER HOUSE
The Strand, Russell
Tel: 09 403 7861
According to the curator recent

renovations have made the garden and ground floor level accessible to those in wheelchairs.

TAIRUA
Popular with holidaymakers for its safe beaches. Its on the Coromandel Peninsula at the base of Coromandel range and the extensive Tairua forest. Forestry is a major industry here.

TAUPO
Settled by the Europeans in the 1860s as a military redoubt, Taupo stands in a bay at the northern end of Lake Taupo (238 sq. miles). It is famous for its trout and is heated in places by thermal activity. The area is rich in Maori legend, very beautiful and now a popular resort, the lake offering swimming, boating and fishing.

TOURIST BOARD
VISITOR INFORMATION CENTRE
Tongariro Street
PO Box 865
Tel: 07 378 9000 Fax: 07 378 9003

The idyllic setting of Hahei Beach, Coromandel.

HOTEL
LAKELAND MOTOR INN (BW)
State Highway 1, Two Mile Bay
Tel: 07 378 3893 Fax: 07 378 3891
No. of hotel rooms: 64
No. of adapted rooms: 16
Facilities: restaurant
Accessible to both airport and beach.

LANECOVE MOTOR INN
213 Lake Terrace
Tel: 07 378 7599 Fax: 07 378 7393
No. of hotel suites: 16
No. of adapted suites: 1
Facilities: restaurant (with steps); full room service for breakfast and dinner is suggested by the hotel for special guests; pool; spa
Two persons per night: 200.00
On the lake front. Spacious suites each with bedroom, lounge with dining area and individual spa pool.

ACCESSIBLE ATTRACTION
CHERRY ISLAND PARK
Waikato Street
Open 0900-1700
Island in Waikato River with good access.

TROUT FISHING
Contact Taupo Visitor Information Centre. Excellent opportunities for river or boat fishing with experienced guides. Charter boats have wheelchair facilities.

ARATIATIA RAPIDS OUTLOOK
10km north of town. At 1000 and 1430 the dam gates are opened to recreate the spectacle of the rapids.

HUKA FALLS LOOKOUT
Loop road just off State Highway 1, south of Wairakei. Falls can be viewed without leaving your vehicle.

WAIRAKEI THERMAL VALLEY
Steaming ground, active fumeroles, curiously shaped geyser craters, steam heated mudpools and silica fossils characterise this area.
The Barn Tearooms are accessible, but the Thermal Valley itself is not because of steps and unsealed paths.

TAURANGA
Centre of the citrus growing area, Tauranga has the best natural harbour on the North Island, many miles of beautiful coastline plus year-round sunshine. Close to the great prime forest and thermal region, Tauranga began as a mission station in the 1830s and one of its attractions includes the Mission House built by the Rev. Alfred Brown. Called The Elms it is set in beautiful grounds. The Monmouth Redoubt occupied by British troops and containing the headstones of those killed at the Battle of Gate Pa is close by.

HOTEL
BAY CITY MOTEL
166 Waihi Road
Tel: 07 578 0588 Fax: 07 578 9335
No. of motel rooms: 14
No. of adapted rooms: 2
Facilities: pool
Two persons per night: 90.00
Five minutes' drive from the city and undulating in its surroundings. All units are on the ground floor.

SEMI-ACCESSIBLE ATTRACTIONS (WORTH THE EFFORT IF POSSIBLE)
ELMS MISSION HOUSE
In April 1864 a number of British officers sat down to dinner around the Oval Table in the Elms Mission House. The following morning they went out to fight the Battle of Gate Pa and all but one were killed. The house is still standing in good repair amid the gardens. Parking is available, but there are no accessible WC facilities.

MONMOUTH REDOUBT
Formerly the site of a Maori Pa. this spot was originally the Mission Cemetery– missionaries being the only Europeans in the locality.
Early settlers are buried here, providing a roll-call of Tauranga's early inhabitants. Parking is also available here, but there are no accessible WC facilities.

BRIAN WATKINS' HOUSE
233 Cameron Road
Tel: 07 576 9804 and 544 2695
Open Sundays only 1400-1600
The house, over one hundred years old, has been restored to its Victorian setting. It is on a main road and has restricted parking and no accessible WC facilities.

ACCESSIBLE WALKING TRACKS
THERMAL WALK, TOKAANU DOMAIN
1km circular walk in thermal area. Small kerb from car park.

TOKAANU
5km northwest of Turangi at the south end of Lake Taupo, featuring thermal pools. Tokaanu was once a port before the days of road transport and is now a popular resort for trout fishermen. The beautiful Maori village of Waihi lies at the foot of the steaming cliffs two miles away.

TURANGI
Excellent fishing in Tongariro River and Lake Taupo. Turangi expanded rapidly in the 1960s following the installation of an hydro-electric scheme.

HOTEL
ANGLERS PARADISE RESORT MOTEL
Corner of State Highway
41 Ohuanga Road
PO Box 130, Turangi
Tel: 07 386 8980 Fax: 07 386 7408
No. of suites: 16
No. of adapted suites: 1
Facilities: restaurant – self catering; pool; spa
At the gateway to the National Park Tongariro. Spacious fully self-contained suites with full cooking facilities. English and Continental breakfast is available as is a hunting and fishing guide. The surrounding area is flat.
All accommodation is on the ground floor and the kitchens are specially adapted.

WANGANUI
Founded in 1840 as a frontier town in the Maori wars. The town is at the mouth of New Zealand's longest navigable river, the historic Wanganui. Flowing over 140 miles, it passes through deep gorges with overhanging foliage-covered strongholds. The river is often referred to as the Rhine of New Zealand, because of its tranquil beauty within the isolation of the Wanganui National Park.
Durie Hill overlooks the city from where, on a clear day, the South Island, Mount Egmont and Mount Ruapehu may be seen.

TOURIST BOARD
VISITOR INFORMATION CENTRE
PO Box 637
Tel: 06 345 3286

ACCESSIBLE TRANSPORT
WANGANUI TAXIS
Tel: 06 345 4444
The company participates in the Total Mobility Scheme. Full details are available from the Visitor Information Centre.

HOTEL
BURWOOD MANOR
63-65 Dublin Street
Tel: 06 345 2180 Fax: 06 345 8711
No. of hotel rooms: 20
No. of adapted rooms: 2
Facilities: pool; spa; sauna
Two persons per night: 80.00
1km from the town centre and 3km from the nearest beach, both the surrounding area and roads are flat.

ACCESSIBLE ATTRACTIONS
SARJEANT ART GALLERY
Civic Centre in Queens Park
Tel: 06 345 8522
Open Monday-Friday 1030-1630
Saturday-Sunday 1300-1620
Delightful domed building featuring a permanent collection. Wheelchair access is at the rear by goods lift, for which PRIOR NOTICE IS REQUIRED. There are no accessible WCs.

WANGANUI REGIONAL MUSEUM
Watt St in Civic Centre
Tel: 06 345 7443
Open Monday-Saturday 1000-1630
Sunday 1300-1630
Largest regional museum in New Zealand

149

featuring an outstanding Maori Court with its famous canoes, collections and natural history displays. Wheelchair access only to the Maori Court.

ACCESSIBLE WALKING TRACK
VIRGINIA LAKE
Great North Road

There is no designated parking. There are some steep paths with accessible WCs up a steep hill, so a companion is needed. There is a circular lakeside walk.
When European settlers first came to the Wanganui region the lake was known as Rotokawau, lake of black shags. It was renamed by settlers who considered it resembled Virginia Water in Surrey. For further information contact:

Parks Department
Wanganui District Council
101 Guton St
Tel: 06 345 8529 Fax: 06 345 3355

The Visitor Information Centre has details of a number of other walks around Wanganui that are suitable for wheelchairs, including Kowhai Park and the riverside along Anzac Parade; Moutao Gardens; Basin Botanical Reserve; Bushy Park and Ashley Park in Waitotara.

PUBLIC ACCESSIBLE WCs
St. Hill Street, between Ridgeway Street and Maria Place
Trafalgar Square Library (Davis Building)
Taupo Quay Wharf

PUBLIC ACCESSIBLE PARKING
Ridgeway Street near Drews Avenue and outside the Cosmopolitan Club.
St. Hill Street near the Opera House and ladies' WC.
Victoria Avenue near Maria Place, and outside Mid-Avenue Post Office.
Wicksteed Street outside the Social Welfare office.
Library Car Park
Wanganui East Shopping Centre.

WELLINGTON
Wellington has been the capital of New Zealand since 1865. Its suburbs cling precariously to its precipitous hills and plunging gullies. Based around the 64 acres of Botanic Gardens, one of the most beautiful parks in the world, Wellington offers an outstanding panoramic view across the Cook Strait.
Cricket may be watched at the Basin Reserve and the home of the world-famous All Blacks rugby football club is at the Athletic Park. Those who enjoy horse racing will find Trentham in the Hutt Valley one of the world's finest courses. Most of the houses in Wellington are made of wood because it is three times more resistant to tremors than brick.

SUPPORT ORGANISATION
DISABLED PERSONS ASSEMBLY
PO Box 27, 186 Wellington
Tel: 04 472 2626

NEW ZEALAND CCS
86-90 Vivian Street
PO Box 6349, Te Aro, Wellington
Tel: 04 384 5677

WELLINGTON DISABILITY RESOURCE CENTRE
55-57 Cuba Street
PO Box 33 084
Petone, Wellington
Tel: 04 568 2890 Fax: 04 568 2896

AIRPORT
WELLINGTON INTERNATIONAL AIRPORT
Tel: 04 388 8500 Fax: 04 388 4912

Facilities
International Terminal: Wall phones are mounted but not too high to prevent access. Low phones are available in Ansett's Golden Wing lounge.
There is a male-female accessible WC on the first floor with lift access.
A restaurant/bar on the first floor is accessible with a lift adjacent to New Zealand check-in on the ground floor. Airbridges are installed in both terminals.

TRANSPORT
COACH

There are several companies operating bus and coach transport with accessiblity, contact:

NEW ZEALAND TOURIST AND PUBLICITY DEPT.
PO Box 95
Wellington
Tel: 04 499 9995

NEWMANS COACHES
Tel: 04 499 3261
Staff will assist person on to the coach and transport their wheelchair.

RITCHES COACHES-GREENHALGE
Tel: 04 833 6053
This company has a 36-seater bus that has a hoist and holds 12 wheelchairs.

RAIL
SILVER FERN; RAILWAY CORPORATION
Tel: 04 794 600 extension 8435
Ramps are available to assist with loading. Staff are trained to assist people in their train seats. Advance notice of journey is required if use of the ramp and other assistance is needed.

TAXI
MAXI-TAXIS
Converted Toyota Hiace vans can carry seven passengers and two wheelchairs, they have a raised roof, a special foldaway chairlift and restraining straps.
Contact Disabled Persons Assembly as detailed above.

PETRON AND LOWER HUTT TAXIS
Tel: 04 567 0057

WELLINGTON TAXIS
Tel: 04 383 8888

SPECIALIST TOUR OPERATORS
SPECIALIST CHARTER SERVICES
1-65 Highbury Road
Wellington
Tel: 04 475 3158

HOTELS
AIRPORT HOTEL
16 Kemp Street, Kilburnie
Wellington
Tel: 04 387 2189 Fax: 04 387 2787
No. of hotel rooms: 120
No. of adapted rooms: 17
Large comfortable rooms. Just a few minutes from Wellington International Airport.

BAY PLAZA HOTEL
40-44 Oriental Parade
Tel: 04 385 7799 Fax: 04 385 2936
No. of hotel rooms: 74
No. of adapted rooms: 1
Facilities: restaurant
Five minutes from the centre of town and two minutes from the nearest beach. The surrounding area is mostly flat but there are some hills.

HARBOUR CITY MOTOR INN (BW)
92-96 Webb Street
Tel: 04 384 9809 Fax: 04 384 9806
No. of hotel rooms: 25
No. of adapted rooms: 2
Facilities: restaurant; pool; spa
Two persons per night: 100.00
One of Wellington's newest motor inns, located in the city centre close to theatres, shops and restaurants.

PLAZA INTERNATIONAL
148 -176 Wakefield Street
Tel: 04 473 3900 Fax: 04 473 3929
No. of hotel rooms: 184
No. of adapted rooms: 14
Facilities: 2 restaurants; cocktail lounge; conference facilities
A five-star hotel in the centre of Wellington with all attractions close by. The surrounding area is flat.

PORTLAND TOWERS HOTEL
24 Hawkstone Street
Thorndon
Tel: 04 473 2208 Fax: 04 473 3892
No. of hotel rooms: 107
No. of adapted rooms: 5
Facilities: restaurant; pool; accessible WC in the lounge, reception and bar.

Two persons per night: 115.00
Note: THIS HOTEL OFFERS A 15
PERCENT DISCOUNT OFF NORMAL
RATES FOR THOSE IN WHEELCHAIRS.
Central location, two minutes from the
Parliament Buildings and close to
Lambton Quay and the Botanical Gardens.

QUALITY HOTEL PLIMMER TOWERS (CHI)
Corner of Boulcott and Gilmer Terrace
Wellington
Tel: 04 473 3750 Fax: 04 473 6329
No. of hotel rooms: 93
No. of adapted rooms: 2
Facilities: restaurant; bar; conference rooms;
sauna.
With direct access to the town centre and
in the heart of the business and shopping

areas. The beach is 10 minutes away by
car and the surrounding area is HILLY.

ACCESSIBLE ATTRACTIONS
CABLE CAR
Owned though not operated by
Wellington City Council the cable cars
run from Lambton Quay to Kelburn and
are designed for wheelchair access. The
bottom station, just off Lambton Quay, is
accessible
The top station, Upland Road, and one of
the entrances to the Botanic Gardens
(details under Accessible Walking below)
are accessible.
There are three intermediate stations and
wheelchairs do have access though the
paths leading away from the stations are

The cable car from Lambton Quay to Kelburn is designed for wheelchair access.

NATIONAL LIBRARY OF NEW ZEALAND
Corner of Molesworth and Aitken Streets
Po Box 1467, Wellington 1
Tel: 04 474 3000 Fax: 04 474 3015
Open Monday-Friday 0900-1700
Saturday 0900-1300

The library was designed with accessibility in mind and there are no obstructions to the three main entrances. All surrounding paths and walkways are accessible, and there are no ramps or curbs to either entrances or exits. There are two designated parking areas located at the rear of the building. Inside there are both ladies' and gentlemen's accessible WCs on the lower ground floor, a lift for access to the different levels, and a cafe, also accessible, on the lower ground floor.

DOWSE ART GALLERY
Laings Road
PO Box 30-396, Lower Hutt
Tel: 04 570 6500 Fax: 04 569 5877
Open every day Monday-Friday 1000-1600
Saturday and Sunday 1100-1700

A fine collection of New Zealand art and craft work. There are designated parking and accessible WCs in the museum. There is a ramped entrance way, and all pathways and walkways are accessible to wheelchairs.

BOTANIC GARDENS
Glenmore Street
Open daily

Entry is possible from Upland Road cable car stop, but only some specific areas are accessible.
The Main Garden (formal bedding, duckpond, Soundshell); the Botanic Garden Education and Environment Centre; the Lady Norwood Rose Garden and the Begonia House are all accessible. There is designated car parking at the top of the Garden, in the Rose Garden and

on slopes of approximately one in five. There is no private vehicle parking available at the top or bottom stations though there is room for vehicles to pull in on the bus turn-round at Upland Road and set down passengers before moving off some distance to locate private parking at the kerb side.
There is an accessible WC at Upland Station.
No restaurant is operated in conjunction with the Cable Car, but there is a tearoom, known as the Skyline, 250m away from the Upland Station Road stop. It is accessible though it involves negotiating a reasonably steep slope from Upland Road. Excellent views over the city.

153

outside the Main Garden.

With prior notice cars may be driven around the Main Garden or down to the Education and Environment Centre for easier access.

There are accessible WCs in the Begonia House and the Education and Environment Centre. By June 1994 there will be another built at the Cable Car entrance to the Garden.

The Teahouse, located in the Begonia House, has suitable access.

The Main Drive, Main Garden paths and Begonia House surrounds are all paved, with no slope above 1:12.

Pathways to the Education and Environment Centre are also at a gradient of 1:12, with a long approach path. The Centre can be reached with moderate difficulty with either a companion or a powered wheelchair. There is provision for a vehicle to approach the Centre to drop off passengers. Entrance to the Centre is from the Founder's Entrance in Glenmore Street. Door upstands are less than 25mm in the Centre and at the Begonia House, with no curbs.

The remainder of the land in the Gardens is rather steep and while the paths are in good condition, help from a companion would be advisable. For further information phone 724 594.

ACCESSIBLE WALKING TRACKS AND PICNIC AREAS IN GREATER WELLINGTON

ORIENTAL BAY
Waterfront walk beside the sea with harbour and city views.

There is an accessible restaurant with parking immediately outside.

AOTEA LAGOON
Picnic areas and fern house and 500m of track. Turn off State Highway 1, 3km north of Porirua. For further information phone 375 089.

ORATI NATIVE PLANT MUSEUM AND WILTON BUSH
Access to this native garden's picnic areas

is from Wilton Bush Road. For further information phone 759 059.

KAITOKE REGIONAL PARK
Picnic area by the river. There ia an accessible one-way bush walk through a locked gate and over a bridge - ring the caretaker, on the number below, to make arrangements. 12km north of Upper Hutt. For further information phone 267 261.

HARCOURT PARK
Urban park and herb garden. The best access to the park is near the substation. 2km north of Upper Hutt on Akatarawa Road off Fergusson Drive. For further information phone 267 400.

TRENTHAM MEMORIAL PARK
On Barton Road, off Ferguson Street in Upper Hutt. This is an urban park with some bush and only some areas are negotiable. For further information phone 286 711.

RIDDIFORD PARK
Laings Rd and Queens Drive. Gardens with an aviary and conservatory in Lower Hutt. For further information phone 660 592.

TAWA GROVE WALK, WAINUIOMATA
700m circular native bush walk in Rimutaka Forest Park. For further information phone 648 551.

PETONE WHARF AND SEAFRONT
There is a footpath beside the sea wall on the esplanade, 1km each way from the Settlers Museum. For further information phone 685 079.

WHAKATANE
A quiet seaside resort that looks out to White Island, an active volcanic island and often described as the safety valve of the North Island.

Whakatane is rich in Maori history and the fabled canoe is said to have landed here from Hawaiki in 1350 AD. At the centre of the town stands the tall Pohaturoa Rock, now a war memorial. The Ngati-Awa chiefs signed the Treaty of

Waitangi in the shadow of the rock. 35km away, on the route towards Rotorua, is Kawerau, a major forestry centre producing over 200,000 tons of newsprint per year and in excess of 12 million board metres of sawn timber. Nearby is Mt. Edgecumbe named by Captain Cook in 1769.

SUPPORT ORGANISATION
DISABILITIES RESOURCE CENTRE
143 King Street
Whakatane
Tel: 07 307 1447 Fax: 07 307 1128

WHANGAREI
Main centre and port of Northland, on a beautiful harbour that Cook visited during his first voyage in 1769. It is now a city of parks and lovely gardens and a busy port. It is situated in a dairy-farming and fruit-growing region.

Explore the fascinating Claphams Clock Museum and the Whangarei and Wairua Falls, that are set in a bushland valley just out of the city. A good view may be had from Parahaki Hill and there is big-game fishing in this area, particularly at Tutakaka, four miles away.

SUPPORT ORGANISATION
NORTHLAND DISABILITIES RESOURCE CENTRE
18 Vine Street
Whangarei
Tel: 09 430 0988 Fax: 09 438 9468
The centre operates two vans converted to wheelchair vehicles. They also have a van with a hoist available through Kiwi Cars.

HOTEL
KINGSWOOD MANOR
260 Kamo Road
Kamo
Tel: 09 437 5779 Fax: 09 437 5780
No. of hotel rooms: 19
No. of adapted rooms: 2
Facilities: All units have cooking facilities; cooked and Continental breakfasts are available; pool; spa
Two persons per night: 75.00
Five minutes north of the city centre on

State Highway 1, close to the Kamo Shopping Centre. The surrounding area is flat.

ACCESSIBLE ATTRACTIONS
CLAPHAMS CLOCK MUSEUM
Water Street
Tel: 09 438 3993
Open 1000-1600
The largest collection of clocks in the southern hemisphere.
Parking is at the Forum North car park, and accessible WCs are in the Forum North Complex.

NZ REFINING COMPANY
Ruakaka
State Highway 1
Tel: 09 432 8194
Open Summer 0930-1900 Winter 1000-1630
20km south of Whangarei. The Visitor Centre has a spectacular free sound and light show and is wheelchair accessible, with a suitable WC also.
The cafe is also accessible, and there is parking available.

ACCESSIBLE WALKING TRACKS AND PICNIC AREAS
For detailed information on the places mentioned below phone 484 879.

WHANGAREI FALLS
Kiripaka Road
There is accessible parking and WC facilities but the tracks for walking are not accessible. There is a lovely view from the top overlooking the falls area.

RAUMANGA STREAM
A concrete path alongside the stream gives access from the end of Te Mai road or West End Avenue.

HATEA DRIVE BROADWALK
A pleasant river walk

BEACH FRONT, ONERAHI
A one-way walk of 4km. following an old railway line through a mangrove forest.

SOUTH ISLAND

SUPPORT ORGANISATION
DISABILITY INFORMATION SERVICE
314 Worcester Street
PO Box 32-074
Christchurch
Tel: 03 366 6189 Fax: 03 379 5939

AIRPORTS
CHRISTCHURCH INTERNATIONAL AIRPORT
Tel: 03 353 7774-7775 Fax: 03 353 7754

Car Parking
There are four designated car parking
spaces.

Facilities
International Terminal: THERE ARE NO
PUBLIC TELEPHONES AT
WHEELCHAIR HEIGHT, but they are
available in Ansett's Golden Wing Lounge.
Airbridges are used for on and off
passengers in both terminals.
Lifts are available between ground and
first floor for all airlines and wheelchairs
are available.
Accessible WCs are located on ground
and first floors. Ramps provide access to
the Cheers Bar and the Marriott
Restaurant. Ramps are also provided for
access to the car park and public
transport, both at ground level.

DUNEDIN INTERNATIONAL AIRPORT
Tel: 03 486 2879 Fax: 03 486 2813

Car Parking
There are four designated parking spaces
in the public car park.

Facilities
International Terminal: Low-mounted
coin and card phones are available as are
one male and one female accessible WC.
The ground floor restaurant has good
access. There is an easy-access lift to the
first floor for boarding. Airbridges are
installed in the domestic terminal only.

WHERE TO GO, WHERE TO STAY

BLENHEIM
Blenheim stands on the wide, open
Wairau plain with a prospect of riverflat,
vibrant with colour except in summer,
when the heat tans the landscape to a
uniform brown. Farming and fruit
growing are the major industries of the
main town of Marlborough.
The town claims 2500 hours of sunshine
per year and is known as the Sunshine
Capital. It has many attractive parks and
gardens. Visit the large memorial at
Taumarina, dedicated to the colonists
who died in the Wairau Affray of 1843.
128km south is Kaikoura, one of the few
places in the world where huge sperm
whales and other cetaceans, such as
dusky dolphins, the rare Hector's dolphin
and fur seals may be viewed at close
range. Although there is activity year
round, there is more to be seen in winter.

HOTELS
AORANGI LODGE HOTEL
193 High Street
Blenheim
Tel: 03 578 2022 Fax: 03 578 2021
No. of hotel units: 14
No. of adapted units: 2
Facilities: breakfast is available and
restaurant meals can be delivered; pool
Centrally located near the
Blenheim/Nelson Highway, the hotel is
only 20 minutes from Picton Ferry
Terminal and five minutes from
Blenheim Airport. It is a short drive to
Marlborough Sounds, the town centre is
1km away and the surrounding area is flat.
The units are one and two bedroomed
with separate lounges and fully self-
contained kitchens. The motel literature
promotes paraplegic units.

CHATEAU MARLBOROUGH
97-117 High Street
Tel: 03 578 0064 Fax: 03 578 2661
No. of hotel suites: 30
No. of adapted suites: 2
Facilities: some suites have cooking facilities;
a cooked breakfast is available; pool

Note: THE HOTEL HAS BEEN INSPECTED AND APPROVED BY THE CCS WHO ALSO ADVISED THAT A MAJORITY OF THE STANDARD SUITES WERE CAPABLE OF ACCOMMODATING OUR DISABLED CLIENTS.

The hotel is situated in the very heart of Blenheim, overlooking Seymoure Square floral gardens. A very attractive building

ACCESSIBLE ATTRACTIONS
BRAYSHAW MUSEUM PARK
Tel: 03 578 7191
Visit the Vintage Farm Machinery Display with rare tractors, engines etc. plus the Modellers Society exhibits and replica of shops at Beavertown.

MARLBOROUGH DISTRICT LIBRARIES
Corner of Arthur and Seymour Streets
Accessible WCs.

CHRISTCHURCH
This very English, very flat, garden city, has as its nucleus the neo-gothic cathedral. There are many museums and galleries, parks and gardens, the largest being the 200-hectare Hagley Park with the River Avon flowing through the centre.

The city boasts many nineteenth century grey-stone buildings. Beside the Botanic Gardens is Canterbury Museum, housing the finest Antarctic collection in the world. Christchurch was planned on paper, right down to the street names, and is quite different from all other towns in New Zealand. Home to the 1974 Commonwealth Games, its facilities are impressive. Near the city on the tip of Banks Peninsula is Akaroa, a former whaling station and quaint picturesque town with reminders of the French attempt at colonialisation in 1840. The town has maintained many historic buildings, museums and craft centres and is well placed for day trips.

AIRLINE OFFICES
AIR NEW ZEALAND
56 Armagh Street
Christchurch
Tel: 03 379 7000

ANSETT NEW ZEALAND
Corner of Worcester Street and Oxford Terrace
Christchurch
Tel: 03 379 1300

MOUNT COOK AIRLINES
91 Worcester Street
Christchurch
Tel: 03 348 2099

ACCESSIBLE TRANSPORT
TAXIS
BLUE STAR TAXIS
Tel: 03 379 9799

GOLD BAND TAXIS
Tel: 03 379 5795

SERCO SERVICES
29-35 Latimer Square
Tel: 03 343 0809
This company has a hand-control unit. It is portable and may be fitted to most vehicles and is available for hire.

SPECIALIST TOUR OPERATORS
HORIZON HOLIDAYS
530-544 Memorial Avenue
PO Box 14-069
Christchurch Airport
Paravan available for hire. Fitted with electric hoists, side mounted and powered by the van's master battery. The rear seat of a usual twin cab has been removed, anchoring down bolts are provided and there is sufficient padded headroom.

SPECIALIST CHARTER SERVICES
92 Nayland Street
Christchurch
Tel: 03 326 6802

HOTELS
NOAHS HOTEL
Corner of Worcester Street and Oxford Terrace
Tel: 03 079 4700 Fax: 03 379 5357
No. of hotel rooms: 208
No. of adapted rooms: 2
Facilities: 2 restaurants

Two persons per night: 235.00
First class, central hotel. The beach is
15km away and the surrounding area is
flat, as is all Christchurch.

QUALITY INN DURHAM ST. (CHI)
Corner of Kilmore and Durham Streets
Tel: 03 365 4699 Fax: 03 366 6302
No. of hotel rooms: 160
No. of adapted rooms: 4
Facilities: restaurant; pool; sauna; spa
This modern hotel is five minutes from
Cathedral Square in the heart of the city
and 20 minutes from the international
airport and the nearest beach.

ACCESSIBLE ATTRACTIONS
AIR FORCE MUSEUM
RNZAF Base, Wigram
Open Monday-Saturday 1000-1600
Sunday 1300-1600
Collection of 16 aircraft including the
classic Spitfire and Mustang. A stairlift is
available for wheelchair visitors.

ROBERT MCDOUGALL ART GALLERY
Botanic Gardens
Open daily 1000-1630
Located behind the Canterbury Museum.
Parking is 500m away, but phone Botanic
Gardens for use of the Gallery car park.

CANTERBURY MUSEUM
Rolleston Avenue
Open 0900-1630
Permanent displays of Antarctic, New
Zealand birds and a 19th-century village.

BOTANIC GARDENS
There are several parking areas throughout
these quiet and peaceful gardens.

CATHEDRAL SQUARE
A level pedestrian area with the cathedral
as the focal point.

ORANA PARK WILDLIFE TRUST
McLeans Island Road
Open daily 1000-1730
New Zealand's leading wildlife park,
includes a kiwi house and Tuatara
enclosure.

FERRYMEAD HISTORIC PARK
269 Bridle Path Road
Open 1000-1630
Museum of Transport and Technology.
Railways, trams and restored Canterbury
township.

ACCESSIBLE WALKS AND PICNIC AREAS
KAITUNA VALLEY SCENIC RESERVE
Ten-minute, one-way walk in a tranquil
bush setting. 45km from Christchurch,
off the Akaroa Highway. For further
information phone 799 758.

MONA VALE
Garden beside the Avon River. The
best month to view the glorious flowers is
October. For further information phone
489 659.

THE GROYNES
Tracks and a picnic area beside the lake.
Groynes to Belfast is accessible and the
return journey covers about 5km.
Located near Belfast. For further
information phone 517 109.

CROMWELL (Central Otago)
Scene of the 1862 Gold Rush. The town
was re-established when the hydro-
electric power dam was built. It is also a
farming and fruit-growing area and the
place where the waters of the Kawarau
River join those of the mighty Clutha,
New Zealand's largest waterway.

DUNEDIN
Retains its Celtic flavour. A gracious city
of grand 19th-century buildings and
beautiful gardens. Like Rome, the city is
built on seven hills and is the home of
New Zealand's oldest university. A short
distance away is Otago Peninsula with
dramatic seascapes and two of the city's

*Christchurch, the very English, very flat,
garden city, relaxes around Victoria
Square.*

famous stately homes, Glenfalloch, surrounded by several hectares of woodland gardens, and the neo-Gothic Larnach Castle.

The beaches of St. Kilda and St. Clair are close by as is the old Maori settlement of Otakou.

SUPPORT ORGANISATIONS

DISABILITY INFORMATION SERVICE INC.
The Foyer, Dunedin Hospital
Gt. King Street
Tel: 03 477 7740 Fax: 03 474 7631

DISABLED CITIZENS SOCIETY
199 Hillside Road

OTAGO MULTIPLE SCLEROSIS SOCIETY INC
8 Baker Street

DUNEDIN CRIPPLED CHILDREN'S SOCIETY
514 Great King Street
Dunedin North

ACCESSIBLE TRANSPORT
TAXIS
DUNEDIN TAXIS
Tel: 03 477 7777
A Maxi Taxi with a wheelchair hoist is available.

CITY TAXIS
Tel: 03 477 1771

GOLD STAR TAXIS
Tel: 03 489 5184

ACCESSIBLE PUBLIC PARKING

Moray Place – UMCA Car Park Building

Filleul Street – Golden Block Building Two Special (W) Parks on ground level

Frederick street – Hospital Car Park Two Special (W) Parks

Hillside Road – South City Mall Car Park One Special (W) Park

Lorne Street Car Park, South Dunedin – rear of the post office

There are two other car parks without designated parking:

Crawford Street Car Park on the corner of Water Street

DCC Great King Street Car Park

ACCESSIBLE PUBLIC RESTROOMS
Frederick Street – male

Athenaeum Building Octagon – female

Gardens Visitors' Education Centre – male and female

New World South City Hillside Road Car Park – male and female

Automobile Association in Moray Place

HOTELS
BENTLEY'S HOTEL
137 St. Andrew Street
Tel: 03 477 0572 Fax: 03 477 0293
Facilities: restaurant; pool; spa
Central location. The town centre is five minutes' drive away and the beach ten. The surrounding area is flat.

LEVIATHAN HOTEL (BW)
65-69 Lower High Street
PO Box 112
Tel: 03 477 3160 Fax: 03 477 2385
No. of hotel rooms: 77
No. of adapted rooms: 1, plus 6 with wide doorways for wheelchair access
Facilities: restaurant
Two persons per night: 80.00
Surrounding area is flat. The town centre is five minutes away, and the beach about ten. The hotel is opposite a bus and train depot.

SOUTHERN CROSS HOTEL (FL)
Corner of High and Princess Streets
Tel: 03 477 0752 Fax: 03 477 5776
No. of hotel rooms: 110
No. of adapted rooms: 3
Facilities: 3 restaurants
NB: THERE ARE FOUR STEPS INTO THE RESTAURANT

Two persons per night: 160.00
A quality hotel with a central location, close to the post office, railway station and airport. The surrounding area is reasonably flat and the beach is 4km away.

ACCESSIBLE SHOPPING MALLS
GOLDEN CENTRE
251 George Street

PLAZA THEATRE MALL
George Street

CENTRE CITY MALL
Gt. King and Cumberland Streets

SOUTH CITY MALL
Hillside Rd

ACCESSIBLE ATTRACTIONS
ROYAL ALBATROSS COLONY
Otago Peninsula
Open daily 1030-1600 Summer hours extended.
This is the only mainland breeding colony in the world where the albatross, the largest of all sea birds, live. There is purpose-built ramp access. The colony is fully accessible and there is designated car parking at the door.

DUNEDIN PUBLIC ART GALLERY
Logan Park
Open Monday-Friday 1000-1700
Saturday and Sunday 1400-1700
New Zealand's most important collection of European fine and decorative arts plus contemporary New Zealand art. Fully accessible with designated car space but a wheelchair is not available.

EARLY SETTLERS' MUSEUM
Anzac Avenue
Open Monday-Saturday 1030-1630
Sunday 1330-1630
Museum of social history of Otago and Dunedin from the early 1800s to the present day. The WC is not fully accessible, there is no designated car space but plenty of parking nearby. There is an accessible WC nearby in Dowling St.

TAIERI GORGE LIMITED
Tel: 03 477 4449
A wheelchair lift onto the train, a special wheelchair carriage and fully accessible WC facilities on board make this train excursion through the Gorge from Dunedin Railway Station worthy of special consideration. Be sure to mention special requirements when booking.

ACCESSIBLE WALKING TRACK
CROSS CREEK WATER RESERVE
A native bush walk located on Malvern Street. For further information phone 774 117.

FRANZ JOSEF GLACIER
Named by Sir Julius von Haast after the Austrian emperor. Until sometime after 1893 the glacier was in steady retreat but, in 1907, in a marked advance, the tourist track was wrecked and in 1909 advances of up to 50m were recorded in 13 months. There is still a pattern of temporary advances that are minor interruptions to a steady retreat up the valley.
This dramatic feature can best be viewed from an aircraft. Hot springs are close by in the Waiho River that leads away from the glacier melt and rises far up in the valley beneath the Franz Josef. Kept in flood for the greater part of the year by frequent rain, the river carves out large caverns between the glacier ice and the valley floor causing occasional collapses.

TOURIST BOARD
DEPARTMENT OF CONSERVATION
Box 14, Franz Josef Glacier

HOTEL
GLACIER GATEWAY MOTOR LODGE (BW)
State Highway 6
PO Box 1
Tel: 03 752 0776 Fax: 03 752 0732
No. of hotel rooms: 23
No. of adapted rooms: 1
Facilities: English and Continental breakfast available; pool; sauna; whirlpool
Two persons per night: 100.00
Opposite Glacier Access Road with commanding views of the Southern Alps

and Glacier Neve and a few minutes from the village.

ACCESSIBLE ATTRACTIONS
PARK HEADQUARTERS
This is the Visitor Centre in Franz Josef and is accessible and has a suitable WC.

LAKE MAPOURIKA
Approximately 9km north of Franz Josef. There is wheelchair accessibility to the lakeside at the jetty bay but not elsewhere along the lake.

OKARITO
A small village on the sea coast 30km from Franz Josef. Okarito Nature Tours conduct guided tours on the lagoon, which is specially designed for bird watching. They happily take people in wheelchairs, but assistance is needed for lifting in and out of the boat. On a clear day there are beautiful views of the mountains from Okarito.

GREYMOUTH
Spanning the Grey River, Greymouth is the major town on the west coast. The economy is now based on coal, timber, farming and some minor industries. The town has its origins in the great Gold Rush of 1865 and has many historical attractions. South of Greymouth in the central west coast region is Hokitika, land of greenstone–New Zealand jade. Beside the Tasman sea and with views to Mt. Cook and the Southern Alps, this former gold mining town is now the craft centre of the coast and a popular base for exploring Westland. Visit the Shanty Town and a greenstone factory.

TOURIST BOARD
GREYMOUTH INFORMATION CENTRE
PO Box 95
Tel: 03 768 5101 Fax: 03 768 0317

ACCESSIBLE TRANSPORT
TAXIS
GREYMOUTH TAXIS
Tel: 03 768 7078

ACCESSIBLE ATTRACTIONS
SHANTYTOWN
Rutherglen Road
Tel: 03 762 6634
Good accessible WC facilities, but no designated parking spaces as such.

MOANA ZOOLOGICAL GARDENS AND NATIVE BIRD SANCTUARY
Main Road, Moana
Tel: 03 738 0009
There are no accessible WCs here, but the tourist board were optimistic about a new installation in what will be a Kiwi House.

ACCESSIBLE WALKING TRACKS AND PICNIC AREA
NELSON CREEK PICNIC AND CAMPING AREA
Riverbank Park, located towards Nelson. Turn off State Highway 7, 2km north of Ngahere. This is an historic goldfield area with a kilometre of track suitable for wheelchairs called Colls Dam Walk. For further information phone 80 114.

LAKE BRUNNER
On the southern shores there is a 90m footbridge over the mouth of the Arnold River. From the car park there is a wheelchair access track to the bridge.

HANMER SPRINGS
The massive trees and comfortable accommodation here are a far cry from the bare tussock in which its well-known thermal springs were first found; pools where, for a number of years, the only amenity was a flagpole on which was hoisted an article of clothing appropriate to the sex of those bathing there. Hanmer subsequently blossomed into a fashionable spa where thousands came to "take the cure". With the passing of that era it has become a mellow mineral spa and holiday resort, with a firm base in forestry. Thermal pools at Queen Mary Hospital are open to the public, with an hydraulic lift available. The soft blend of fairly saline water contains a little alkaline carbonate and some lithium. The principal ingredients are sodium chloride and sodium borate, prolonged immersion

being considered beneficial for chronic arthritic diseases. Particularly fine in winter with snow-capped mountains, it was the first exotic forest in the South Island and thus boasts more arboreal species than any other in New Zealand.

ACCESSIBLE WALKING TRACK
WHEELCHAIR WALK
1km one-way walk through the exotic forest. There are also a couple of other suitable walks. For further information contact the Department of Conservation at the Visitors Information Centre listed above. For access to the roads of the forest contact:
Carter Holt Harvey Forests
PO Box 214
Tel: 03 315 7218

HOKITIKA
Famous for its Greenstone factory, Hokitika is the gateway to and from the west coast of the island and boasts a fine airport. Capital of the Goldfields, the town now has an economy based on the trees of Westland's vast forests, on the grass of neighbouring alluvial flats and the processing of minerals (including greenstone). Firms in the town process local greenstone into jewellery, bringing blocks in by helicopter from mineral claims in the exceptionally rugged mountains, or by quarrying the stone in old river terraces.
A symbol of the town is the romanesque tower of St. Mary's Catholic church, rising to dominate the town-scape and embody the predominantly Irish nature of the goldfields.
Lying at the mouth of the Hokitika River, the town had one of the country's foremost ports, remembered now only by a long disused lighthouse on the cliff at Seaview and by disintegrating timberwork past the river mouth.
Three miles away is Lake Kaniere that has a heavily wooden shoreline and calm waters reflecting the surrounding mountains. Visit the West Coast Historical Museum.

TOURIST BOARD
WESTLAND DISTRICT COUNCIL
VISITOR INFORMATION
Private Bag
Tel: 03 755 8322 Fax: 03 755 8026

ACCESSIBLE TRANSPORT
TAXIS
HOKITIKA TAXIS
Tel: 03 755 8437

HOTEL
SOUTHLAND HOTEL (FL)
111 Revell Street
Tel: 03 755 8344 Fax: 03 755 8258
No. of hotel rooms: 10
No. of adapted rooms: 2
Facilities: restaurant—award-winning "Tasman Views" overlooking seashore; some rooms have a spa
Two persons per night: 85.00
In the town centre on the shore of the Tasman Sea, family-owned for 105 years.

ACCESSIBLE ATTRACTIONS
MOUNTAIN JADE FACTORY
Weld Street
Tel: 03 755 8007
No accessible WC or specific parking, but ample parking space in the vicinity. From April 1994 there will be two accessible WCs and parking.

SEASIDE JADE FACTORY
Revell Street
Tel: 03 755 6228
At present there is no accessible WC or specific parking, but there is ample parking space in the vicinity.

WESTLAND GREENSTONE
Tancred Street
Tel: 03 755 8713
No accessible WC or specific parking, but ample parking space in the vicinity.

WEST COAST HISTORICAL MUSEUM
Tancred Street
Tel: 03 755 6898
Accessible WCs.
Accessible WCs are also available at the RSA building in Sewell Street.

GIBSON QUAY AREA

Now landscaped, the area is an Heritage Area and is accessible with a lovely view of the Hokitika River and of the nearby mountains.

BEACH STREET

There is a grassed area off this street from which there are good sea views and it is accessible.

INVERCARGILL

Strong Scots roots and named after Captain Cargill, founder of the Otago Settlement. As Dunedin rose to prosperity on gold the province of Southland found a more enduring asset in grass, hence its fame as a centre for sheep farming and for well laid out gardens, parks and elegant buildings. This coastal town has the lowest national average of bright sunshine and highest number of rainy days. Pastures do not dry out in summer. Nearby, the Catlins forest Park offers fine coastal scenery.

TOURIST BOARD
INVERCARGILL VISITOR CENTRE
PO Box 1012
Tel: 03 218 9753 Fax: 03 218 9753

ACCESSIBLE TRANSPORT
TAXIS
BLUE STAR TAXIS
Tel: 03 218 6079

HOTELS
BALMORAL LODGE MOTEL
265 Tay Street
Tel: 03 217 6109 Fax: 03 217 6109
No. of hotel units: 28
No. of adapted units: 2
Facilities: Self-catering with all amenities; whirlpool is some units, but not specified.
Opened in 1985, this hotel is part of a modern, architecturally designed complex that uses much local timber. The motel actively promotes paraplegic units in its brochure. Located right on State Highway 1, five minutes from the town centre and 15 minutes from the nearest beach. The surrounding area is flat.

TOWNSMAN MOTOR LODGE
195 Tay Street
Tel: 03 218 8027 Fax: 03 218 8420
No. of motel units: 20
No. of adapted units: 1
Facilities: cooked and Continental breakfasts available
On State Highway 1 and close to CBD. Self-contained motel units include a kitchen. The nearest beach is 7km away and the surrounding area is flat.

ACCESSIBLE ATTRACTIONS
SOUTHLAND MUSEUM AND ART GALLERY
Queens Park
Victoria Avenue
Tel: 03 218 9753
Open Monday-Friday 1000-1630
Saturday and Sunday 1300-1700
Displays of local and national artifacts, including the Tuatara, a slow-moving reptilian descendant of the dinosaur. Accessible WCs and lift access.

ST. JOHN'S ANGLICAN CHURCH
Tay Street
Tel: 03 218 9805
Side door access

FIRST CHURCH
Tay Street
Tel: 03 218 6340
Side door access. No accessible WC.

ST. MARY'S BASILICA
Corner of Tyne and Ninth Streets
Tel: 03 218 4123
Side door access. No accessible WC.

ANDERSON PARK ART GALLERY
Waikiwi
Tel: 03 215 7432
Open daily, except Monday and Friday, from 1400-1630
A Georgian mansion with 24 hectares of grounds including a traditional Maori meeting house. The house is now a public art gallery.
Fully accessible, with two wheelchairs available on site if required.

ORETI BEACH
Accessible.

STEWART ISLAND
Stewart Island Marine
PO Box 99
Tel: 03 212 7660 Fax: 03 212 8377
Stewart Island has a rich Maori history.
The first European residents were
whalers and sealers. Brown kiwi are
common.
The ferry service between Stewart Island
and Bluff is accessible.

MARLBOROUGH SOUNDS
Waterways and secluded bays, myriad
islands and intricate coastline at the
north part of the island. The area was
named in 1857 after John Churchill,
Duke of Marlborough, in the belief that
the new province should, like Nelson and
Wellington, bear the name of a great
fighting hero. Blenheim was named at
the same time to honour the Duke's most
famous victory. Long hot summers bake
the land almost white and with frosty
clear winters this is an ideal grape
growing area.
Small craft fill the harbours in the sounds
and the wooded and rugged scenery
sweeps down to the shore. The area caters
for sea-fishing, hiking, climbing,
sunbathing and bird watching.

MT. COOK
Mt. Cook and Fox Glacier are only 35km
apart, but the fastest land journey takes
eight to nine hours.
Mt. Cook is the highest peak in the
Southern Alps at 3,764 metres.
Frequently covered in cloud, it is best
seen in winter. As New Zealand's most
popular scenic wonder it has become a
little commercialised.
Sadly neither the Hermitage Hotel nor
the Mt. Cook Travelodge are accessible.

NELSON
Lying snugly at the head of Tasman Bay,
and named the sunshine city, Nelson is a
garden town with spectacular beaches,
safe swimming and a mountainous
backdrop. The town looks over Nelson
Haven and across the broad curve of
Tasman Bay to the tall Tasman
Mountains. There is a strong nautical
flavour about the town with its streets
and parks echoing the exploits of the
admiral after whom it was named, as well
as those of ships that bought the pioneer
settlers. The city's charm is further
enhanced by many imposing old timber
buildings.
Hops, tobacco and a range of fruits are
cultivated in its mild climate. There is
also a good crafts centre with
glassblowers, potters, weavers and
carvers, all drawn to the town by its
climate. Kaiteriteri Beach, one and half
hours' drive from Nelson, on the opposite
side of Tasman Bay, is typical of coastal
scenery in these parts.

HOTELS
RICHMOND MOTEL AND HOLIDAY PARK
29 Gladstone Road
Richmond
Nelson
Tel: 03 544 5218 Fax: 03 544 4597
No. of hotel units: 11
No. of adapted units: 1
Facilities: restaurant — self catering; pool
Close to the Richmond shopping centre
and restaurants. Near the crossroads to
Abel Tasman National Park and Nelson
Lakes National Park, Golden Bay and the
West Coast. The beach is 6km. and the
surrounding area is flat.

QUALITY HOTEL NELSON (CHI)
Trafalgar Square
PO Box 248
Nelson
Tel: 03 548 2299 Fax: 03 546 3003
No. of hotel rooms: 114
No. of adapted rooms: 3
Facilities: restaurant; pool; sauna; whirlpool
Note: LIFT-CALL BUTTONS, DOOR
HANDLES AND LIGHT SWITCHES IN
BEDROOMS, AND DOOR HANDLES AND
LIGHT SWITCHES IN WCs ARE 160cms
ABOVE FLOOR LEVEL, NOT 140.
The town centre is 300 metres flat access,

and the beach five minutes by car. The surrounding area is flat.

ACCESSIBLE ATTRACTIONS
FOUNDERS PARK
87 Atawhai Drive
Tel: 03 548 2649
Open daily 1000-1630
A collection of historical buildings laid out as a village, including the Harbour Board Museum. Fully accessible. Designated car parking and accessible WCs.

SUTER ART GALLERY
208 Bridge Street
Tel: 03 548 4699
WCs and restaurant are accessible. There is no off-street parking.

NELSON CATHEDRAL
Church Hill
Trafalgar Square
Tel: 03 548 8574
Open during the summer months from 0700-2000
There are accessible WC facilities below steps, but no special designated parking. Parking is available in Trafalgar Square.

NELSON PROVINCIAL MUSEUM
Isel Park
Stoke
Tel: 03 547 9740
There are accessible WCs and a car park.

ACCESSIBLE WALKING TRACK AND PICNIC AREA
TAHANANUI BEACH
Access to the beach is from the car park at Natureland. Most broadwalks are rather steep. For further information phone 60 2000.

OAMARU
Famous for a Wallaby Park, public gardens and grand 19th-century buildings of creamy white limestone, mined in local quarries that reflect the wealth of the gold rush era.
The town lies in the crook of Cape Wanbrow, a knuckle on the North Otago coastline. Sheltered to the south by this high headland and to the west by low hills, this chief town of North Otago enjoys a warm, dry climate evidenced by its luxurious gardens. Sheep farming, fruit growing and cereal crops dominate the landscape.
Oamaru lies exactly half way between the equator and the South Pole and boasts an excellent port. Do not miss the Botanical Gardens originally laid out in 1876.

TOURIST BOARD
VISITOR INFORMATION CENTRE
19 Eden Street
PB 50058
Tel: 03 434 8060 Fax: 03 434 8442

HOTEL
ARMADA MOTOR INN
500 Thames Highway
Tel: 03 437 0017 Fax: 03 437 0297
No. of hotel rooms: 20
No. of adapted rooms: 2
Facilities: restaurant; pool; sauna; spa
Two persons per night: 75.00

ACCESSIBLE ATTRACTIONS
TYNE/HARBOUR STREET
An area of 19th century whitestone buildings within a conservation area. No designated car space, but plenty of parking. There is a new accessible WC nearby in Eden Street (opposite the art gallery).

OAMARU PUBLIC GARDENS
Severn Street
Established in 1876, and including Wonderland Gardens and the Summerhouse. Mostly flat. Designated car space. Accessible WC nearby in the aviary/rose garden.

OAMARU WALLABY PARK
Chelmer Street
Open daily 0900-1800
The park offers visitors the opportunity to touch and feed wallabies and alpacas. Accessible WC and designated car spaces.

MOERAKI BOULDERS
Fully accessible tearooms and WC.

NEW ATTRACTIONS
Yellow-eyed penguin and Little Blue penguin watches take place on the beach at night. There is an accessible viewing area, but no accessible WC.

OTEMATATA
The name means place of good quartz or flint. The town, by the Waitaki River, was created in 1958 as a construction town for the Aviemore and Benmore hydro projects. Crib owners have filled much of the void left when the workers moved on, enjoying the facilities offered by hydro lakes for boating and fishing.

QUEENSTOWN
Local folklore tells of gold prospectors pronouncing the town as "fit for any Queen" and then formally christening the settlement "Queenstown" on a blacksmith's anvil. On the shores of Lake Wakatipu, Queenstown is renowned for bungy jumping over Kawarau River. The visitor is unaware that the lake rises and falls three inches every five minutes, and another characteristic is its refusal to freeze over during even the harshest of winters.

Places of interest on Wakatipu Lake, the country's third largest, include Frankton, Kingston, Halfway Bay, Cecil Peak, Eflin Bay, Kinlock and Paradise.

The town is surrounded by the most dramatic Southern Alps scenery, and is a year-round resort with many attractions including Te Anau, gateway to Fiordland. There is a daily bus service to Milford Sound, with the mile-high Mitre Peak, one of the most famous and spectacular of all New Zealand views. The Tourist Board advises that the Milford Bus Service will take wheelchairs in its luggage compartment, but contact the Tourist Board for fuller details and the timetable.

Many of the towns 3000 residents are New Age believers, and the spiritually inclined flock here, claiming Queenstown as a new Mecca for spiritual energy. Scene of a goldrush, the area is now more renowned for its activity holidays and boat trips although gold mining continues around Queenstown where miners can make NZ$1000 a day. It is a local tradition to mine enough gold to make your own wedding ring.

TOURIST BOARD
VISITOR INFORMATION NETWORK
Clocktower Centre
Corner of Shotover and Camp Streets
Tel: 03 442 8238 Fax: 03 442 8907

HOTELS
GARDENS PARKROYAL
Marine Parade
Tel: 03 442 7750 Fax: 03 442 7469
No. of hotel rooms: 150
No. of adapted rooms: unknown
Facilities: restaurant
In the centre of town, and close to the beach, the surrounding area is flat.

HOLIDAY INN (HDI)
Salisbury Road, Fernhill, Queenstown
Tel: 03 442 6600 Fax: 03 442 7354
No. of hotel rooms: 150
No. of adapted rooms: 7
Facilities: 2 restaurants; pool; spa; sauna
Two persons per night: 240.00
Overlooking Lake Wakatipu and the Remarkables Mountain Range from high on the slopes of Fernhill. Amazing views from the hotel that is 20 minutes from the local airport and two minutes from the centre of Queenstown. The beach is 500m. away and the surrounding area is HILLY.

ACCESSIBLE ATTRACTIONS
THE STONE LIBRARY
Stanley Street
Tel: 03 442 7668
Wheelchair access to the top floor, but no accessible WC.

EARNSLAW PADDLESTEAMER
Steamer Wharf
Tel: 03 442 7500
An 80-year-old working steamer chugs

out onto Lake Wakatipu several times each day. Wheelchair access onto the boat, but no accessible WC, but there are accessible facilities at Farm-Walter Peak.

ST. OMER PARK
Accessible WC and wheelchair access into the park.

QUEENSTOWN GARDENS
There is wheelchair access, but no accessible WC.

ST. ARNAUD
Farming locality and holiday resort at NE head of Lake Rotoiti, within Nelson Lakes National Park. The park preserves in perpetuity the rugged, mountainous country that surrounds the slender,

beech-fringed glacial lakes of Rotoiti and Rotorua. Lake Rotoiti has good swimming, a host of picnic places along its eastern shore and few sandflies.

HOTEL
ALPINE LODGE ROTOITI
St. Arnaud
Nelson Lakes
Tel: 03 521 1869 Fax: 03 521 1868
No. of hotel units: 20
No. of adapted units: 2
Facilities: 2 restaurants; accessible bar
20 units with full facilities. Situated at the edge of Nelson Lake National Park, and a five-minute walk from Lake Rotoiti.

TE ANAU
Lake Te Anau is glacial, some 40 miles

Breathtaking beauty and scenic splendour all around at Lake Wakatipu.

Two persons per night: 150.00
Situated near Lake Te Anau's shore, the hotel is close to the town centre and all amenities. The beach is within walking distance on good footpaths with ramps at intersections. Accessible.

ACCESSIBLE WALKING TRACKS
MIRROR LAKES
200m track to the lakes with their mountain reflections. Mostly accessible. On State Highway 94, 56km from Te Anau. For further information phone 249 7921.

THE CHASM
A 250m track to a spectacular river gorge. Care is needed on the ramped access. On State Highway 94, 106km from Te Anau. For further information phone 249 7921.

TIMARU
Timaru is built on a lava flow from nearby Mt. Horrible. Originally this was the only haven for Maori canoeists making passage along an unfriendly coastline between Oamaru and Banks Peninsula. The name probably began as Te Maru (the place of shelter).
Today it is the major bulk-handling port of the South Island and also has a thriving fishing industry, in addition to sheep, dairy and arable farming and forestry.
Timaru has one of the world's largest tanneries, and one of the biggest breweries in the southern hemisphere.

TOURIST BOARD
SOUTH CANTERBURY PROMOTIONS
Corner of Stafford and George Streets
PO Box 194
Tel: 03 688 6163 Fax: 03 688 6162

ACCESSIBLE TRANSPORT
TAXIS
TIMARU TAXIS
Tel: 03 684 8899

long with very different shorelines. To the east, where Te Anau town is located, trees are few; in the west the dens are part of the impenetrable beech forest of the Fiordland National Park. Surrounded by mountains and covered by beech forests, it is a centre for walkers and nature lovers. It is also a generally popular summer resort and the gateway to Fiordland country. Milford Sound is a must.

HOTEL
VILLAGE INN
Mokoroa Street
PO Box 195
Tel: 03 249 7911 Fax: 03 249 7033
No. of hotel rooms: 50
No. of adapted rooms: 1
Facilities: restaurant; pool; spa

ACCESSIBLE ATTRACTIONS
SOUTH CANTERBURY MUSEUM
Pioneer Hall
Perth Street
Tel: 03 684 8199
Open every afternoon, except Monday and
Saturday, 1330-1600

Operated by Timaru District Council.
Displays include everything from whaling
relics and examples of pioneering life to a
library of early newspapers.

There are steep steps at the front, but
there is flat access from the back of the
building from the grounds of St. Mary's
Church.

ST. MARY'S ANGLICAN CHURCH
Church Street
Tel: 03 688 8377

Built in 1880 of locally quarried
limestone and famous for its spectacular
pinnacled tower.

There are one or two steps into the main
porch, but a side door near the tower is
more easily accessible.

AIGANTIGHE ART GALLERY
49 Wai-iti Road
Open Tuesday-Friday 1100-1630
Saturday and Sunday 1400-1630

The name is Gaelic and means welcome
to our home. The original homestead and
gardens were presented to the city in
1956, with a modern extension added in
1978.

Situated in lovely gardens, Aigantighe
offers a changing programme of
exhibitions and events throughout the
year. There is also a permanent collection
of New Zealand artists. The gallery is
easily accessible on the ground floor, and
there seems to be no accessibility
problems with the main display areas.
Operated by the district council. For
further information phone 03 684 8199.

TIMARU BOTANIC GARDENS
Queen Street and Domain Avenue
19 hectares set aside in 1869. Features
include a conservatory, herb garden, rose
gardens, statues of Robert Burns and of

Queen Victoria. No problem for
wheelchairs although there is a steepish
hill leading down to the duck ponds and
there are steps into the Education Centre,
that the tourist board advise is usually
fairly congested.
Operated by the district council. For
further information phone 03 684 8199.

SACRED HEART BASILICA
Craigie Avenue
Tel: 03 684 4263

Built in 1911, with some of New
Zealand's finest stained glass windows.
Wheelchair access is through side doors.

WANAKA
A popular lakeside resort, famous for
beautiful scenery and watersports. Also
the base for Mt. Aspiring National Park.
Steam launches cruise around the lake.
This attractive alpine area is dominated
by Mt. Aspiring (9957 feet), and the Lake
covers 75 sq. miles with an attractive
shoreline suitable for picnics and shore
parties.

HOTEL
FAIRWAY LODGE (BW)
Highway 89, Wanaka
Otago
Tel: 03 443 7285 Fax: 03 443 9178
No. of motel rooms: 16
No. of adapted rooms: 1
Facilities: self-catering; outdoor pool
Two persons per night: 100.00

All paraplegic units are on the ground
floor. The surrounding area is hilly and
flat.

ACCESSIBLE ATTRACTION
MOUNT ASPIRING PARK
PO. Box 93, State Highway 89
Tel 03 443 7660 Fax: 03 443 7660

The park headquarters does have a
suitable access at the rear of the building
and is clearly signposted.

*The giant Kauri tree "Tane Mahuta" in
Waipoua Forest.*

SUGGESTED ITINERARIES

AUSTRALIA

Apart from Sydney and Canberra, all capital cities can be reached only by domestic flight.

15 DAYS, SYDNEY, CANBERRA, MELBOURNE, ALICE SPRINGS, DARWIN, CAIRNS.

Day 1. Sydney
Day 2. Sydney
Day 3. Sydney - Canberra - Melbourne
Day 4. Melbourne
Day 5. Fly to Alice Springs
Day 6. Alice Springs
Day 7. Alice Springs - Ayers Rock
Day 8. Ayers Rock - Alice Springs
Day 9. Fly to Darwin
Day 10. Darwin - Kakadu National Park
Day 11. Kakadu - Darwin
Day 12. Fly to Cairns
Day 13. Cairns - Dunk Island - Carins
Day 14. Cairns - Kuranda - Cairns
Day 15. Cairns and departure

5 DAYS SOUTHWEST MONKEY MIA & PINNACLES

Day 1. Perth
Day 2. Perth - Denham (Monkey Mia)
Day 3. Monkey Mia
Day 4. Denham - Cervantes (Pinnacles)
Day 5. Cervantes - Perth

6 DAYS RED CENTRE

Day 1. Darwin
Day 2. Darwin - Kakadu
Day 3. Kakadu - Darwin
Day 4. Fly to Alice Springs
Day 5. Alice Springs - Ayers Rock
Day 6. Return to Alice Springs

8 DAY TOURER

Day 1. Adelaide
Day 2. Fly to Alice Springs
Day 3. Alice Springs - Ayers Rock
Day 4. Ayers Rock - Alice Springs, fly to Cairns
Day 5. Cairns - Kuranda - Cairns
Day 6. Cairns - Port Douglas and Outer Barrier Reef.
Day 7. Port Douglas - Cairns.
Day 8. Depart Cairns.

13 DAY GREAT BARRIER REEF

Day 1. Sydney - Armidale
Day 2. Armidale - Coolangatta
Day 3. Coolangatta - Brisbane
Day 4. Brisbane - Fraser Island - Brisbane
Day 5. Brisbane - Gladstone
Day 6. Gladstone - Hamilton Island
Day 7. Hamilton Island
Day 8. Hamilton Island - Mission Beach
Day 9. Mission Beach - Dunk Island
Day 10. Dunk Island - Townsville
Day 11. Townsville - Cairns
Day 12. Cairns - Kuranda - Cairns
Day 13. Depart Cairns

16 DAY FROM COAST TO COAST

Day 1. Perth
Day 2. Perth - Denham
Day 3. Denham - Perth
Day 4. Fly Perth to Melbourne
Day 5. Melbourne
Day 6. Fly Melbourne to Sydney
Day 7. Sydney
Day 8. Sydney
Day 9. Fly Sydney to Cairns
Day 10. Cairns
Day 11. Cairns
Day 12. Fly Cairns to Brisbane
Day 13. Brisbane
Day 14. Brisbane - Surfers Paradise
Day 15. Surfers Paradise - Brisbane
Day 16. Depart Brisbane

15 DAY HIGHLIGHTS

Day 1. Sydney
Day 2. Sydney
Day 3. Fly Sydney to Alice Springs
Day 4. Alice Springs - Ayers Rock
Day 5. Ayers Rock - Alice Springs
Day 6. Fly Alice Springs to Darwin
Day 7. Darwin - Kakadu
Day 8. Kakadu - Darwin
Day 9. Fly Darwin to Cairns
Day 10. Cairns
Day 11. Cairns
Day 12. Fly Cairns to Brisbane
Day 13. Brisbane - Noosa Heads
Day 14. Noosa Heads - Brisbane
Day 15. Depart Brisbane.

NEW ZEALAND

12 DAYS AUCKLAND TO CHRISTCHURCH

Day 1. Auckland -Rotorua
         (Travel south through rich farmland,
         the Waikato Province, known for
         thoroughbred horses)
Day 2. Rotorua
Day 3. Rotorua - Wellington
         (Continue south, see Huka Falls and
         Lake Taupo)
Day 4. Wellington - Nelson
         (Take a look at Wellington and cross
         from Wellington to Picton, and on to
         Nelson)
Day 5. Nelson - Greymouth
         (Drive via the Buller Gorge to the
         west coast and Greymouth)
Day 6. Greymouth - Franz Josef/Fox Glacier
         (Visit Shantytown, a factory at
         Hokitika and on to Franz Josef
         Glacier at the Westland National Park)
Day 7. Fox Glacier - Queenstown
         (Continue across the Haast River
         Bridge, along shores of Lake Wanaka
         to Queenstown)
Day 8. Queenstown
Day 9. Queenstown - Milford - Te Anau
         (Shores of Lake Wakatipu and Te
         Anau to Milford Sound)

Day 10. Te Anau - Invercargill -
         Bluff - Dunedin
Day 11. Dunedin - Mt. Cook (Tour Dunedin,
         travel north through the coastal town
         of Oamaru, then inland following
         Waitaki River to Lake Pukaki. Mt.
         Cook is at the head of the lake).
Day 12. Mt. Cook - Christchurch

3 DAYS AUCKLAND TO AUCKLAND - BAY OF ISLANDS

Day 1. Auckland - Bay of Islands (North
         through farming towns of Warkworth
         and Wellsford, through Dargaville and
         the Waipoua Kauri Forest Reserve and
         east to Bay of Islands)
Day 2. Russell - Paihia
Day 3. Bay of Islands - Whangarei - Auckland
         (Treaty House, Whangarei and via
         coastal road to Auckland)

9 DAYS CHRISTCHURCH TO AUCKLAND - HIGHLIGHTS

Day 1. Christchurch to Queenstown
Day 2. Queenstown
Day 3. Queenstown - Milford - Te Anau
Day 4. Te Anau - Invercargill - Bluff - Dunedin
Day 5. Dunedin - Mt. Cook
Day 6. Mt. Cook - Christchurch
Day 7. Christchurch - Wellington
Day 8. Wellington - Taupo
Day 9. Taupo - Auckland

8 DAYS CHRISTCHURCH TO CHRISTCHURCH - FIORDLAND

Day 1. Christchurch - Greymouth
Day 2. Greymouth - Franz Josef Glacier
Day 3. Glacier - Queenstown
Day 4. Queenstown
Day 5. Queenstown - Milford Sound - Te Anau
Day 6. Te Anau - Invercargill - Bluff - Dunedin
Day 7. Dunedin - Mt. Cook
Day 8. Mt. Cook - Christchurch

INDEX

AUSTRALIA

NEW ZEALAND